YORKSHIRE –
ANCIENT NATION,
FUTURE PROVINCE

YORKSHIRE –
ANCIENT NATION,
FUTURE PROVINCE

COLIN SPEAKMAN

GRITSTONE
PUBLISHING

Copyright text and photographs Colin Speakman © 2021
except where otherwise credited

Published in 2021 by
Gritstone Publishing Co-operative
Birchcliffe Centre
Hebden Bridge
HX7 8DG
www.gritstonecoop.co.uk

British Library Cataloguing-in-Publication data
A catalogue record for this book is available from the British Library

ISBN: 978-1-913625-05-4

Designed and typeset by
Carnegie Scotforth Book Production

Printed and bound by Cambrian

Front cover image: Whitby Abbey – Tim Barber

CONTENTS

Acknowledgements

My warmest thanks and appreciation are due to the efforts of several individuals whose work has made this book possible.

To Lucy Frontani of Carnegie Scotforth Book Production whose creativity and designing skills have turned this manuscript into a handsome book.

To Tim Barber and Dorian Speakman for use of some superb photographs that have helped the book come alive.

To John Grogan and his colleagues on the One Yorkshire Committee whose commitment to the project and much appreciated financial support have been essential.

To Michael Bradford whose advice and 1988 book *The Fight for Yorkshire* have been an inspiration.

To my colleagues Andrew Bibby, Chiz Dakin, Christopher Goddard, Eileen Jones, Andrew McCloy and Laurence Rose of the unique Gritstone Cooperative whose constant practical support and advice are hugely appreciated.

To Phil Bell and The Yorkshire Society whose sharing of ideas and passion for everything Yorkshire have been a driving force behind its writing.

And finally, and perhaps above all, to Fleur Speakman whose constant personal support and sharing of thoughts during a somewhat frenzied period of research and writing, plus some extremely important text proofing, have been vital.

It goes without saying that any errors, misinterpretations and omissions are entirely my own.

Colin Speakman   August 2021

Part One:
A Yorkshire Identity

Foreword

Born and raised in West Yorkshire, I am humbled to be the first ever Metro Mayor of this wonderful region.

Our fantastic landscape, coastline and history as the engine room of the Industrial Revolution is a continuous source of pride.

And I know we have an even more glorious future ahead of us as the centre for a green revolution where we harness our experience in manufacturing to create a sustainable future in environmental management and technology.

As Colin's book so eloquently argues, to be the best, we must also work together. Devolution gives us the opportunity to take hold of the levers of power, working on our own, with business and government to set the pace and control our destiny.

The past has lessons for us all and this fascinating story of an ancient kingdom can help us articulate, understand and build a better, more prosperous future English province.

Tracy Brabin
Mayor of West Yorkshire

1

Introduction: A Sense of Identity

This is a very different book about Yorkshire.

It is about celebrating many aspects of the Region's history, beauty, diversity and variety in the early 21st century. But is also about the challenges and the opportunities people of Yorkshire are facing at a time of perhaps momentous change.

Britain has left the European Union after 45 years of being closely entwined economically and politically with the other democratic nations of Europe. We are only just starting to recover from coronavirus pandemic, perhaps the worst natural disaster to affect the world for over a century. In addition, the impacts of Climate Change are now resulting in the need to make fundamental changes in how we organise our lives and our society, most especially in terms of energy and use of fossil fuels. These three factors could mean that we are now facing what could be the greatest series of economic, social and structural transformations that have occurred since the first Industrial Revolution.

The world as it was in 2019 will never return. Town centres will have less shops, less offices, less commuters, less pubs and cafes to serve these commuters. Many businesses will have disappeared. New Information Technologies accelerated by the pandemic – Zoom is but one example – will change the way we do things. People may travel abroad less but take more domestic or stay-at-home holidays. Many younger people in particular will, at least for the immediate future, see their incomes decline. Local authorities, squeezed for cash, will no longer be able to maintain some services which for decades we have taken for granted. It could be a tougher, meaner future.

But it could also be a greener future, one in which people get out of their cars and walk, cycle and use trains and buses more, and appreciate the environment and natural world that exists all around them. The pandemic has also revived an amazing spirit of community and social awareness which suggests a realisation that materialism and the acquisition of ever more consumer goods are not the purpose of life. Community values and the need to have an empathy for others, both our own families and friends, but also other people in wider society, are things that the hardships and isolation of the pandemic has taught us. Volunteers may have to take over jobs once done by paid employees. We have also learned the value of the natural world, the beauty and power of nature so evident all around us.

To meet the new world we are now entering, society has to change. We need new forms of "green" and community-led localism in every aspect of our lives – transport, food production, the environment, the economy, jobs. Think globally act locally is a powerful guiding slogan.

Perhaps most challenging possibility of all, is that there is now a distinct possibility that even the four hundred-year-old idea of "Britain" as a centralised state and focal point of a once mighty Empire may have to change radically.

The very word "Britain" is itself a misnomer. It is actually a shorthand. The sovereign state we currently live in is correctly known as the United Kingdom of Great Britain and Northern Ireland. One unforeseen consequence of Brexit has been to create a new customs border across the Irish Sea. This could create a new relationship between Northern Ireland and its close culturally and ethnically linked neighbour, the Republic of Ireland. If as seems likely Ireland prospers with new ferry links to France and UK businesses moving their offices to Dublin to access their EU clients, many people in Northern Ireland could be seeking a closer relationship with their fellow countrymen on the island of Ireland.

Scotland, irrespective of that sovereign nation's future membership of the EU, may well also seek ways of loosening its ties with England. The Welsh, remembering Edward I and the years, when even as late as the 19th century when the English tried to ban their language, could soon follow. That would leave England a nation on its own.

If we cease to be a "United Kingdom", the label Great Britain (which refers to the largest island of the British archipelago) also becomes meaningless. The term "Great" doesn't refer, as too often glibly assumed by some politicians, to the unique superior qualities of its inhabitants.

What will happen should any, or all, of the other nations choose to leave this political union? Where does that leave the English and England, the nation that occupies the southern part of this large island of Great Britain?

A fundamental problem is that most English people use the term "British" when they actually mean "English". For many English people, including many decision takers in London and the Home Counties, by "Britain" they actually mean London and the Home Counties. What happens in other parts of England, including anywhere north of Watford, is simply off their radar.

Over decades this has resulted in serious inequalities within England and between the English Regions. The comparisons are bleak. To take just one major example, transport. In 2018/19 transport spending in London by central Government, was £903 per head; for Yorkshire & Humber Region it was £276 – less than a third. Even that represented a cut of 9.9% since 2017.

Unlike in Scotland or Wales, not a single new rail line has been opened in Yorkshire since the Beeching closures of the 1960s savaged the region's rail network.

Bus services in rural Yorkshire have fared just as badly. In the urban areas of West and South Yorkshire, and in the larger towns and cities such as York, Hull, Middlesbrough and Harrogate, most of the public bus network is commercial and has survived reasonably intact, especially in areas with large student populations.

However, in rural North Yorkshire in particular, the situation is far worse. Because of Government austerity cuts, subsidy available to support non-commercial rural bus services in North Yorkshire was slashed between 2010 and 2017 from over £6 million per annum to £1.7 million, taking no account of inflation.

Yet the comparison with Greater London could not be starker. Londoners of all ages enjoy frequent services and bargain travel cards. From the age of 60 onwards Londoners enjoy free travel on frequent buses, trains, tubes and trams, either with the TFL-60 Oystercard or the Freedom Pass, whilst people in Yorkshire must wait until the age of 67, and if you live in rural North Yorkshire, you may have few if any buses left to use your pass on.

Poor rural transport means out-migration of young people and those on lower incomes, as fares become unaffordable and services hopelessly infrequent. This creates a spiral of rising fares, worsening services, and poorer patronage as people move back into towns or buy a car – adding to congestion and pollution. Things might get even worse post-pandemic after months of urging people not to use local buses and trains for fear of the virus.

The only way to ensure genuine equality of opportunity and reduce congestion and pollution is to transfer responsibility for public transport away from cash-starved County Councils whose priorities lie elsewhere, to new regional transport authorities. These must be directed and funded, as in Wales or Scotland, if not by a Parliament or Senedd, by a regional body, capable of investing in genuinely integrated, cross-boundary travel opportunity for local communities and their visitors within both urban and rural Yorkshire. Only by giving the whole community realistic and affordable travel choices will we reduce the massive carbon footprint and congestion nightmare of the now dominant private car.

But the need for a new Regional agenda is about far more than transport. According to the Government's own Department of Communities & Local Government, in 2015 Hull and Middlesbrough were near the top of the list of the ten UK towns and cities with the highest proportion of neighbourhoods among the most deprived in the United Kingdom, with Bradford only a short distance behind.

A recent European Union report[1], confirms that in 2019 the average GDP per person in the Region was around 20% less than the UK average, and 17% less than the EU average. Given the wealth of natural resources and the skilled population of the Yorkshire Region, this is a deplorable situation. It reveals in more ways than one, how the provinces of England are still treated as outposts of the Home Counties.

A fundamental issue perhaps is that England has an ageing population. Many older people, with triple locked pensions, especially those living in the better off rural parts of the South, East and West, but also the rural North, are enjoying continuing increases in their personal wealth thanks to rising property prices. It has been estimated that one person in five aged 65 or over is now a millionaire[2]. Such people are more likely to also vote for political parties which defend their interests.

Young people do not share such perceptions. The great cities of the North contain a far higher proportion of younger people whose world is very different. If they are fortunate enough to get into higher education, they face significant, long term student debt, and when graduating many have wretched job prospects, leading to part time jobs in the gig economy and wages that make home ownership and access to the "property ladder" enjoyed by their parents and grandparents almost impossible to achieve.

Disenchantment means less young people than older people take the trouble to vote, but when they do their votes are less likely to transform into parliamentary seats, rather increase the majorities of many MPs in heavily populated city wards. Allowing a whole generation of disaffected young people to in effect become disenfranchised is a serious failure and could well lead to social unrest and even violence in our cities. Neither recent nor present national Governments have any incentive to change this situation. Local politicians are, on the other hand, more likely to respond sympathetically and intelligently to such situations by dealing with root causes.

As a result, many people now believe that change will only be achieved by devolving power from what is essentially an over-centralised state whose structure and attitudes have changed little since the days of Empire, to a more federal structure for the United Kingdom including the English Regions. Such Regional structures might better reflect the very different needs and wishes of their constituent communities, in what are very different parts of the nation.

But national Governments of whatever political colour, will not easily concede power even though, as countless examples from many parts of the world testify, decision making in many aspects of life is most successful and relevant when taken at local and regional level by the people who are directly affected by those decisions. There is still and always will be, a role for the central state in key areas such as taxation, defence, national (as opposed to local) travel infrastructure, international affairs and the wider environment. As the governance of many very successful countries in the world demonstrate, including most of our European mainland neighbours in Germany, Netherlands, Italy, France, Austria, Switzerland, Regional Government works in ways that are both more efficient and more sensitive to local cultures. Put simply they are more democratic.

This can only happen in England if there is strong support for such devolution of decision making from among people living within the English Regions themselves. It will also only happen if people of differing backgrounds and political views are united and prepared to work together and are prepared to bury differences within a greater cause to achieve mutual benefit and the greater good for all the people living within their Region.

For this to happen, there needs to be an awakening of a sense of local and regional identity and pride. This needs to reflect an understanding of what it is to be both Yorkshire and English in the early twenty first century.

It also needs a sense of history. England as a nation is itself a union of several individual Anglo-Saxon and Anglo-Norse kingdoms that didn't really fully unite as a single nation under successive Anglian and Danish kings until the tenth century, prior to the Norman Conquest.

One of those kingdoms was that part of Northern England between the Humber and the Tees we now call Yorkshire. This history is a part of our identity, both metaphorically and for many inhabitants, even part of our DNA.

So the purpose of this book is very simple. To explore what Yorkshire as a place actually is, physically, historically, and above all culturally.

First, we need to explore what we mean by identity.

Our identity, our sense of who we are, is an important, indeed an essential part of what makes up our individual and collective personality and psychology. Our self perception is a complex mixture of memories and recollections, often strongly mixed with a sense of place – where we came from or where we feel we belong.

At least in the days before the Internet took over our lives, many children around the ages of 7 or 8 played a game usually on the inside cover of an exercise book which involved identifying who they were and where they lived – Johnny or Jenny Smith, 3 Blankshire Terrace, Woodhurst village, Bradford, Yorkshire, England, United Kingdom, Europe, the World, the Solar System, The Universe. The important thing being that Johnny or Jenny's bedroom was of course the centre of the Universe.

But it is a game, whether consciously or not, we all still play. The centre of our personal Universe is often a place which is very special to us – either because it is where we live, where we grew up, spent time as a teenager, or where we first fell in love, had our first home, spent time on holiday.

The poet W.H.Auden – born in York – once memorably described such places as being:

> *"wherever your heart directs you most longingly to look – wherever you were as a child or had your first affair / There it stands amid your darling scenery"* **(The Summer Holds).**

The Germans have the word *Heimat*, which is difficult to translate – meaning on one superficial level "homeland". But *Heimat* means far more than that – somewhere you love, feel at home, feel you belong to, which is part of your soul.

The further you are away from that special place, the stronger that feeling, though for most people (to take the Yorkshire Dales example) that feeling may cover also the surrounding area such as along the length of an entire Yorkshire Dale or the Yorkshire Dales as a whole, widening out in a less intense form to the Yorkshire region.

It is a love of place that can and often is shared between family, friends and neighbours, a collective enthusiasm for that special space, so valued and treasured. It will include an area's distinctive landscape, its flora and fauna, its architectural features both vernacular and grand, but also its history – its archaeology, its older and more recent history, but also the lives of the people who lived or came to the area, wrote about it, painted, photographed it, or used it as a setting for a book or a film. It can be therefore described as a kind of patriotism – so well defined (*Wikipedia 2021*) as

> *"a feeling of love, devotion, and sense of attachment to a homeland and alliance with other citizens who share the same sentiment. This attachment can be a combination of many different feelings relating to one's own homeland, including ethnic, cultural, political or historical aspects".*[3]

In so many ways such feelings are therefore both engendered and encouraged by creative people who do just that – the artists, poets, writers, topographers, journalists, photographers who share their sentiments by shaping our understanding of an area and our response to its special qualities. We see it through their eyes, even without being fully aware of it. But equally important are the scientists – geologists, palaeontologists, botanists, archaeologists, amateur and professional, who have over generations interpreted and explained the area we know and love to local communities and visitors alike.

To some extent this process of communication and education is something now undertaken by educational institutions, primary and secondary schools, and universities. But throughout Yorkshire in particular there is a long and continuing tradition of voluntary organisations, including local naturalists or civic societies, U3As, and even walking groups, who through regular outdoor visits, field trips and talks have stimulated and shared research into exactly what makes their area and local environment special.

This process of awareness raising includes explaining how local experience and historical processes relate to the wider regional, national and even international story, whether this is about local flora and fauna, monastic settlement, political and religious struggles, the growth of the wool industry – or the impacts of climate change on the landscape. This educational activity also includes the many museums and galleries within a given area or region of Yorkshire. Their professional and voluntary curators have selected, conserved and interpreted their area's archaeological and cultural heritage including local or industrial history in many different ways.

The purpose of this book is to explore this theme of belonging to one part of England where a sense of regional identity is particularly strong – Yorkshire. This is not to say that it is better or stronger than in other parts of England. Yorkshire just happens to be the region I know best and feel most qualified to write about.

But it is also about looking to the future. What will be the role of what could and should be a strong and vibrant Region of England, within the British Isles and even in Europe (which inescapably we are part of) in the difficult and perilous years of the mid twenty first century?

So I want to start by looking at an inevitably over-simplified history of Yorkshire as it emerged from the conflicts and contradictions of the early Middle Ages, for a time an independent state before merging with the new unified nation of England. This continues with an examination of how Yorkshire's identity changed, yet survived, through the turbulent years of Norman Conquest, Plantagenet and Tudor and Stuart Kings, to the time when it became part of the one of the world's first industrial nations during the four centuries or so of the British Empire. Finally how the Region has an opportunity to find a new identity as the certainties of what constitutes the United Kingdom of Great Britain and Northern Ireland shift.

Yet to understand the present, and shape the future, we need to understand our past – this is as true for nations and regions as it is for individuals. Just who are we as a people and how does the culture in which we live determine our values?

Such considerations must inevitably influence the current debate for the Devolution of certain powers and responsibilities within a transforming United Kingdom, changes that have happened to some significant degree for three of the four constituent countries. Such changes are still notably absent within the English Regions. In fact, over the last decade, they have been put into reverse with the abolition of eight of the nine English Regions as administrative units – London hardly surprisingly, being the sole survivor.

But as I shall argue, to be effective such change has to come from the grass roots, from individuals and communities, and not be something imposed by politicians with their own limited agendas – as the muddle and contradiction of local Government changes over the last half century in Yorkshire have revealed all too clearly.

Real change therefore comes from building on that powerful sense of localism, a pride in a community's shared values, a process that moves outwards from neighbourhood to district, from district to region, from region to nation.

Such an individual and community awareness may not respect or respond to often arbitrary, and clumsily drawn, local government boundaries, lines on a map, but are more like to follow more complex, more difficult to define, cultural areas or sub-regions, which may often overlap or have subtle cross currents. Yorkshire is large and populous enough to be a free-standing nation. Yet it can only be fully understood as a geographical and cultural entity by recognising what are its nine very different sub-regional **cultural landscapes**, separated by their contrasting geology, geomorphology and human settlement, and ever-changing cultural activities.

However, these nine varied, contrasting and distinctive cultural landscapes, considered in greater depth in the second part of this book, still share a common, powerful unifying identity, symbolised, I suggest, by the simple mechanism of a Yorkshire emblem contained within a Yorkshire flag.

These are themes to be explored in the next two chapters.

Notes

1 https://ec.europa.eu/growth/tools-databases/regional-innovation-monitor/ base-profile/yorkshire-and-humber
2 Self Alex 2021 *De-Generation: How the age divide is tearing society – and politics – apart* Prospect magazine, May 2021 pp30–34
3 https: wikipedia.org/wiki/Patriotism

2

Yorkshire: A Nation within a Nation

To understand why Yorkshire is a region of England with such a special and strong cultural identity, it is important to understand a little of the tumultuous history of early medieval England.

After the ending of the Roman occupation of the island of Great Britain in the early 5th century, in the eastern part of Northern England we now recognise as Yorkshire, several Romano-Celtic tribal kingdoms survived in the former Roman colony of Britannia. These included the Brigantes in the Pennines and Vale of York, the lands of the Parisi around the Yorkshire Wolds and the kingdom of Elmet in the Aire valley, which with its smaller dependency Loidis, continued in existence well into the 7th century.

By this time successive waves of Germanic tribes were occupying and settling the eastern side of England. These primarily were Angles from the narrow neck of land between the North and the Baltic Sea, south of Denmark, an area that includes what is now the Region or "Land" known as Schleswig Holstein in northern Germany. They settled in a huge area of north east England, north of the Humber, eventually creating their own Kingdom between the Humber and the Tees known as Deira. Its capital was established in the old Roman provincial capital and garrison of Eboracum, at the highest navigable point of the River Ouse, at its confluence with the little River Foss. Eboracum was renamed by the Saxons as Eorforwic. North of the Tees, as far as the borderlands occupied by Scottish Pictish tribes, was another Anglian kingdom, Bernicia, its capital at Bamburgh on the coast where a mighty defensive castle was later constructed.

These new Anglian settlers brought with them their own version of the old Teutonic languages, a West Germanic language we now recognise as Anglo-Saxon or Old English – the root of modern English, and one shared with that of the Saxon invaders occupying the southern part of the island.

Deira and Bernicia were eventually united within one larger Anglo-Saxon kingdom – Northumbria, stretching from the Humber to the much disputed and constantly shifting Scottish border north of the Tweed. King Edwin, the first Christian ruler of Northumbria, was baptised in 627AD, in a little wooden church dedicated to St Peter in Eorforwic. This church was eventually rebuilt in stone to become York Minster.

But it was later invasions, primarily of Norse-speaking Viking warrior-sailors and merchants, that were to create what was initially a colony and finally an independent kingdom in what is now modern Yorkshire. The Great Heathen Viking Army of 866, consisting of several thousand warriors, primarily from what is now Denmark, invaded eastern "Aengle-land" reaching and capturing Eorforwic in 867 and establishing, no doubt with their followers and relatives, the town and inland port on the confluence of the Ouse and Foss as their main regional capital, now renamed Jorvik. Jorvik was a term used both for the city itself and for the wider province, largely covering the former Anglian kingdom of Deira, extending from the Humber to the Tees and from the coast to the high Pennines in the west; much of the land in the less fertile uplands of western Dales was settled in later years by mainly Norwegian Viking invaders from their established colonies in Dublin and on the Isle of Man.

Though the kingship of Jorvik varied between Danish and Anglian monarchs, until the last independent monarch, the tyrannical adventurer Eric Bloodaxe was assassinated in 954, Jorvik prospered as major Viking port and international trading centre.

After the death of Bloodaxe, peace treaties with the predominantly Saxon Kingdoms of Wessex and Mercia finally brought England together as a single United Kingdom, though the North of England always retained its distinctive Anglo-Norse identity.

This is evidenced by the wealth of Norse place names, predominantly Old Danish in origin to the east, but of Norwegian to the west. This was a result of centuries of constant settlement, intermarriage and trading activity by Anglo-Norse immigrants prior to the Norman Conquest.

Even to the present day, Yorkshire dialect reflects a rich heritage of words and phrases of Norse origin, many but not all of which have passed into mainstream modern English.

Crucially it was during the early Viking period that the Kingdom of Jorvik was divided into the three great "thrithings" – old Danish for "thirds" – later anglicised to "Thridings" then to "Ridings" – East Riding, West Riding and North Riding. The Three Ridings remained in existence as administrative divisions of the ancient kingdom for over a thousand years, until abolished by the less than entirely successful local Government reforms of 1974. To a significant extent, historic Yorkshire also reflected a region that was remarkably well defined by its great natural physical features – the coast to the east, the Pennines to the west, the Humber and its headland marshes and tributaries to the south and the Tees to the north.

The three ancient Ridings were only later given the Norman title of "counties". York, the capital, and for many year's England's second city – plus the Wapentake of Ainsty – remained an ancient borough outside the county jurisdictions. Though Yorkshire in popular and even scholarly parlance is still often described as a "county", it is strictly not correct to describe Yorkshire as a "County".

One useful definition of a county (Royal Historical Society) is:

> Counties are geographic entities whose origins reach back into the pre-Conquest period. They were derived either from Anglo-Saxon kingdoms whose size made them suitable administrative units when England was unified in the tenth century, or as artificial creations formed from larger kingdoms. The number of 'shires' (the Anglo-Saxon term) or 'counties' (Norman term) varied in the medieval period, particularly in the north of England.

Yorkshire's Three Ridings are a perfect example of just such "artificial creations formed from a larger kingdom", with the thriving Anglo-Viking port and city of Jorvik as the Kingdom's capital and administrative centre.

Local Government at that time existed primarily through a system of Norse "Wapentakes" which corresponded to the "Hundreds" of southern (Saxon) England and consisted of 100 "hides" of land – a hide traditionally corresponding to the amount of land sufficient to feed a family (and in later times four families).

Once a month each owner of a hide had to turn up to a gathering – literally taking their weapons as an act of loyalty – in what were simple courts, traditionally at an ancient oak tree (or Skyrack), a sort of primitive democracy to resolve disputes under common law, collect taxes and maintain order, if not quite carrying out the functions of local Government. The residue of this remained in the legal system of the names of courts and place names well into the 20th century, as a map of the Yorkshire Wapentakes dating from 1832 testifies.

It is interesting to note how close Jorvik came to remaining a Norwegian colony rather than a part of England. The battle of Stamford Bridge in East Riding – the last great victory of the Anglo-Saxons – took place in September 1066 when the Norwegian King Harald Hardrada tried to reclaim the Kingdom of Jorvik for the Norsemen. Hardrada was narrowly defeated by the King Harold Godwinson (Harold II) a few weeks before he and his army were in turn defeated by William the Conqueror at Hastings. Had the Stamford Bridge battle gone the other way, people in Yorkshire might all now be speaking a version of Old Norwegian.

William would have still invaded Kent when opportunity arose to claim the disputed English throne, and sooner or later would have been in armed conflict with the Norse colonisers.

Yet those 80 or so flourishing years of the independent Kingdom of Jorvik were hugely important in terms of the Kingdom becoming a major cultural and trading centre, for a time part of Danelaw – subject to the rule of Danish kings – which covered most of eastern England. This period had a massive influence on Yorkshire's subsequent history, no doubt reflecting the scale of Norse settlement and linguistic domination, a heritage which survives in terms of dialect and place names and in the genetic and cultural make-up of the local populations of Yorkshire to this day. At the end of this period York was England's second city, a pre-eminence which remains in ecclesiastical terms, with York's Archbishop being second only in authority to Canterbury. The name "Yorkshire" first appears in writing in the Anglo-Saxon Chronicle for the year 1065.

After Jorvik was absorbed into the rest of England and was ruled by successive Wessex and Danish Kings of England, each King appointed a local Jarl or Earl as his deputy. This continued into Norman times. By the 14th century this Earl was replaced by the Dukedom of York.

Massive changes were to occur to the region as a result of the Battle of Hastings and the imposition of martial law throughout England. William's close allies and relatives formed a quasi-military elite who were awarded huge areas of land in reward for their support for the new monarch. Periodical – and temporarily successful – rebellions against Norman rule, were brutally suppressed, most notably with the Harrying of the North during the winter of 1069–70, an act of genocide against Anglo-Viking communities in Jorvik and Northumbria. However, evidence is that most of the population of the former kingdom, impoverished and thrust off their land, survived and eventually prospered, albeit subservient to their Norman overlords. A network of massive heavily fortified castles was built in what were to become prosperous market towns to serve their military masters. Many, but by no means all, survive in Richmond, Scarborough, Skipton, Pontefract, Sandal, Conisbrough, Pickering, Helmsley, Middleham, and in the city of York itself.

The Norman Barons, who were given freedom by their monarch to suppress and totally control their local communities, soon became enormously powerful. This reached a point when the authority of later monarchs could be challenged. Indeed the 15th century Wars of the Roses were largely a series of inter-family feuds and power struggles, that had little to do with the actual counties of Lancaster or York, despite the subsequent adoption of the White Rose as the symbol of Yorkshire. Kingdoms of Anglo-Saxon England also had their earls, men of noble birth or rank, and local supporters of the King, who were also major landowners, and administrators of local justice. The Normans kept the term, but only for a third-tier ranking – below Dukes and Marquises and equating to a Count. A Duke could also be the son of a monarch. Of course, Yorkshire had and still has its single Duke of York – traditionally the second son of the monarch. But noteworthy he is called Duke of York as denotes the capital, not Yorkshire its hinterland.

Landowners or Lords of the Manors created during Norman times and continuing throughout the succeeding centuries, enjoyed an extraordinary degree of freedom and autonomy. Governments passed laws, raised taxes and armies, but most local Government law enforcement mechanisms to deal with law breaking or legal disputes were handled by local manorial courts.

The Normans brought with them their own language, Norman French, which for a couple of centuries was the language of the ruling elite. It was only gradually replaced by English, the language of the common people of England. But medieval English absorbed many hundreds of Norman French words and phrases from that culture as English has continued to do from other cultures over centuries. Likewise, the growth and success of the monasteries, encouraged by their Norman overloads, brought a highly sophisticated new economic as well as religious and educational system to the region. The great Benedictine, Cistercian, Augustinian and Premonstratian Abbeys, Nunneries and Priories laid the foundations, among many other things, for the Yorkshire wool industry. This was initially through the export of wool produced from the great sheep walks of the Pennines and Wolds to Flanders and Italy via the flourishing port of York, but in later centuries through the weaving of that wool into cloth and tailoring into garments.

But patterns of rural landowning, in terms of the great rural private estates established by the Normans, have survived with remarkably little change into the twenty first century.

Much of our experience and understanding of governance goes back to even earlier roots. Some of our basic laws and governance have pre-Norman origins. It is a well-known fact that the Normans (sensibly) took over many largely Anglo-Saxon legal structures and laws, adapting them to their own use and in most cases renaming them.

For example, the important unit of Norman local Government that still survives are our parishes – again based on the ancient Saxon and Norse townships or "tuns" or "burghs" but formalised by the Normans – hence the word Parish from old Norman French "parashe". These were initially the areas controlled by a local church and its priest, but over the centuries the secular aspects of the old ecclesiastical structures –whose ancient boundaries can still be traced on modern maps – have morphed into the civil parish structure we have today.

Parishes had a lot of powers, including the repair of highways and looking after the poor, but one reason for the setting up of independent turnpike trusts in the 18th century was to raise sufficient money for new road building to replace the appalling ill-maintained muddy tracks that were crippling the development of Britain. New turnpikes roads were the first major step in the Industrial Revolution.

The role of what became the three Counties or Ridings of Yorkshire was also primarily legal. From the time of Henry VIII Lord Lieutenants were appointed in each to represent the King and be responsible for organising the local militia. The Sherriff (literally "The Shire Reeve") was a legal officer appointed to represent the King and ensure the enforcement of Law and Order. From 1870s onwards these became largely purely ceremonial roles. Tellingly the fact that Yorkshire's three County Ridings each had a Lord Lieutenant and a High Sheriff is an indication of their full formal County status.

The ancient boroughs (burghs) of Yorkshire including York but also historic towns like Wakefield, Halifax, Dewsbury, Richmond, Ripon, Scarborough, Hull, Beverley, each had their own councils, mayors and powers and Parliamentary representation, but the new industrial cities that developed from the 18th century onwards were woefully underrepresented in Parliament until the 1832 Reform Act. The 1888 Local Government Act established the modern system of County Councils (including the three historic Yorkshire Ridings) and urban County Boroughs that by then included the relatively recently established major industrial cities of Leeds and Bradford. This structure survived until 1974. The implementation of the 1972 Local Government Act changed forever the Victorian system of County Councils, Rural and Urban District Councils and County Boroughs. What was removed in 1974 for good and for ill was a local Government system in Yorkshire which in many fundamental respects went back to the ancient Anglo-Norse Kingdom of Jorvik.

Yorkshire, with its extensive coastline, has also always looked east and outwards. Ports at Whitby, Scarborough, Bridlington, Selby, York, and above the eventually dominant port of Kingston-Upon-Hull, built on land purchased by King Edward 1 in 1293 from Meaux Abbey alongside the River Hull where larger vessels could be berthed for access to the Humber estuary, ensured constant trade and cultural exchange with mainland Europe. These links were most notably strong with the Baltic States, Prussia (now part of modern Germany) and the Netherlands. For many years Hull and York were both members of the Hansa League, a flourishing free trade association of North Sea ports, a pre-cursor of the EEC and EU.

Contrary to popular perception, the North Sea was not a barrier for travel and trade to Continental Europe, but the equivalent of a busy superhighway, bringing communities, ideas and trading partners from the east coast of England and the Continent closer together. Until the coming of the turnpike roads and railways in the 18th and 19th centuries, it was easier, quicker and cheaper for people and goods to travel by water, whether by river or sea, than by land. The Humber estuary and its river tributaries, particularly the Ouse to York, the Don to Doncaster, and the River Hull from Beverley, and the east coast ports, Whitby, Scarborough, Bridlington and in later years most prominently Kingston-upon-Hull, could trade far more quickly and conveniently with Hamburg, Amsterdam, Antwerp and the Baltic than with London. If London and southern ports looked towards France and southern Europe, Yorkshire looked towards Northern Europe – the Netherlands, Germany, Scandinavia and the Baltic. The wealth of York and Beverley was created by the massive export trade of wool and high-quality textiles to Flanders and beyond, whilst the Baltic iron and timber trade, as well as whaling and other forms of deep-sea fishing lay behind the success of Whitby and from the 14th century onwards, Hull.

It was common, for example, to import cheap but good quality Dutch pantiles as ballast to fill the empty holds of trading ships returning from the Netherlands and these have become a characteristic and defining feature of cottage roofs throughout East and North Riding coastal towns and well inland. Architectural styles, such as Dutch gables, continued even when it was cheaper to manufacture tiles locally. Dutch engineers, most notably Cornelius Vermuyden (1595–1677), changed the lowland landscape when they brought new methods of land drainage to claim marshland for agriculture.

From Tudor times onwards the lead mines of the Yorkshire Dales brought in skilled miners from Cornwall and from Derbyshire, with much of the lead exported via the river Ouse to York and Humber to London and beyond. But it was the growth of the new initially water, then steam-powered, textile mills, and the building of the canals and the railways from the late 18th century onwards, bringing unlimited cheap energy in the form of transported coal, that accelerated the continuous process of immigration from rural areas of Yorkshire into the rapidly expanding towns and cities of the West Riding. The rapid growth of coal mining, steel production and heavy industry to serve a growing

Empire also meant attracting tens of thousands of new workers to build the canals and the railways, hew coal from the new deep mines and man the forges and the looms. Irish immigrants in particular provided much of the vital labour force required for the Industrial Revolution.

By the late 19th century, improved communications led to the beginnings of mass migration. Hull became the crucial entry port for many thousands of refugees from central and eastern Europe fleeing from poverty, starvation and frequent pogroms.

Most were using Yorkshire as a land bridge, heading for Liverpool Docks by train and a passage to the New World. Others chose to stay and fill labour shortages in England or bring new skills to exploit new trading opportunities. Leeds, for example, benefited from many East European Jewish communities who were to lay the foundations of the city's great tailoring and clothing industries, and in later generations came to form the core of the city's intellectual elite. A whole area of central Bradford warehousing became known as Little Germany.

In 1909, Fritz Bützner, a penniless young Swiss baker arrived in Bradford to seek work at a local confectioners. By 1919 he was able to set up his own elegant tea shop in Harrogate to which he gave an English name Betty's. This is now a great Yorkshire institution with branches in Harrogate, Northallerton, York and Ilkley.

In the post-war years of the 20th century, significant numbers of immigrants from the former British colonies were to provide the low-cost labour Britain desperately needed for its industrial recovery, initially from the Caribbean and later from South Asia. The Bradford, Dewsbury and Huddersfield Worsted and Wool mills in particular suffered from major labour shortages in the 1950s and 60s which immigrants from India, Pakistan and Bangladesh in particular were able to resolve. In this way these South Asian immigrants were able to make a major contribution to the region's economy and help bring about Yorkshire's urgently needed post-war economic revival.

In the latter part of the 20th and early 21st century migrant workers from eastern Europe countries within the EU were again providing essential labour, for example for agriculture and the hospitality and care industries, working long hours of physically demanding work in the fields, in care homes or hotels that few English-born people were able or prepared to tackle.

It is also worth noting that according to the 2011 census 44% of NHS staff in the UK were of BAME (Black and Minority Ethnic) origin – possibly an even higher percentage within Yorkshire.

But this new cultural diversity has added to, not diluted Yorkshire identity. The parallel might be to regard human occupation and settlement of Yorkshire as a great river. The different sources of the river from moorland streams – be they Celtic, Anglian, Viking, with their languages and customs – combine to form the main river. Over centuries other tributary streams have joined and enriched but not altered the core character of that main river. Yorkshire remains, fundamentally, culturally the province of those early Anglo-Viking settlers. We share, to this very day, close cultural links, as well as our DNA, with our European cousins particularly in northern Europe – with German, Danish, Swedish, Norwegian, and Dutch communities who share so many common values and attitudes and a common ancestry. Several hundred of the most common words in English, such as man, bread, butter, house, stone, water, most especially in Yorkshire dialect (kirk, beck), are similar to those used by modern Germans and Scandinavians. People in Friesia, a cross boundary Region of northern Netherlands and northwest German islands and mainland, still speak a local language or dialect which is remarkably close to modern English. It is all part of our common European heritage.

More recent immigrants have added new vibrant elements, not just in terms of cuisine, to our culture, but an important new dual identity opportunity and cross-fertilisation of ideas through being proudly of Yorkshire-Asian or Yorkshire-Caribbean heritage. There are huge numbers of words in the English language of Indian origin, reflecting the many close political and cultural contacts in the days of Empire reinforced by links of trade and by recent immigration.

Identity, as we have suggested, is both a personal issue and about the place where you feel you belong. It is not just a matter of birth and ancestry. For recent immigrants from other parts of Europe, Asia or Africa, every bit as much as those of parents, grandparents or great grandparents who first came to the welcoming towns or cities of Yorkshire, combining their ancestral culture with that of the place that is now their homeland, especially when intertwined with faith, that dual identity is a source of enrichment and strength. You can be

Jewish Yorkshire, Irish Yorkshire, Afro-Yorkshire, Muslim Yorkshire, Hindu Yorkshire, Sikh Yorkshire and draw huge strength from your dual identity.

Take one lovely recent example. Gurcharan Jagdev arrived at the port of Tilbury in England with his mother and sister in 1956 and travelled by train to join his father in Bradford. The family prospered and soon moved to a street in a suburb of the city in which they were the only Indian family. When playmates invited him to come along to their local Sunday school, though his family were Sikhs, he was given permission by his parents to attend. But far from seeing Christianity as a threat to Sikh beliefs, he saw many parallels with the two faiths. In later years when he became a father and grandfather, Gurcharan, a true adopted Yorkshireman, fell in love with the Yorkshire Dales. Once their family owned a car, they were frequent visitors to Knaresborough, Malham and Bolton Abbey.

As he writes:

> My favourite and perhaps most visited place in the Dales is Bolton Abbey. As well as a place of open spaces, flowing water and fresh air, the Abbey is a place where I can find peace and tranquillity and also offer a quiet prayer in another place that is as important to me as a Gurdwara.

The archetypical Yorkshireman or Yorkshirewoman is popularly deemed to be someone who is reliable, hard-working, stoical, honest, shrewd, slow speaking with a recognised accent. Silences between sentences can be as full of meaning as words used; but at times Yorkshire people can seem blunt, direct, obstinate and slow to change traditional ways of thinking. They also have a dry sense of humour, a sharp wit, based on experience, that can quickly deflate all that is over-blown and pretentious. In his novel **Good Companions** J. B. Priestley's hero Jess Oakroyd from "Bruddersford" embodies exactly these traits.

This is a cliché perhaps, and maybe less applicable to the majority of present-day Yorkshire people, especially younger people and those from different minority ethnic backgrounds who may have very different characteristics, including speech. But enough of the stereotype remains to distinguish slow talking, sometimes even dour Yorkshire people from their faster talking Lancastrian neighbours, or people from faraway places such as London or Wales.

However, language, and how people use it, remains an important distinguishing feature of a nation. Unlike Wales, Ireland or Scotland, Yorkshire does not of course have its own language. But it does have its own distinctive dialect.

Dialect differs from accent purely in degree. A Yorkshire accent has long been associated with some very positive qualities – honesty, reliability, wisdom, maturity. Since the early days of broadcasting, voices like J. B. Priestley and Wilfred Pickles have been used for their strongly reassuring qualities, and this has continued into the age of television with well-known voices of people such as Michael Parkinson, Geoffrey Boycott, former House of Commons Speaker Betty Boothroyd from Dewsbury, Sheffield's Roy Hattersley, Leeds-born playwright Alan Bennett or TV Countryfile's John Craven. A wonderful recent example of a Yorkshireman who has captured the nation's heart with plain speaking is the late Captain Sir Tom Moore from Keighley.

A dialect however has significant numbers of words and grammatical structures, some archaic, some belonging purely to a particular region or occupation, that will not be familiar to standard English speakers or someone from another region of the UK. It will also have its own intonation, grammatical variations and patterns of speech, which can easily become unintelligible to outsiders. Written down it can require footnotes or even a dictionary to make it intelligible to outsiders. Someone who speaks a very strong Yorkshire dialect is deemed to be speaking "Broad Yorkshire."

Dialect is also the language of the common people and generally for this reason has been ignored by national commentators as somehow being low class or vulgar. This exception to this narrow perception is when it has produced, in the case of Robert Burns, a poet of genius, whose Lowland Scots is revered throughout the world. His poem "Auld Lang Syne" is sung by English speaking people worldwide, every New Year, even though most have no idea what these words mean, though the emotion communicates powerfully enough.

Yorkshire Dialect, with its deep Anglo-Norse roots, flourished right through into the twenty first century, especially in more isolated parts of the region, among older speakers and in less affluent older industrial areas where the population is less mobile. It also varies between different parts of the region.

There are different varieties of Yorkshire Dialect – East Riding, Cleveland (essentially north-east Yorkshire), West Riding and North Riding, the division (as evidenced by pronunciation and some key identification words such as that for a barn, such as "shippon", "cow-house" "laithe". Even indeed within individual cities local patois develop – Leeds speakers can easily be distinguished from Bradford (the words for an alleyway – "ginnel" and "snicket" – have slightly different meanings in the two cities). Locals can easily distinguish the difference between natives of Halifax and Huddersfield or between Sheffield and Barnsley. A local bus company created outrage when announcements on buses in Airedale were made by a speaker from Barnsley.

Dialect enjoyed a great flowering of intellectual interest in the early 19th century with the growth of both romanticism and nationalism, as the language of the people, with the publication not only of collections of poetry but what were known as "Almanacs" – miscellanies of prose and poetry celebrating this traditional form of speech combined with local history, wit and wisdom.

The **Yorkshire Dialect Society**, established in 1897, with the support of some leading academics from Leeds and other Universities, and Society members such as Frederick Moorman, Joseph Wright, Harold Orton, Stanley Ellis, and Arnold Kellett has done much to preserve and celebrate this vibrant subculture. The Society arranges regular meetings of speakers and publishes annual Transactions, including much original work by dialect writers, many of them (unlike the earlier dialect speakers) well educated standard English speakers who are also bi-lingual. Despite its pioneering Survey of English Dialects undertaken in the 1950s, dialect studies are no longer a part of mainstream English language teaching at Leeds University. However the University's new Dialect and Heritage Project is currently updating the Survey and linking it to a study of present day vernacular culture. In 2019 the Borthwick Institute at the University of York published a new dictionary of older dialect words and phrases, the **Yorkshire Historic Dictionary**, based on work by the late Dr George Redmond and edited by Alexandra Medcalf. Several new research projects are also under way via the YDS and other academic institutions to record current dialect and socio-linguistic trends. The outcomes of this research will be awaited with interest.

As Professor Moorman claimed in the Preface to his influential 1916 anthology of **Yorkshire Dialect Poems** "in volume and variety the dialect poetry of Yorkshire surpasses that of all other English counties"[1] and indeed more has been recorded and collected from earlier times than in most other areas, from as far back as the 17th century. This was followed by the equally fine anthology of 1949 **White Rose Garland**[2] collected by Wilfrid Halliday and Stanley Umpleby.

As has so often been predicted, will Yorkshire dialect die out in the twenty first century with the advent of the internet, social media and increasing, all-pervasive trans-Atlantic influences? Why bother to preserve or even revive what might be considered to be anachronistic and doomed?

There are several reasons for doing so. Recording dialect and even teaching it to new generations has exactly the same justification as preserving the Welsh or Gaelic tongues which now flourish, or even Cornish, now being revived. They are the languages, the collective memory of a people. Yorkshire Dialect also has a unique strength not easily recreated in standard English, an ability to convey humour and tenderness in a remarkable way. Unlike most other European languages, English has lost its second person singular, the more intimate "tu" or "du" form, the "thee" and "thou" so familiar from the King James Authorised translation of the Bible. This was a pronoun you use for your children, your inferiors, but also your close friends and family. It survives in modern Yorkshire dialect and you'll still hear it used, albeit in snatches, in parts of both rural and urban Yorkshire – usually among men in informal gatherings like a football match, at work or in the pub, and at least until recently in school playgrounds in Dales villages.

Dialect can express moods and emotions in a vivid, compressed and powerful way. And there are no standard English words which can convey so effectively the meaning of words like "nithering", "fettle" or "thoile".

The hugely successful Ken Loach film **Kes**, set in a South Yorkshire mining community, gained enormously from several bits of dialect slipped into the script, even though it then required subtitles in the USA and other parts of the (standard) English-speaking world.

Sadly, these often prolific dialect speakers and writers never included a poet or novelist of stature to equal Burns, nor even in more recent times Hugh MacDiarmid.

There is one undoubtedly great anonymous Yorkshire dialect poem that is, along with **Dream of the Rood** and **Gawain and the Green Knight** a masterpiece of English medieval literature – the **Cleveland Lyke Wake Dirge**, a ceremonial poem first recorded in the 17th century but probably dating back to the 14th century or even earlier, with images that are both pre-Reformation and Pagan. Its hauntingly beautiful setting by Benjamin Britten as part of his **Serenade for Tenor, Horn and Orchestra** has brought this great piece of Yorkshire dialect poetry to international audiences.

However, many very fine Yorkshire writers over the last two centuries have chosen to use Yorkshire dialect as their prime means of expression. These include such figures as John Hartley, Ben Preston, Tom Twistleton, Tommy Blackah, William Wright (Bill o'th Hoylus End), John Thwaite and in more recent times Fred Brown, Stanley Umpleby, Bill Cowley, John Castillo, Dorothy Unna Ratcliffe and Ian Dewhirst, and many others whose work deserves to be better known.

Isn't it time perhaps that these Yorkshire authors and their work and dialect, a rich variety of English, should be taught with other aspects of English language in our Yorkshire schools, rather than the rote learning of irrelevant anachronistic Latin-based so-called grammar, from Victorian ideas of English teaching, disinterred from the distant memories of politicians' public schools?

Frederick Moorman even suggested there should be an annual "Yorkshire Eisteddfod" to celebrate the region's unique literary and linguistic heritage. Music would be a part of this. Another dimension to the whole issue of Yorkshire dialect is the remarkable survival of so many fine popular folk songs written to traditional tunes, usually played on the fiddle or accordion. This heritage is wider and deeper than the widely recognised part-dialect but part ironic, unofficial national anthem of Yorkshire, **Ilkley Moor Baht 'At** – which also has a distinguished history of its own skilfully told by Arnold Kellett[3].

Though no longer enjoying the wide popularity of the 1960s, a time when the legendary Hull-based family group The Watersons enjoyed national acclaim, Yorkshire folk music survives through regular gatherings and festivals throughout the region, from Hull to

Cleveland, and as far west as Ingleton and Saddleworth, with new generations constantly adding to this rich heritage. One particular group of Yorkshire folk music performers, recorders and collectors, the **Yorkshire Garland** have put together a huge audio album, freely available on-line to the public, of recordings going back to the 1950s of original singers from different parts of Yorkshire available on their website (www.yorkshirefolksong.net.). Many of the songs are powerful social documents in their own right, even protest songs, reflecting the hardship of the singers' lives and pressure for change going back well into the 19th century. The collection represents a priceless source of oral social history and inspiration for later generations.

To a significant extent in the modern world, sporting activity also plays a key role in regional identity. This is especially true in Yorkshire. It has been pointed out that if Yorkshire had been an independent sovereign state in the 2016 Rio Olympics, it would have ranked 17th in the world[4], in terms of the all-important medal tables. Gifted and successful athletes such as Jessica Ennis Hill, Nicola Adams, the Brownlee Brothers, and Ed Clancy are heroes of Yorkshire as well as national heroes.

Cricket in Yorkshire also has a symbolic force way above its participation levels among players or spectators. Yorkshire County Cricket Club has, more than any other in England created a sense of identity to unite three counties of Yorkshire into what has been usually assumed to be a single "county"[5]. Headingly Cricket Club is for many cricketing aficionados, a sporting shrine, reverentially recalling the long history of supremely gifted Yorkshire batsmen over several generations, legendary figures such as Herbert Sutcliffe, Len Hutton, Geoffrey Boycott and captain of England Joe Root. Where else in England but in Yorkshire is there a life size sculpture of a great fast bowler – Fred Trueman, now immortalised, in bronze, in action, on the canalside wharfe in Skipton?

Soccer, perhaps supremely, has created its own powerful tribal loyalties. After all Sheffield Football Club the first such club in the world, was founded in 1855. This loyalty is especially true in towns or cities with their clubs in higher divisions of the Football League – Sheffield United and Wednesday, Leeds United, Huddersfield Town, Rotherham United and Barnsley – whose nickname The Tykes is carried with pride. But even those clubs not touching the top flights such as York City, Bradford City, Hull City, Doncaster Rovers, and Harrogate Town have their devoted fans. The wearing of the scarf, the shirt, the logo is an affirmation of that loyalty, a loyalty that most politicians would die for. To some extent this is replicated in both Rugby Union but most especially in the more northern-based Rugby League, including the Super League.

There is every hope that this success and involvement will also extend to the womens' game in both modes.

But many of the top teams now belong to their local communities in name only. Soccer in particular has become very big business. Football clubs in the Premier and Championship Leagues are highly commercial financial institutions able to survive only by buying top players at astronomic prices. They are often owned by very rich and powerful American, Russian or Arabs oligarchs, over whom the local fans have no control. Managers are hired and fired at whim and survive only as long as the team is winning. Football clubs are now increasingly becoming "products" sold to "customer" fans, and divorced from their original communities and locations.

This business model contrasts with the German equivalent, the Bundesliga, where with only a few exceptions, the major clubs are still controlled by their local supporters. Ultimately highly commercialised sport can do little to support personal identity and, vitally, our sense of place.

The other defining aspect of a nation and a province is food. Yorkshire is rightly establishing itself as one of the places in which to both live and visit for the fine quality of its locally produced food, with towns like Malton, self-proclaimed Yorkshire food capital, and Leyburn and many other centres of excellence, many with outstanding restaurants, food markets and artisan bakeries.

What are Yorkshire's signature food products? Yorkshire Pudding, which used to be a simple cheap meal to fill empty bellies as a substitute for meat, has been taken over by the world usually accompanied by roast beef, as has York Ham, often spelt in peculiar ways. Havercake – oat cake – once produced in every farmhouse kitchen as simple, basic fare, still thrives as popular form of sustenance in Scotland but is no longer typical of Yorkshire. But an interesting variant, devised in the 19th century in and around industrial Leeds, is created by adding black treacle to the mix, and known as Parkin, most certainly is. It remains very distinctively Yorkshire, and a wonderful delicacy in the dark winter months.

Cheese, in particular Wensleydale Cheese rescued so heroically by Kit Calvert in the 1930s and the people of Hawes in the 1980s, is now a part of the Yorkshire brand, reflecting its great dairy tradition. But there are other locally produced farmhouse cheeses from the Yorkshire Dales in particular, that deserve to be far better known and enjoyed – Blue Wensleydale, Coverdale, Swaledale, Ribblesdale and several fine goat cheeses. Yorkshire lamb, including the celebrated Barnsley Chop, has long enjoyed a fine reputation as has Yorkshire beef, though Whitby Scampi, a ubiquitous listing on pub menus, may well have originated somewhere a little further east than the cold North Sea.

And finally beer. Beer in the sense of real ale isn't specially Yorkshire, and even the once ubiquitous Tetley's Bitter that once defined a man from Leeds has long disappeared. Great beers, it has to be conceded, also come from other parts of England, Scotland and Wales. But beers also define a nation and a region.

The best known, nationally famous Yorkshire brand is Timothy Taylor's of Keighley, whose classic Landlord is regarded as one of the great beers of Britain, followed by national award winning Boltmakers, but not to be forgotten is that rare Pennine pale mild known as Golden Best. But Yorkshire is now rather like Bavaria, the German state in which almost every small town seems to have its own monastery and attached small brewery. Yorkshire may lack the monasteries but has the wonderful network of local breweries, all encouraged by Gordon Brown's change to beer taxes to encourage small back lane breweries, which in some cases have prospered mightily, each with their own distinctive flavour and taste. They include such favourite local small breweries as those in York, Settle, Dent, Ilkley, Wharfedale, Ossett, Barnsley, Bradford, Newton on the Wold (Wold Top), Hull, Sheffield (Abbeydale, Kelham Island) Leeds (Leeds Brewery, Kirkstall Brewery), Theakston (Masham) Naylor's (Cross Hills), Bingley, Todmorden (Little Valley), Askrigg, Yorkshire Dales (Bellerby) Cropton, Helmsley, Bradfield (Sheffield), Whitby and many more besides. And say it quietly, there is now even a flourishing Yorkshire wine industry.

Yorkshire even has its own national newspaper – **The Yorkshire Post**. Founded in 1754 by Griffith Knight as a successful four-page weekly newssheet known as the Leeds Intelligencer, in 1866 it was taken over by a group of Conservative supporters, and republished as a daily paper they named as The Yorkshire Post.

The Yorkshire Post continues to flourish as a traditional, conservative-leaning daily newspaper offering high quality journalism and coverage of national and regional events but keeps a very strong sense of commitment to the region, celebrating and championing Yorkshire in every possible aspect of its work.

A far more recent product of the digital age is **Yorkshire Bylines** (yorkshirebylines.co.uk.). This is a digital newspaper producing news articles and blogs by voluntary contributors again with a strong Yorkshire slant. It is an initiative of March for Change, a campaign group whose prime aim is "Citizen empowerment in the political issues of the Day."

There are now two key voluntary organisations who are also championing Yorkshire's distinctive and regional special culture. The first, based at York St John University, is **PLACE Yorkshire**, the acronym standing for People, Landscape, Culture and Environment of Yorkshire. PLACE, an educational charity, works to achieve a greater recognition and understanding of Yorkshire's distinctive landscape and culture through a variety of activities – lectures, research, publications and site visits for its members.

The Yorkshire Society established in 1980, is a not-for-profit body. Its mission is to be a champion for all good things Yorkshire. It has a wide, non-party political remit "to bring the people of Yorkshire together for business and pleasure"

It works to support the social, environmental and economic aspects of Yorkshire as a semi-autonomous region within the United Kingdom. It does so by working with local authorities, civic leaders, and other voluntary bodies and agencies to celebrate the special and distinctive quality of the region. This includes organising annual Yorkshire Day events every August 1st, with a different town or city within Yorkshire acting as host each year for annual festivities. In addition, the Society organises annual Yorkshire Awards that recognise outstanding contri-butions that individuals have made to the life of Yorkshire, places Blue Plaques on buildings associated with such individuals historically, and initiates fund raising events to support local and regional good causes.

Welcome to Yorkshire is the region's commercial tourist agency, supported by the local authorities and the tourism industry, that works to promote the region as a visitor destination on the national and world stage. W2Y also sponsors the hugely popular annual **Tour de Yorkshire** cycle race, watched on television screens throughout the world. It also promotes, in various ways, the region's rich and complex landscape and cultural heritage.

How do we define that cultural heritage?

In his seminal book **Yorkshire – a Lyrical History of England's Greatest County**, Professor Richard Morris provides a scholarly and entertaining account of how Yorkshire has emerged as perhaps England's most remarkable cultural province. In pursuing several different themes of "Yorkshireness", Morris divides the historic county into four sub-regions – York & Ainsty, the North, the East and the West. Themes in each individual area are explored in fascinating detail.

But the factors that create the differences between these subdivisions, geology, landscape, natural and human history and local culture, that also create such immediately recognised, identifiable more local cultural landscapes, are not explored to the same extent.

Most peoples' understanding and love of Yorkshire are actually triggered by a recognition not of the whole complex Region that is historic Yorkshire, but their knowledge and awareness of one or more of what are in fact nine contrasting subregions – the nine **Cultural Landscapes of Yorkshire**. These differ from each other, in some cases dramatically, in geological, landscape, social and industrial history and therefore cultural terms. But they all share a common, over-riding strong identity as part of Yorkshire.

Each is an essential part of "being Yorkshire". All have strongly identifiable names; some like York, the Yorkshire Dales, the North York Moors, are known nationally and internationally. Most have been the home of some remarkable personalities who have changed English history or have been celebrated by nationally known writers, artists and dramatists.

This variety and unity are all part of what should be recognised by its communities, its politicians and ultimately our national Government and legislators, as the Cultural Province of Yorkshire.

Notes

1 Moorman F.W. (ed.) 1916: *Yorkshire Dialect Poems* ppxix Sidgwick & Jackson London
2 Halliday W.J. and Umpleby A.S. (ed.) 1949 *White Rose Garland* Dent
3 Kellett Arnold 1998: *On Ilka Mooar Baht 'At* Smith Settle Ilkley
4 Yorkshire Post 22nd August 2016
5 Morris Richard 2018: *A Lyrical History of England's Greatest County* p26 Weidenfeld & Nicholson London

3

Steps towards a Cultural Province
of Yorkshire

So where does all this leave Yorkshire today? With further changes to the structure of local Government in Yorkshire now under way, what possible relevance, if any, has the historic former kingdom of Jorvik and its Three Ridings for its 21st century inhabitants and for the Region's future governance?

In his important book on Yorkshire identity, **The Fight for Yorkshire**[1] the writer and academic Michael Bradford outlines the sense of anger and loss which occurred when in 1974, the historic three counties of Yorkshire were effectively abolished. In the minds of many people these changes were as much about politics as administrative logic. The mighty West Riding, long celebrated for its far sighted and efficient County Council, was effectively carved into three. In the south, the old industrial heartlands of the Yorkshire coalfields and steel mills, dominated by Sheffield, became South Yorkshire Metropolitan Council; the area noted for wool, the clothing industry, heavy engineering and financial services dominated by Leeds became West Yorkshire Metropolitan Council. But the rest of rural West Riding, including the Yorkshire Dales and most of the deeply rural North Riding, were thrust into a new, amorphous two tier (County & Districts) County of North Yorkshire, administered from the small market town of Northallerton in the Vale of Mowbray. So tightly were the boundaries drawn that some of the suburbs of the towns of Ilkley, Otley and Wetherby in Wharfedale were sliced off for planning and administrative purposes, even including dustbin collections, into the Harrogate District of North Yorkshire. The western parishes of the old West Riding in the South

Pennines, Forest of Bowland and Yorkshire Dales were handed without due ceremony to the new counties of Greater Manchester, Lancashire or Cumbria.

The north Cleveland part of the old North Riding including such North Riding towns as Guisborough and Middlesbrough (but mercifully not Whitby after vigorous local protest) was duly handed over in 1974 to a new unitary authority, Cleveland County Council. Cleveland didn't last long. In 1996 it was abolished and the former once proud towns and villages of the North Riding of Yorkshire south of the Tees, Yorkshire's historic northern boundary, are now subdivided within three separate unitary authorities: Middlesbrough, Redcar & Cleveland and Stockton. Little wonder that many people living in these areas must sometimes feel seriously disorientated and perhaps wish they still lived in Yorkshire.

East Riding was served equally badly, thrust unwillingly into a new Unitary Authority known as Humberside, which was divided into North Humberside and south of the river, South Humberside.

These changes were achieved with little or no consultation and actually contradicted much of the Government's own Redcliffe-Maud Report 1969 which was totally set aside by the Local Government Act of 1972. In some cases, they made sense but in other cases they were absurd and caused significant upset. Postcodes are, in fact, a useful, if not infallible, clue to genuine lines of communication and affiliation, as are local newspapers.

The 1974 changes had a prime result – the breaking of the historic bonds between urban and rural parts of Yorkshire, so that better-off community charge payers no longer had to subsidise or pay for services, through their Community Charge, needed by poorer urban communities of cities and towns such as Bradford, Batley or Barnsley. With a population of only 618,000 compared with the combined population of West and South Yorkshire of 3.66 million, better off rural dwellers or those living in the outer suburbs of Harrogate or Knaresborough in North Yorkshire, would not be "burdened" by high charges to meet the needs of poorer members of urban communities.

But things didn't end there. When it was discovered by central Government that the voters living in the towns and cities of West and South Yorkshire voted for politicians who would oppose many central

Government policies and protest about cuts in public services and lack of investment, the Metropolitan Counties were summarily abolished in 1986, again without consultation. This left much smaller Metropolitan Districts and Boroughs for Government to deal with rather than the powerful Metropolitan Counties, a classic case of Westminster divide and rule.

In 1996 the unpopular Humberside County was also abolished and replaced with a Unitary Authority for North Humberside which has reclaimed the ancient name of East Riding. Hull remained as an independent unitary authority, Hull City Council, established in 1972 to replace the old Corporation of Kingston upon Hull whose origins dated back to 1440. To the immense relief of most of their inhabitants, South Humberside became the new Unitary Authority of North Lincolnshire. The name Humberside still however exists in the local Police and other cross-boundary services.

Michael Bradford has outlined[2] how many people living in the area of former West Riding and East Riding felt deeply betrayed, especially those tipped into Greater Manchester, Lancashire, Teesside or Cumbria, a grievous loss of birthright and identity. For many people, the 1972 Local Government Act was a violation of their sense of who they were and where they came from.

Further local Government changes now planned are due to remove the awkward two-tier system of Governance in North Yorkshire and replace it by a simpler, clearer single unitary authority which is to be welcomed. But there is no chance the old local structures will ever return.

The really important debate still to be had is the future of the structure of Regional Government in the English Regions. Between 1992 and 2011 England did have at least some kind of skeletal regional democratic structure with nine official Regions, with Regional Government Offices manned by civil servants, tasked with representing the interest of their Region to central Government. The Yorkshire & Humberside Region included the three major post-1974 counties, of North, West and South Yorkshire, plus Hull, York and North Lincolnshire. It is now more usually referred to as Yorkshire and the Humber, bizarrely adding the name of a river to the great traditional name of our region, and thereby including that disputed strip of North Lincolnshire.

Whilst this was a significant step forward, in 2011 the new Coalition Government took an equally significant step back towards centralisation and abolished all the Regions apart, highly significantly, from London, which was allowed to keep its elected Mayor – one Boris Johnson – and an Assembly. The other Regions survived in name only, purely for statistical purposes and as constituencies of the European Parliament, a requirement now removed by Brexit.

So what, if anything might replace the over-centralised English state?

When the English Provincial Regions were summarily abolished there was little or no protest in the media. Six of the Regions, including Yorkshire have since formed their own purely advisory, all-party Leaders' Boards, two of the Regions being too apathetic even to retain such modest residual credentials.

The cross-party Yorkshire Leaders' Board, now firmly united, are now pushing ahead to secure greater devolutionary powers for the people of the Region, including strategies for what has been called One Yorkshire, an informal grouping or Committee for cooperation, mutual support and the devolution of more powers for the people of the Region.

A fine example of what can be achieved by working together as a Region is the new **Yorkshire & Humber Climate Commission**, an independent group of experts, established in 2021. The Commission brings together some of the region's leading academics, environmentalists, voluntary, private and public sector representatives and politicians into a single body which focuses on the need to adapt all aspects of life in Yorkshire to reduce our carbon emissions from whatever sources. It is dedicated to working closely with the One Yorkshire Group.

Its aims for the Region are:
- *to foster climate resilience and adaptation to climate risks and impacts*
- *to support rapid progress towards net zero carbon emissions*
- *to encourage a just and inclusive transition and climate actions that leave no-one and nowhere behind*
- *to promote sustainability and climate actions that also protect nature and biodiversity.*

But the move towards creating a new Regional identity has been made even more complex over the last decade, by Government supported "City Regions", each planned to have their own elected Mayor. This has paved the way for sub-regional Mayors, so far achieved for Sheffield/

South Yorkshire and West Yorkshire, with Hull & East Riding and York & North Yorkshire to follow. The Mayors will have some significant new regional funding within their control, and powers relating to such key issues as local transport, police, social housing and green investment.

Very welcome as this is, it is vital that the four new Yorkshire Mayors, when all are finally elected, support people across the urban/rural divide, suspend their political differences, and work and function together as a mutually supportive quartet for the benefit of all the people of Yorkshire. This the only way, pending further devolved powers to the Region, to ensure the best possible deal from the Westminster Government irrespective of political affiliation.

To add to the sense of confusion there is now a network of business-led Local Enterprise Partnerships (LEPs) to encourage business investment into the region – but again divided into competing areas and also frequently changing their names and the areas they cover. In 2021 these are designated as being West Yorkshire, Sheffield City Region, York & North Yorkshire, and Hull & East Yorkshire LEPs. These are unelected bodies and what degree of control the new elected Mayors will have over their decision making and priorities over the decades ahead is far from clear. However the new Mayoral elections are an important and welcome step forward.

But it is still rather unsatisfactory. Dividing up a Region of England like Yorkshire with a strong sense of history and identity, into four, potentially competing smaller local dominions reflects the classic divide and rule tactic of Governments throughout the ages.

The recent pandemic crisis has, for the first time, exposed the differences between the separate "four nations" of the United Kingdom in the UK news media. We have become used to the leaders of the three smaller nations appearing on our television screens. But the English Regions, despite their vastly greater population of 51 million, have no separate elected leaders to represent their interests – except the British Prime Minister who is also, by default, the English Prime Minister.

But where does that leave the English Regions? It took an irate Andy Burnham, Mayor of Greater Manchester, to protest and articulate what he regarded as inadequate financial support for the people of Manchester at the start of the first pandemic lockdown. Overnight he became a local hero.

Added to this has been the generally admirable, cautious way the Devolved Nations of Scotland, Wales and Northern Ireland have dealt with the pandemic crisis for their own populations. This has provided a powerful case for Devolved English Regions, with at very least, a democratically elected Regional Assembly to determine key priorities for the Region's population.

This has now become a clear objective, regionally and nationally, of several of the main political parties. There is now the **Yorkshire Party**, established in 2014 with the prime objective of securing a Scottish or Welsh-style Yorkshire Parliament, within the UK but with a similar range of devolved powers. In the 2021 West Yorkshire Mayoral elections, the Yorkshire Party candidate secured 58,851 votes and came third in the poll, ahead of the Greens and the Liberals.

Even though there are many issues still to be resolved, with the distinct possibility of full Scottish independence and a recalibration of the relationships of the two parts of Ireland, many people in Yorkshire have reason to envy the existing greater degree of democratic control the people of these devolved nations have over so many of their own affairs.

Yorkshire is not like Scotland or Wales. Since the 10th century, Yorkshire has been part of the English nation and most of its people would want to continue to have a say in English, not just UK affairs. Most people would also wish to stay in some form of United Kingdom.

This should not be an issue. An ideal outcome would be to develop something not unlike the structure ironically the UK Government helped create for what is now the Federal Republic of Germany in the immediate aftermath of the Second World War to help the recovery of a crushed and defeated nation state. It was also undertaken to avoid the re-appearance of another over-centralised military dictatorship in the decades that were to follow, another interesting issue for a future United Kingdom.

The German system is one of 16 semi-autonomous regional States or "Länder". It is a system something we have every reason to envy, given the huge success of Germany economically, socially and culturally over the last seventy years. But Germany is not unique – a federal or regional structure is normal in many other European nations – Austria with its Länder and Switzerland with its Cantons being two extraordinarily successful examples that contrast with the over-centralised, bureau-cratic oligarchy that England has become since the abolition of its even limited Regional Government offices a decade ago.

As has been frequently pointed out, with a population of over 5.4 million people, Yorkshire is the same size as Scotland (5.4 million) but larger than Wales (3.15 million) or Northern Ireland (1.2 million), all of which enjoy an important degree of autonomy within the United Kingdom, a Parliament in the case of Scotland, Senedd for Wales and Assembly in Northern Ireland. Yet in terms of population, Yorkshire is only slightly smaller than many independent European states such as Denmark (5.8 million), Finland (5.5 million) and Norway, (5.4 million). But Yorkshire is significantly larger than Estonia (1.3 million) Latvia (1.9 million) or Lithuania (1.9 million).

The difference is that all these nations have a far greater degree of control over their own lives than the people who live in the Regions of England. Compared with these nations, which in the case of those in Denmark and Norway (also outside the EU) are signifi-cantly more prosperous, Yorkshire suffers from a serious democratic deficiency.

For Yorkshire to be recognised a semi-autonomous English Region clearly would have huge implications in terms of its Governance, not by a Government appointed Civil Service "Office", but by a democratically elected Regional Assembly with delegated powers over the Region as a whole. Such an Assembly is more likely to be aware of and be able to respond to the issues that affect the lives of the people it serves.

Devolution, at whatever level this may operate, whether as the semi-autonomous level of a full German/Austrian or Swiss Land or Canton, or a more modest Regional Assembly, would give people more control over their lives. It would also give people in the Region a stronger voice, not only within the UK but with other regional and national Governments. It would enable greater cultural exchange and ultimately greater economic success.

The cautious devolution of certain central Government powers or budgets to a group of elected Mayors is at least an important step forward, however modest.

As Professor Paul Salveson of The Hannah Mitchell Foundation, an all-Party campaigning group that *"works for a fair and prosperous*

North of England through devolution to local and regional government"
has suggested:

> *"In the North we need to develop a regional culture and consciousness*
> *which includes an alternative body of thinking that is both progressive and*
> *inclusive"* [3]

The first step in achieving greater autonomy for the people of Yorkshire therefore is to celebrate their unique identity by adopting a symbol which truly belongs and reflects the best of the Cultural Province of Yorkshire. If this can complement the Union Jack, without all the positive and negative political baggage and imperial and authoritarian overtones of our perhaps tired national symbol, it could create a focal point for a growing movement among people of our region not for full autonomy, but to have some significant influence on the many decisions that affect their daily lives and future prospects.

An ancient symbol does exist and already enjoys huge success – the White Rose of York.

Its regular use and association with Yorkshire go back to medieval times.

Some commentators now suggests that the symbols, the Red Rose of Lancaster and the White Rose of York, were only adopted in the latter part of the baronial 15th century civil wars (1435–1487), popularised by writers such as William Shakespeare and Sir Walter Scott. It was Scott who actually coined the romantic term "Wars of the Roses" for what was a sordid and extended baronial feud. The Tudor Rose of the English Crown was a blending of the two competing rose emblems, first used by Henry VII to signify the unity he wished to be seen to achieve after the defeat of Yorkist Richard III at the Battle of Bosworth in 1485.

The White Rose of York is however a far more ancient symbol of purity, frequently used throughout the Middle Ages. The white rose – "the mystical rose of Heaven" – with its religious connotations, was used by many people not just the Plantagenet supporters of the House of York in the 15th century.

The "white double heraldic rose with green sepals and gold centre" design we see today as the symbol for Yorkshire is based on the stylised emblem used in tapestries and illustrated manuscripts throughout medieval and Tudor times. This in turn was almost certainly based on the ancient Rosa Alba Semi-Plena, a white shrub rose, still grown in gardens in Yorkshire and elsewhere. It has been used in flags and heraldic representations of Yorkshire for generations.

White roses were also reputedly worn by soldiers of the King's Own Yorkshire Light Infantry at the Battle of Minden on August 1st in 1759. It is believed they each fastened a white rose in their caps in memory of their fallen comrades after the battle. This makes what is now the Yorkshire Rose a potent symbol not of military aggression, but of peace, sadness and memory.

Appropriately, it is now the proud symbol of the Yorkshire Regiment, based at Catterick, as part of their regimental badge, the rose featured prominently under the British Lion.

The story of the blue and white Yorkshire flag has a more recent but equally powerful history. The flag itself, on its bright or pale blue background, was designed sometime in the 1960s, but only adopted in 1975 when the newly formed Yorkshire Ridings Society made use of the flag to help safeguard the name and identity of Yorkshire and of the ancient Yorkshire Ridings, abolished in those controversial local Government boundary changes in 1974. Thanks to the Yorkshire Ridings Society, August 1st is now recognised throughout the "ceremonial counties" of Yorkshire as Yorkshire Day.

After a Yorkshire farmer was summoned, but not prosecuted, sometime afterwards for displaying the Flag, allegedly without planning permission, on July 29th 2008 the Society had the Flag officially registered by the UK Institute of Flags. From then onwards it has become the official Flag of Yorkshire, adopted by The Yorkshire Society. It can be legally displayed in public on any occasion, just as you can the Union Jack or the red and white cross of St. George. You now see it, not just on Yorkshire Day, but everywhere, on civic buildings, churches, pubs, garages, cafes, private houses.

So why has the flag become so popular in Yorkshire?

First of all, it is not political – and unlike the Union Jack or St George's flag, has not been hi-jacked by any political group for their own purposes, nor is it used in any authoritarian, menacing way. Secondly, in a very real sense it is the Peoples' Flag, suggesting the immense pride that whoever displays it has, in belonging to and being part of Yorkshire, a special region of England.

You are not compelled to show it to prove your loyalty. It is not shouting defiance at your enemies or indicating hostility. You wave the flag because it is your choice to belong. It has in a real and valued sense become part of our Yorkshire identity and togetherness, celebrating our rich, shared culture, one which is not about exclusiveness, but one which, whatever our background or birth heritage, is about belonging to a special part of England – to Yorkshire.

The White Rose flag is also a sign of the need for change. It symbolises all that is strong about Yorkshire and its people, the beauty and variety of our region, but also its inclusive character and its resilience.

It therefore is truly a symbol of hope to help the people of our Region emerge from these most difficult and troubled times of the pandemic and its aftermath.

As we have suggested, what ultimately matters during a process of change is not bureaucratic lines on a map, but how people identify with the place where they feel they belong.

So, if it is not a nation but more than a mere single county, what term can be used to describe Yorkshire? The one which seems to most clearly describe the rich and varied area in which I and over five million other people live, is a Cultural Province.

Michael Bradford has suggested that "Yorkshire", as defined historically as that part of Northern England that lies between the Humber and the Tees, the Pennines and the North Sea, and recognised by the ancient boundaries of York and its three Ridings should be regarded in a radically different way – as a Cultural Province of England. Bradford cites Normandy in France as an internationally recognised European Cultural Region[4] which has no legal or administrative structure as such, yet has enormous cultural resonance, recognised, like Yorkshire, internationally.

Other suggestions of semi-autonomous Regions within larger nation states which have the same kind of powerful cultural identity include Texas within the USA, or Bavaria in Germany, or Tyrol in Austria. Tyrol is especially interesting because its cultural identity extends across the borders of two nation states, Austria but also Italy (Süd Tirol). Just as in Ireland (until recently), the open borders of the EU have helped reduce tensions and conflicts yet allowed Tyrol to retain its unique identity.

Normandy is perhaps the most interesting and helpful comparison.

Covering an area of Northern France 11.8k square kilometres and a population of 3.3 million compared with the 15.4k sq.km and 5.4 million population of Yorkshire, the two areas are broadly compatible. But in local Government terms Normandy has six constituent administrations – Calvados, Eure, Manche, Orne and Saint Maritime, names, with the possible exception of Calvados, which are largely unknown to people outside Normandy itself.

But Normandy is a powerful brand, which for obvious reasons also is also intertwined with English history. It also has equally strong associations of natural beauty, a dramatic coastline, a fine cultural heritage and a rich history. In short, like Yorkshire, it is a perfect Cultural Province.

Cultural Province is therefore a useful term to use for Yorkshire. It is defined by the leading American archaeologist and anthropologist Elizabeth Prine Pauls in her Encyclopaedia Britannica entry (2014) in the following way:

> *Culture area, also called **cultural area, culture province,** or **ethno-geographic area**, in anthropology, geography, and other social sciences, a contiguous geographic area within which most societies share many traits in common. Delineated at the turn of the 20th century, it remains one of the most widely used frameworks for the description and analysis of cultures.*

It is easy to see therefore that a first step in that critical process of Devolution for an area like Yorkshire is a recognition, perhaps intuitive, by its inhabitants and not by distant bureaucrats, of these "traits in common" that its population shares – all the many different aspects of what it is to be part of a wider community that is Yorkshire.

A process of voluntary self-identification is therefore the best way to bring Yorkshire people together into a Cultural Province of Yorkshire. This will ensure that, sooner or later, legislation to formalise this recognition will follow. Yorkshire is a state of mind as well as a place, something and somewhere people can opt into, to choose to belong to, not be ordered to by fingers on a bureaucrat's keyboard. Ultimately that will be its appeal and its power.

So what are the key elements to support the identification of Yorkshire as a cultural province using Prine Paul's criteria:

Geographic. Apart from Cornwall (which has a similar strong sense of cultural identity) no Region of England is so clearly defined by physical features – the coast, the Humber estuary and Tees valley, the Pennines; but also its extraordinary geological diversity, from the most ancient to the most recent deposits of rocks, provides an astonishing variety of different landscapes, perhaps unique in any other European region, yet united within its physical geographic framework. It also has powerful contrasting cultural landscapes shaped by centuries of human activity, farming, forestry, quarrying, railway building, heavy industry, architecture as well as service industries such as financial services, tourism and education in both urban and rural settings.

Anthropological The Anglo-Norse Kingdom of Jorvik, which occupied that part of England now known as Yorkshire brought a different people from Northern Europe to those who settled in the former Saxon kingdoms to the west and south. Even in the 21st century, after centuries of further immigration, these differences remain, as evidenced by the DNA of much of the population, but also by place names, by dialect, still distinguishable in their East, North and West Riding variants and accents, and even manners and customs.

Other social sciences This must include its constant patterns of population movement, immigration, industry, but also a recognition of the poverty and deprivation suffered by much of the population especially in the early years of the Industrial Revolution and indeed the two World Wars, and maybe even the amazing spirit of resilience shown in the recent pandemic, that made Yorkshire people as tough and as adaptable as they are. Yorkshire has a rich and powerfully evocative history, dating from the Anglo-Viking Kingdom of Jorvik to the present day, which shapes its communal memory.

Traits in common These are the qualities to be recognised both inside and outside the region about the special qualities of Yorkshire people and the communities that unite them.

In the second part of this book therefore, I want to explore and attempt to define in more detail what I believe to be the central characteristics of these nine, widely recognised, great cultural landscapes of Yorkshire. I shall look in turn at each one with their own special distinguishing landscape features, their environment, economy, history, stories, politics, and above all noting just a few of the many remarkable personalities, landowners, scientists, industrialists, writers, musicians whose energy and creativity has created the Province of Yorkshire we know today.

These nine distinctive cultural landscapes of Yorkshire are:
1. The City of York
2. The Vale of York and Mowbray
3. The North York Moors and Cleveland
4. The Yorkshire Wolds and Holderness
5. The Yorkshire Dales
6. The South Pennines
7. The Forest of Bowland
8. West Yorkshire
9. South Yorkshire

These are based not on current, and frequently changing, local Government boundaries, but on these essential cultural factors. They are based on areas within the three historic counties which are still largely within the Region of Yorkshire, within what the Office for National Statistics has defined as *a stable, unchanging geography which covers the whole of Great Britain*[5]

The second part of this book, therefore, sets out to briefly summarise just some of the elements in each of these cultural landscapes that make Yorkshire so distinctive and special, in some cases better known nationally and internationally than the region itself. Together and combined, they form the unique English Province of Yorkshire.

It also sets out some of the challenges and perhaps opportunities for the future, which communities within a Cultural Province of Yorkshire, will be best able resolve or take forward. They will only be able to so if they have a strong sense of their own local and regional identity, supported by effective governance, based within the Province, controlled and determined not by Whitehall bureaucrats, but by the people of Yorkshire.

Notes

1 Bradford Michael 1988: *The Fight for Yorkshire* Hutton Press, Beverley
2 Ibid pp52–107
3 Salveson Paul 2021: *Another England is possible – Lancashire Loominaries* (lancashireloominary.co.uk)
4 Bradford Michael 1988: Op. Cit. pp126–7 Hutton Press, Beverley
5 Office for National Statistics 2016: Index of Place Names of Great Britain (IPN) 2016 User Guide

Part Two:
The Nine Cultural Landscapes
of Yorkshire

1

The City of York

Capital of a Roman Province

The city of York spans 2,000 years of English history. It owes its existence to being on a raised glacial moraine at the confluence of the tidal River Ouse and the little River Foss, being the highest point where supplies of men and equipment could be brought in sea-going vessels from the North Sea via the Humber to service the Roman garrison established there in 71AD. This was a strategic location to secure their conquest of the Celtic kingdom of Brigantia. There may well have well been a Celtic settlement nearby – the Roman name, Eboracum, is linked to a Celtic term for Yew trees.

It was also close enough to the network of paved military roads that the invading army was building to secure the conquest of Brigantia, initially using Ricknield Street, the prehistoric highway through the centre of Yorkshire which followed the magnesian limestone ridge and glacial moraines above the marshland that covered the lowland areas. Roman military engineers also created Dere Street. This linked Eboracum with a shallow crossing of the Humber where a small defensive fort at Pretoria (Brough) was built to protect the crossing. A ferry, probably operated by shallow barges, linked Winteringham in modern Lincolnshire, with Ermine Street, their more direct road to Londinium (London) via Lindum (Lincoln).

At Eboracum a large military base and supply centre was established on the north east bank of the Ouse, as headquarters of the Sixth Legion. By the time of the arrival of the Ninth Legion in 120AD the fortress covered around 50 acres of land and had accommodation for over 5000 soldiers. Among early users of the fortress was the Emperor Hadrian in

122 with his army heading towards Scotland and the site of the Wall he was constructing to keep out warring Pictish tribes.

The initial wooden buildings and turf ramparts of the fortress were soon replaced by more robust stone. A flourishing civilian community or Civitas developed to service the garrison was established across the river, to the south west on adjacent land, close to where there was a bridge built across the Ouse carrying the Via Praetoria, the main entrance road to the Garrison from the south. The line of Via Praetoria survives to this day under what is now Stonegate, the Roman bridge being where the Guildhall stands today, with a link from Micklegate. This was for many centuries the only crossing of the river, but after its collapse a new wooden bridge was built at what is now Ouse Bridge by the Vikings, which survived, after several rebuilds, well into the 19th century. Before being replaced by the present structure, it was little more than a narrow stone humped back bridge linking the walled city on both sides of the river.

By the third century, Eboracum had grown to become the most important military and civil centre in the north of Britannia and was given the honorary status of a Colonia. Emperor Septimius Severus made his headquarters here between 208 to 211, in order to lead his military campaign against the Caledonian tribes, bringing with him both his family and his own elite protective Praetorian Guard. He died in York in 211.

Eboracum, the recognised capital of northern Britain (Britannia Inferior), was soon to attract an even more influential figure – Constantine the Great who was in York in 306 with his father Emperor Constantius, when his father died. The Sixth Legion stationed in the garrison promptly proclaimed Constantine as Emperor of the Roman Empire. Constantine the Great, as he became, went on to unite the Empire, bringing it under the control of a single ruler. He is thought to have converted to Christianity in 312. He is justly celebrated for granting all Christians the freedom to worship. In 314 Eboracum was given its first Christian Bishop.

Given the importance of Eboracum in Roman history, it is surprising there is so little evidence of that long and event-filled part of York's history visible above ground, apart from the great column opposite the south door of the Minster, one of thirty-six columns of the long vanished Great Cross Hall in the fortress. In the gardens of the Yorkshire Museum Gardens there is the great Multangular Tower and sections of the original Roman Wall that initially fully surrounded the fortress and later the part of the civitas. A visit to the Minster's Crypt and Undercoft Museum indicates how the present Minster was built on the foundations of the army barracks. Pieces of Roman masonry, including columns, survive, together with some interior plasterwork and other artefacts. An audio-visual display also suggests with some justification, that this might have been the exact spot where Constantine the Great was declared Emperor. Appropriately enough, a statue of Constantine has been placed directly outside the Minster close to the spot where he was proclaimed Emperor.

However, within the several metres of soil and deposit that have accumulated in the city over the last two millennia, much fascinating Roman material has been excavated and unearthed, but there is certainly much more sealed under existing buildings for future generations to find. This is a massive time capsule containing intriguing parts of the Roman city only revealed after future excavations to allow modern development. Many existing finds such as pottery, coins, jewellery, glassware are displayed in the Yorkshire Museum. A considerable number of Roman lead and stone coffins have also been discovered, close to the city walls in what were Roman cemeteries.

Eorforwic

When the Legions were forced to leave Britannica after 410, it is likely that for the Roman-British civilian population, life in the city went on much as before, until waves of Anglian invaders came as conquerors, stayed as settlers, intermarrying with those Romano-British citizens of the Empire who had not already fled west. Having first colonised the fertile lands around the Yorkshire Wolds, these Anglian warrior-farmers moved west and northwards searching for more land, soon capturing Eboracum, re-purposing the surviving buildings and wharves, building their own wooden homes and workshops in the ruins and foundations of the Roman city. It soon developed into the strategic capital of their new kingdom of Deira, which extended between the Humber and the Tees. Eventually Deira became part of an even greater Kingdom, Northumbria, that extended, as its name implies northwards from the Humber to the Scottish border. The name Eboracum was changed by rough Anglian tongues to Eorforwic, "wic" meaning port or trading centre. One telling surviving relic of late Roman or Anglian occupation of the city is the so-called Anglian Tower, built against an original section, as a possible repair and refortification of the Roman Wall. It is still visible on the section of wall behind Explore York, the City Library. It was probably constructed between the 5th and 6th centuries, perhaps to improve or strengthen the fortifications as the Roman garrison was abandoned.

Northumbria became a Christian Kingdom in the 7th century when their charismatic king, Edwin, was baptised in 627. It became a centre in the 7th and 8th centuries of that great flowering of Anglo-Saxon culture exemplified by the magnificent Lindisfarne Gospels and the writings of Bede. This influence was equally evident in Eorforwic when Ecgbert, the brother of King Eadbert of Northumbria, and a disciple of Bede, became Archbishop of York in 732. The little church of St Peter where King Edwin had been baptised in 627 was rebuilt as a fine stone Minster. No physical remains of that building survives, though it was probably sited to the north of the present Gothic Minster near the Chapter House. Contemporary accounts described it as a large and imposing structure. Attached to the Minster was a School or College which soon enjoyed a reputation throughout England for its scholarship, not just in theology but in the liberal arts, literature and science. One of Archbishop Ecgbert's most gifted pupils was a local boy from southern Deira, probably the Yorkshire Wolds, an area of early Anglian settlement. Alcuin (c735–804) soon proved himself a brilliant scholar. In his twenties he became a teacher at the College, renowned for his learning and eloquence as theologian, poet and a scholar. His reputation was such that he was sent by King Elfwolf on a mission to the Pope in Rome to confirm the status of Eorforwic's archbishopric.

On his journey home via Parma, Alcuin met Charles I, King of the Franks, Lombardy and later of Rome, better known as Charlemagne. Latin, the lingua franca of medieval Europe, facilitated communication between the two men, as it did between theologians and scholars of all nations. Charlemagne, who reigned over the nations of what became the Carolingian Empire, was so impressed with the young theologian, he invited Alcuin to his court in Aachen, in what is now modern Germany, to join his court of scholars and intellectuals. He soon appointed him head of the Palace School in Aachen. This was for all intent and purposes one of Europe's first universities.

In what was a great flowering of European civilisation during the late eighth century, Alcuin's writing and teaching becoming known throughout Europe for its eloquence and scholarship. This created a direct link between the great Northumbrian tradition of art and learning flourishing in York and the intellectual life of mainland Europe.

Tragically, Ecgbert's Minister, the School and its magnificent Library, which may have had illuminated manuscripts to rival Durham and Lindisfarne, and many precious books and manuscripts relating to Anglian Eoforwic, were destroyed by fire, first by ninth century pagan Viking invaders, and later William the Conqueror's brutal Harrying of the North in 1069. But one precious relic of that rich Northumbrian civilisation is the York Helmet, a superb Anglian helmet dating from the mid 8th century, the time of Alcuin. Richly decorated, it was unearthed in Coppergate and is now displayed in the Yorkshire Museum.

Jorvik

As we have already seen, in 867 life had totally changed for the people of Northumbria. Invading Vikings came to eventually transform Deira into that remarkable dynamic and successful trading Anglo-Viking nation of Jorvik.

The new inhabitants of the city of Jorvik soon rebuilt and repaired the 2½ miles of city defence wall, covering the Roman walls with earth and adding new wooden palisades. They also added to the surviving paved Roman streets with a network of their own roads, lanes and alleyways, many of them retaining the Viking word "gata" for a street or lane – Micklegate, Gillygate, Stonegate, Petergate – as a strong indicator of their origin. But perhaps the most evocative direct link with Viking York is to be sensed in King's Square in the centre of the city, the probable site of the regular Viking "Thing" or open-air parliament attended by King, Earls and Thanes (Knights) – a tradition which continues to this day in the Isle of Man, also settled by Vikings, with their Tynwald or ancient Parliament, part of which takes place in the open air. By the 9th and 10th centuries the Vikings were also converting to Christianity, if for no other reason than it was good for encouraging trade with neighbouring nations. But they often retained some of their pagan beliefs and iconography.

To really understand Viking culture, you need to visit the **Jorvik Viking Centre** in Coppergate. Between 1976 and 1981 the York Archaeological Trust carried out some extraordinary excavations in that immediate area, and many of their finds have been used in a highly imaginative recreation of urban life as it was in the Viking era, using original or carefully constructed objects, and even authentic smells, to give the visitor an impression of life in those cramped streets and workshops. Many superb finds – ceramics, glass, jewels, coins, leatherwork, can also be enjoyed in the **Yorkshire Museum** which includes the Vale of York Hoard, discovered by metal detectors in a field east of Harrogate in 2007. Dating from the tenth century, the undisturbed collection consisted of 617 silver coins and 65 other items, including jewellery, ingots, and a beautifully engraved gilt silver vessel, lined in gold. Many of the precious objects originated from far corners of Europe and beyond, including Afghanistan and Samarkand in what is now Uzbekistan. The Hoard and a similar mainly silver Hoard unearthed in Bedale in 2012, gives some insight into the extent and sophistication of the international trade to and from York in the tenth century.

In the **Treasury of the Minister** is another item which gives insight into the extent of Viking trade – the Horn of Ulf. The richly decorated horn is made from elephant tusk with Arabic carvings which probably originated in north Africa. It was transformed and decorated into a horn in the city of Salerno, in what is now Italy. It was presented to the Dean and Chapter of York Minster in the early 11th century by Ulf, a local Thane and wealthy landowner, as part of a deed for a gift of land to the Minster.

So what happened to the city of Jorvik after the Conquest and the disastrous Harrying of the North in 1069–70?

St Mary's Abbey and the Minster

It was not all bad news. The city seems to have recovered remarkably quickly from the disaster. In 1088, within months of the death of his father, William Rufus, the new king William II of Norman England, gave additional land on the riverside just outside the city walls and alongside a little Anglo-Viking church dedicated to St Olaf or Olav. King Olaf II of Norway (995–1030), canonised in 1031 as St Olaf, was a Viking saint, making York's St. Olave's church a rare example of an English church dedicated to a Norwegian King and Norway's patron saint. The church was rebuilt in the 15th century and heavily restored in later years.

This enlarged area of riverside land outside the city walls was then offered to a group of Benedictine Monks and dedicated to St Mary. Within a few decades the Abbey prospered as a centre of scholarship and learning, becoming one of the most wealthy and influential Benedictine Abbeys in the North. Adjacent on the other side of the building was St Leonard's Hospital. For hundreds of years St Leonard's served the people of York, becoming the largest hospital in the north of England. When it was closed down by Henry VIII at the Dissolution of the Monasteries in 1538, it took more than two centuries before York again had a purpose built hospital of its own. Henry also took over the Abbot's House for his own use, renamed it the King's Manor, in what is now Exhibition Square. It was also the location for meetings over the next century of the Council of the North, which was less to do with giving power to the people of the North, more a question of keeping a watch over any subversive or rebellious activities such as occurred in Yorkshire in 1569 with the pro-Catholic Rising of the North. The present building now forms part of York University.

But only a short distance away an even more momentous building than the Abbey was gradually to appear. Close to the site of the ruins of the Anglo-Saxon Minster of St. Peter, William I offered land to Thomas of Bayeux, York's first Norman Archbishop, for a fine new Minster or Cathedral. This was given perhaps in atonement for the damage caused to such a holy place by his own troops. When it was finally built in 1095 on the ruins of the Roman fort, it was on a massive scale. It was designed in Norman style 365 feet in length with a commanding tower, a dominating feature in the landscape. The building survived another disastrous fire in 1137. However, this Norman Cathedral was eventually replaced by an even grander structure on the same site, now in the fashionable new Gothic style. The construction was initiated in 1220 by Archbishop Walter de Grey and incorporated much of the Norman structure and masonry in its rebuilding. Remains and models of the Norman building are to be seen in the Undercroft Museum.

This was the building we see now, added to and shaped over the next 250 years. Despite constant setbacks of accidents and fires, it grew to become one of the great Gothic cathedrals of Europe, the largest cathedral north of the Alps and a glorious celebration of both Christian faith and humanity, and in particular a brilliant testament to York's craftsmen – masons, joiners, wood carvers, glaziers, with 128 stained glass windows overing a period of over 800 years. The 14th and 15th century stained glass are among the finest to be seen anywhere in the world.

Everyone who comes to **York Minster** will have a favourite part – the great, recently restored West Window with its amazing Biblical scenes, the Five Sisters Window in the North Transept, the wonderful Rose Window dating from the end of the Wars of the Roses and decorated with the newly combined Tudor Rose, the stunningly engineered Chapter House, not to mention the three magnificent towers. The Central Lantern Tower at 231 feet is the highest point in York, and a landmark for miles around, as well as, for those capable of climbing the 275 steps, a magnificent viewpoint across the city, and the Vale of York, and on to the Wolds, Moors and high Pennines.

But York Minster is far more than a building. It is both a religious and a cultural centre, with a range of activities linked to its core function as a place of Christian worship. It has also produced some remarkable Archbishops, none more so than Dr., now Lord, John Sentamu, a forceful personality whose energy and compassion has reached out to people beyond even his own large congregations.

The medieval city

York continued to prosper throughout the Middle Ages as the most important city in the North, the only comparable cities in England outside London being Bristol and Norwich which in terms of trade and wealth matched the Northern capital. The walls were soon extended eastwards to protect the growing city from marauding Scots.

One measure of its wealth and success was the number of churches built to serve its growing population. By 1330 there were around 45 parish churches in existence in the city, of which 20 survive today.

Though many of them now serve different purposes, such as small museums or art centres, twelve of them still provide religious services to their local congregations.

There are still recognisable medieval streets and alleyways, and even houses, such as Lady Row in Gillygate built in 1316, and inns occupying at least the same sites since perhaps even the days of Jorvik. Few that that survive are in fact older than the 17th century and most are Victorian or rebuilt in later times. Many claim to have ghosts.

Barley Hall, in Coffee Yard, off Stonegate in the centre of York, is a carefully, fully restored medieval house, dating back to 1360. Though only the outer fabric of the building is original, details of the interior and furnishings have been recreated to give an impression of what a 14th century house in York would have looked and felt like.

The Guilds of York

One aspect of the city which is perhaps insufficiently celebrated is the influence of the system of Guilds. Guilds were either secular, linked to specific crafts or trades, or religious, facilitating the work or activities of the church.

A Guild is a cross between a trade union and a consumer protection society. It enables particular trades and crafts in a city to flourish. From Viking times onwards York was a major manufacturing centre, for example for metalwork, glass, masonry, leather, ceramics, textiles and tailoring, as well as butchers and bakers, but also merchants. The Merchant Adventurers were vital for England's prosperity by building international trade and revenues from a huge variety of goods, though the main export product from Yorkshire for many centuries continued to be wool, particularly to Flanders or Italy. The Guilds ensured high standards of workmanship. They developed the still highly regarded system of apprenticeships, most young men (and occasionally women) having to serve an apprenticeship of five years or more to learn a craft or trade, before graduating to the status (and pay) of a Journeyman, before finally, after the production of a piece of work described with the word we still use, their test-piece "masterpiece", they achieved the status of a Master or a Master Craftsman and full member of the Guild.

Evidence of the importance of the Guilds in the story of York comes from the surviving Guildhalls. The city's magnificent Civic **Guildhall** in Coney Street, dates from 1449–59 and has been a focal point of civil life ever since – Richard III was entertained there in 1483, St Margaret Clitheroe the Catholic martyr was tried in 1586 and the meeting by Northern leaders to raise the ransom money for Charles I took place in 1642 within its walls. Tragically it was the victim of a Nazi "Baedeker" bombing raid in 1942 when much of the interior of the building, including the great medieval stained-glass window, was destroyed. Much has been meticulously restored and the historic hall is now used for a variety of civic meetings and events.

Just as fine is the **Merchant Adventurer's Hall** in Fossgate with its great hall and attendant rooms, now open to the public and used for a variety of events and activities. The **Merchant Taylors' Hall** was originally built for a 12th century religious guild which became secular in later years. Part of the present building dates from the 17th century. **St Anthony's Hall** in Peasholme, built in the 15th century, was originally the home of St Martin's Guild but has had many uses including a workhouse, and a school for the poor, and for the University's Borthwick Institute. The Butchers' Guild had their headquarters close to what was the dingy and filthy Shambles, the narrow medieval street which is now such an iconic feature of tourist York.

Two other outstanding houses of medieval origin can also be seen close to the Minster. **St William's College** was first developed as accommodation for chantry priests in the 15th century but later converted to a school, shops, and fine private accommodation. **The Treasurer's House** close by originated in the 12th century but was extensively rebuilt in the 17th and sympathetically restored, with its gardens in the 20th century. It is now owned and managed by the National Trust and open to the public with displays that tell its history, complete with an appropriate ghost story.

But perhaps the most important surviving inheritance of the Guilds is the **York Cycle of Mystery Plays** based on Biblical themes – traditionally performed each year in June during the feast of Corpus Christi, each Guild taking turns to perform part of the Cycle in a different location in the city. The plays are still performed regularly, usually on a four yearly Festival cycle, their texts based on a precious surviving 15th manuscript now kept in the British Museum.

Nine Guilds in York still survive, no longer as trade associations, but as charities focusing on different areas of charitable activity in the city. Three of them – the Guilds of Freemen, Cordwainers and Buildings now have their base in another interesting survival from medieval York – **Bedern Hall**, dating from 1370 and used by Canons and Vicars Choral of the Minster for a variety of purposes, but over ensuing centuries for a variety of other purposes, only escaping demolition in the 1970s. It is now beautifully restored, with the support of the three Guilds, and is used for public meetings and gatherings.

Jewish murders – and expulsions

But medieval York had its darker side. By the end of the 12th century York had the largest Jewish community outside London. Their work as moneylenders and financiers, in effect early bankers, was a vital part of York's international trading success. Around 40 families were living in Coneygate in the centre if the city. They had a burial ground just outside the city walls in an area still known as Jewbury. But something all too familiar in the 20th and 21st centuries was to occur. "False facts" propaganda, stories about the alleged atrocities committed by people of non-Christian faith – particularly Jews and Muslims – were used to justify the Crusades. The same lies were circulating even among the people of York, leading to local unrest. This was encouraged by five powerful and ruthless local Norman landowners, who coincidentally all owned money to the financiers – William Percy, Richard Malbisse, Alan Malekale, Marmaduke Darell and Philip de Faucenberg. On 16th March 1190 rioting and plundering were tacitly encouraged. Terrified all members of the Coneygate Jewish community fled as a group to seek safety in what was still the wooden Norman Castle on Castle Hill. The mob, infuriated, set fire to the castle, and faced with imminent death, most of the Jewish community committed mass suicide rather than fall into the hands of the mob, fathers killing their wives and children, the last men alive being killed by the rabbi. A small group who had agreed to be baptised Christian to save their lives left the castle on that promise but were treacherously butchered by the mob outside.

This dark stain on York's history was only partly relieved when those that owed money to the murdered Jewish moneylenders were still forced to pay their debts. Within a few years however, such was the need for their services, that the Jews were invited back to the city and in 1218 formed one of England's specially protected Jewish communities. In 1290, Edward I, in another bout of anti-Semitism, banned all Jews from England.

It took several more centuries before Jewish people came back to York; the one small synagogue in the city closed in 1975 and whilst there is once again a small Jewish community in York able to celebrate their faith in partnership with other groups such as the Quakers, orthodox believers must travel to Leeds to the nearest synagogue.

Defending the city

Clifford's Tower is the only surviving part of the great Norman motte-and-bailey castle that together with a similar structure on Bail Hill on the opposite side of the river, guarded the other river entrance into York between the walls, restricting access by boat along the river with chains. A similar arrangement was put in place at Lendal (Lendal Bridge was only built in the mid-19th century – until then Lendal was served by a ferry) where towers and chains controlled the northern entrance to the town via the river.

The defensive fortification needed constant reinforcement during the 13th, 14th and 15th centuries, the threat coming from constant invasions and even, as in 1322, an entire army of marauding Scots. As well as strengthening and improving the walls to their present height, the four heavily fortified gateways or Bars were built at Micklegate Bar, Bootham Bar, Walmgate Bar and Monk Bar – which has kept its portcullis.

Clifford's Tower was totally redesigned and rebuilt as a fortified tower by Henry III, to a unique design in England, in the later 13th century, a time of constant danger from Scottish invaders. It was also used as a secure treasury store and a gaol and saw some military action in the Civil War. By the 18th century, no longer needed for defence, it was in a ruinous state, regarded as little more than a picturesque folly. Now in the ownership of English Heritage it is being beautifully restored. A small plaque outside recalls the massacre of the Jewish population that took place at the site.

The **Castle Museum** has somewhat less grim memories. Built on the site of the Bailey or outer part of the Castle, these elegant Georgian buildings in a now restored square, once contained the city's Debtors and Female Prisons but are now the home of this award-winning Museum. Its collections focus on the last 400 years of York's social and economic history, including a carefully re-created Victorian street.

England's second city and centre for trade

York flourished as a trading and manufacturing centre from the tenth to the sixteenth centuries, in effect the capital of the North and England's second city, with a population, in spite of the Harrying of the North and the Black Death of 1349–50, rising to over 10,000 by 1377 and to 12,000 by 1600. King and Parliament were based in York on five occasions between 1298 and 1338 during the time of the wars against Scotland and again in 1392, the town receiving Royal charters in 1393 and 1396 to give it full status as a County Borough.

As already indicated York was also, for several periods of later medieval history, host to the Council of the North. This was first established in 1472 when Edward IV set up the Council with an aim of keeping the peace and ensuring the King's laws were kept, but also encouraging economic prosperity, appointing his brother, Richard Duke of Gloucester (later Richard III) who spent part of his childhood at Middleham Castle, as its Lord President. The Council was revived by Henry VII and continued to meet sporadically in the period 1536–1641. It was based at King's Manor, the former home of the Abbots of St Mary's Abbey, a building that dates from the 15th century. This Council, consisting of local trusted supporters of the King, was less about devolving power to the Northern Barons, more about keeping a watchful eye the activities of recalcitrant Catholic sympathisers.

The city's gentle decline from Tudor times onwards, from being one of the principal trading centres of England, was less due to any failings of its own, rather the decline of the wool export trade and the rise of competition elsewhere. Hull became the region's thriving port capable of taking far larger sea-going vessels than could find their way up the meandering Ouse, even when a new lock at Naburn south of the city ended the restrictions for boats at low tide. Improved turnpike roads in the 18th century also connected that rapidly expanding city with its hinterland for waggon as well as coach traffic. London was now increasingly dominant in overseas trade to an expanding empire. Ports like Bristol, Liverpool and even Lancaster were now also beginning to benefit from the lucrative but evil slave trade. Textiles were now being manufactured with speed and skill in the scattered communities of the Pennines where abundant, fast flowing streams could provide the waterpower for the new mills, with Halifax, Wakefield, Bradford and Leeds rapidly emerging as hugely successful new textile trading centres. Perhaps too the system of Guilds was acting as a protectionist brake on innovation and the truly entrepreneurial spirit.

But York was still the focal point of much local trade and commerce in the North and East Ridings. From the years of the late 17th century and the Restoration onwards, the city became a fashionable social centre for a wide catchment area across and along the Vale of York as far as the coast.

Fine Georgian houses were built within the walls including the Judge's Lodgings, the Assembly Rooms, De Grey Rooms, the Mansion House. **Fairfax House** in Castle Street, home of Charles Fairfax, Viscount Emsley (1700–72) and his family was elegantly remodelled in the mid-18th century and is now a remarkable museum of Georgian interior design, furnishings and middle-class life.

Science and scholarship

By the early 19th century, many people in York realised the city was missing out as a centre of intellectual activity compared with growing importance of centres in the new manufacturing cities of Leeds, Manchester, Newcastle and Hull. A scientific or Philosophical Society was formed in the town in 1822 to deal with matters of local antiquity and scientific enquiry. Members were soon to play a leading role in saving the city's historic walls, and within a decade, in 1830, the Society opened their magnificent **Yorkshire Museum** on the site of the ruins of St Mary's Abbey. With astonishing vision, the Museum founders actually incorporated some of the ruins, which their members had helped to excavate, within the basement of the grand neoclassic building erected to house the museum's collection.

They also built a library and a lecture theatre in which to hold public lectures.

Thanks to two remarkable individuals who held office with the Yorkshire Philosophical Society for many years, York became a national important centre for intellectual energy, learning, scientific enquiry and scholarship. These two people were William Vernon Harcourt (1789–1871), son of the Archbishop of York, Chairman and later President of the YPS, and the great geologist, palaeontologist and topographer John Phillips (1800–1874) who arrived in York in 1824, as a penniless apprentice surveyor with his uncle, the great pioneering geologist and mapmaker William Smith (1769–1839). Phillips left York 30 years later to become Professor of Geology at Oxford University, one of the top scientific academic posts in the British Isles. Phillips was an early professional scientist and museum curator, serving as paid secretary of the Society and the first professional Keeper of the Yorkshire Museum[1].

The Museum Gardens were carefully laid out as a resource for education and botanic and other research and opened to the public for this purpose. An Observatory was built for astronomical research. In 1831 Harcourt and Phillips used their new Museum as the centrepiece of the first meeting of the British Association for the Advancement of Science in York. Later called the "Parliament of Science" the Association brought scientists from all over Britain together for an annual conference and sharing of research. Phillips was the Association's Secretary for many years.

Phillips' work pioneering the interpretation of the geology of the Yorkshire Coast and the Yorkshire Dales, and in encouraging both professional and amateur science throughout the region, makes him one of the intellectual giants of the 19th century, especially in his adopted home city of York. When he left to take up one of the most prestigious academic posts in British science at Oxford University, he continued to publish, teach and support the work of others. When he died in 1874 following a tragic accident after a university dinner, he was brought back by train from Oxford to York, in line with his wishes, to be buried with his beloved sister, and fellow geologist, Anne, in a simple grave in York Cemetery. The Minister's great bell was tolled and the whole city turned out for his funeral cortege.

His home for many years in York was in the former Lodge to St Mary's Abbey, at what is now the Marygate entrance to the Museum

Gardens. It was from the private garden of this house that Phillips took what at that time was only the second ever, close-up photograph of the moon by telescope. A blue plaque on the building commemorates his occupancy of the house, now appropriately the home of the Yorkshire Museum Trust.

The Museum that John Phillips did so much to help to establish in 1830 now houses collections of national importance, but especially outstanding Roman, Viking and Medieval artefacts, including the famous Middleham Jewel, using modern techniques of interpretation, education and communication to bring both palaeontology and natural history to newer, younger audiences in ways which also relate to current issues of ecology and climate change.

The Railway Age

Phillips also published in 1853 what was perhaps the world's first popular railway guidebook to the newly established North Eastern Railway in Yorkshire[2], aimed at the newly literate audiences, then able to travel quickly and cheaply across Yorkshire for the first time in human history. It was the coming of the railways in the late 1840s that was to rapidly change life in England by dramatically improving speed of communication. True, turnpike roads of the late 18th and early 19th century had allowed the journey to London to shrink from several to less than two days, but stagecoach travel was still slow and totally unaffordable for most people. Even more significant, railways enabled the fast interchange of ideas, not just for travel and meetings, for example of embryonic trade associations, political parties and unions, but for newspapers, books, a national standard "railway time", eventually an electric telegraph system, soon used even as a way of catching criminals

York was to benefit like few other cities in England from the new railway age – largely owing to the brilliant, if unscrupulous, entrepreneur George Hudson of York (1800–71) the so-called Railway King[3]. Hudson's York and North Midland Railway gave him the opportunity for extraordinary and not always legal wheeler dealing of the railway boom. Though he ended up bankrupt and disgraced, what Hudson achieved was to make "all railways come to York". York became the major rail hub it remains to the present day, a key point both on the

East Coast Main Line between London and Edinburgh, but also the equally important Trans Pennine routes linking Liverpool, Manchester, Leeds, Hull, Darlington and Newcastle and Scarborough.

York Station, the second to serve the city, with its great train shed, a huge 800 feet long span of curving arches, supported on iron columns, has been described as "one the great iron cathedrals of the railway age". It was designed by Thomas Elliot Harrison, Chief Engineer of the North Eastern Railway in partnership with company architect Thomas Presser and opened in 1877 and is still fulfilling its primary role over a century and a half later.

A walkway extension of the station overbridge leads almost directly to the entrance to the **National Railway Museum**, housed in former railway buildings and workshops. The NRM is one of the world's great museums, winner of countless national and European awards. Though its collection of magnificent steam locomotives, from George Stephenson's iconic Rocket to the world steam record holding Mallard and the last great steam giants of the 1930 and 50s will always grab the headlines, the Museum is about far more than steam, or even diesel and electric locomotives, including the legendary Japanese bullet trains. Using a variety of exhibits and interpretive techniques, the Museum tells an epic story of technical, economic and social change, worldwide. This railway age transformation applied not just to travel but to industrial production and exchange of ideas and information; a transformation of society during the 19th and 20th centuries that can only be compared with the more recent impacts of the internet age. Much of the Museum is devoted to social history, the railway carriages used by royalty and ordinary commuters, the memorabilia which indicate the impact of the railway on every aspect of our lives and of that of our recent ancestors, and indeed the future.

One of the most popular corners of the Museum is the observation veranda where the visitor can watch the passing of trains, from the latest Azuma Scottish expresses heading for Edinburgh or London, to humble local commuter trains clashing their way over the complex points.

It is sad to reflect that with all this railway heritage, the city is no longer a manufacturer of railway equipment or rolling stock or centre of railway engineering. The once busy former NER/LNER/BREL

Holgate Road Carriage Works finally closed in 2002, apart from some minor maintenance and repair workshops.

Victorian York – cocoa and social reform

From the 1840s onwards the railway brought industry and trade to York on a hitherto unimaginable scale. It allowed the city to develop and population expand as rows of Victorian workers terraced housing outside the city walls testify. The local railways and later trams, trolley and motor buses also allowed the city to extend into the Vale of York to create outer commuter suburbs.

One of the major industries to develop and prosper in York because of the railway was the manufacture of sweets, most especially cocoa and chocolate. The oldest of these manufacturers was Terry's. The company started in 1767 as a small enterprise in Bootham, owned by Robert Berry and William Blaydon, making cough sweets and glazed fruit. Joseph Terry (1793–1850), a chemist born in Pocklington, joined the firm in 1825 helping it to expand. After the death of Blaydon and retirement of Berry the firm took Terry's name. The enterprise was so successful it opened a new factory in the hamlet of Clementhorpe, downriver from Skeldergate Bridge. This was in a prime position close to a large riverside wharf to receive supplies of imported cocoa and sugar, twice weekly, by steamboat along the River Ouse.

But Terry's was also shrewd enough to use the newly created North Eastern Railway to get their products sold throughout England, especially to the Midlands and to London and to develop his business nationally.

Rowntrees came later but became even more successful. Joseph Rowntree was born in 1836. As a Quaker, denied access to universities and many traditional careers, he used his energy and creativity to join his brother, Henry Isaac Rowntree, in developing the company that Henry had set up. It was soon to become one of the great confectionary manufacturing enterprises of England. As well as chocolate and cocoa, the Rowntree brothers developed a popular form of fruit pastille which was cheaper and better quality than the imported French equivalent. By 1863 production was such that they had to take over a former foundry at Tanners Moat, close to what was then the new Lendal Bridge.

Rowntrees were soon investing in the latest technology for cocoa and chocolate making. Such was the demand throughout Victorian England, even with minimal advertising, that production to meet that demand had to soar. But Joseph and his son Seebohm Rowntree (1871–1954), who became Chairman in 1923, were not only shrewd industrialists, but great philanthropists, developing a carefully planned village at New Earswick, on a greenfield site two miles outside the city. The Rowntrees understood that a healthy and happy workforce was a more efficient and productive workforce. In 1899 Seebohm also initiated the first of many detailed surveys of poverty in the city which led to the setting up of what are now the Joseph Rowntree Charitable Trusts. These are now among Britain's greatest anti-poverty, social housing and democratic research organisations[4]. Typical of Rowntrees, in 1921, the company bought land and dedicated a beautiful and still extremely popular public park on the banks of the Ouse south of Clementhorpe, in memory of the Rowntree employees who had lost their lives in World War I. This is a wonderful, living memorial that has benefited so many later generations.

So successful were Rowntrees that by the latter part of the 19th century, they had outgrown their Tanners Moat premises. In 1890 the decision was taken to locate their confectionary production into a purpose-built fine new factory at a new 20-acre greenfield site on Haxby Road in what at that time was the edge of York, but within walking distance of New Earswick. The factory site even had its own railway branch line.

Success continued throughout the twentieth century with Rowntree's becoming a household name for its cocoa, chocolate, pastilles and fruit gums. By 1988 Rowntrees had grown to become the fourth largest chocolate manufacturer in the world.

Unbelievably, these two bright jewels in Yorkshire's crown were soon to be threatened – a problem of success. Such is the nature of predatory capitalism, that in 2005 Terry's was sold to a multinational corporation Kraft, who now outsource the manufacture of chocolate by this famous British and Yorkshire brand in Slovakia, Poland and even Switzerland.

To rub salt in the wounds, Terry's great Chocolate Works factory, built in 1926 overlooking the Knavesmire has been transformed to luxury apartments, as developers' brochures stated, purchasers enjoy great views across the famous racecourse.

Likewise, Rowntrees was bought by the Swiss-based Nestlé

Corporation who now source the manufacture of most of the world-famous brands elsewhere in the EU.

But Rowntree have fared somewhat better than Terrys. Though the Rowntree name has vanished from many products, manufacture of many of them continues in York. Around 2,000 people are still employed by Nestlés in manufacturing, plus a further 170 in the company's key research and development unit in the city, making the company still one of the largest employers in the city. The biggest single item produced in terms of quantity is the ever-popular KitKat bar, of which 4 million per day are produced for the world market, and also Polo Mints, Aero, Milkibar and Yorkie Bars.

With an inevitable symmetry, Joseph Rowntree's 1890 model factory on Haxby Road where in the 1920s 6,000 people were employed, has been converted to fashionable apartments, a story all too familiar as Britain de-industrialises.

The modern city

So, what has happened to York during the first quarter of the 21st Century?

In a curious way, the city is like a giant doughnut. The central hole in the doughnut, like a dab of rich cream, is the Roman, Viking and Medieval city contained within the great City Walls, with so much of Yorkshire's story contained within that small area.

It is all so compact, even compressed. So much is within easy walking distance, and therefore for good and for ill, a perfect tourist destination.

But the real, working city where most of the 193,000 people who call the city their home, live and work, extends around and outwards from the ancient heart.

York is, by any measure, an extremely pleasant city in which to both live and to work. It has attractive suburbs, and satellite villages which in some cases have been absorbed into the main fabric of the city and in others are separated from the city by areas of precious Green Belt. Like any city of its size, it has its poorer districts and drab inner and outer areas of featureless housing. It also has a high measure of social deprivation and, sadly, much needed foodbanks, even in the city of Rowntree. It also has its quota of car-served city edge supermarkets for everyday shopping and even a "designer-outlet" shopping centre on the city edge.

Greener York

Yet it is also a green city, within its wider boundaries, fine areas of green space, often known as Strays, where the city's inhabitants can enjoy access for informal outdoor recreation – to walk, stroll, cycle, exercise a dog, or simply enjoy the natural world. Many of these Strays are ancient commons with public access rights. The most famous of these is **Knavesmire**, which is also used as York's Racecourse, with nearby **Micklegate Stray**. To the south of the city centre there is also **Walmgate Stray**, **Hob Moor** whilst to the north lies **Clifton Park, Bootham Stray** and **Monk Stray**. There is also a network of good walking and cycling routes along the banks of the river, or which link the city centre with outlying suburbs and the now rapidly expanding satellite villages for example along the banks of both the Ouse and the Foss as far as Haxby. There are several routes which use former rail lines, such as out to Huntington and Osbaldwick, but most notably the 15-mile Sustrans route between York and Selby using the disused sections of railway trackbed between York and Riccal, linked to sections of cycleway and riverside path into the centres of both York and Selby. This includes the elegant Millennium Bridge at Nunthorpe which provides a traffic free route from the University at Heslington, joining cycle paths and walking routes alongside both sides of the river, past Rowntree Park and into the city centre.

In terms of controlling traffic which still congests and pollutes much of the old city centre, York Council has made valiant efforts. Many of the narrow streets were the first in Britain to be pedestrianised. Various measures to reduce private cars at least in daylight hours have been of enormous benefit to the city, its inhabitants, and its visitors. Predictably, resistance from motoring lobbyists is still a constant threat to any traffic management scheme. An experimental closure of Lendal Bridge and Coppergate to daytime traffic in 2014 came to grief despite scientific evidence of much reduced air pollution and less delays to buses. With a greater understanding of how traffic pollution contributes to premature death and illness, it was a sad reflection how the convenience of vociferous motorists to save a few minutes' journey time, instead of walking, cycling, or using a bus, is so often allowed to triumph over the life-threatening pain and suffering of thousands of others, and at vast cost to the National Health Service.

On the more positive side, York has been one of the pioneering cities in the UK in the use of electric buses, and reintroduction of street trams has also been suggested. There is also a very efficient, highly successful park and ride bus service several points on or near the outer Ring Road into the city centre, and an exceptionally good network of local bus services feeding into the city centre from the outer suburbs and also connecting the city with other towns in Yorkshire. These supplement the excellent network of rail services that link the city with neighbouring cities and towns of Yorkshire, such as Leeds, Sheffield, Doncaster, Scarborough, Harrogate, Knaresborough and even (though sadly no longer by the much-lamented direct rail route via Market Weighton) to Hull. In rail terms, York is the centre of Yorkshire.

Two universities

York also enjoys the status, and the employment opportunities, of two fine Universities.

The University of York was established in 1963 as one of a new generation of post-war Universities created at that time to meet the growing needs of the country for highly qualified graduates in both the science and the humanities. The University was established on a greenfield site near the village of Heslington, some two miles to the east of the city. It operates on the collegiate system, with purpose-built teaching, research, library and accommodation blocks in carefully designed, tree-lined green spaces, yet only a few minutes' (frequent) bus or cycle ride from the city centre. This allows students to enjoy the best of both worlds, and with ample space for the university for expand. Such has been the success of the University which enjoys an international reputation for its teaching and research, that it has now joined the elite Russell group of British Universities.

York St Johns University is in one way newer, but in another way older that its larger sister. The University emerged from the merger of two well respected Yorkshire institutions, the York Diocesan College founded in 1841, and the Ripon College of St John, which was established in 1974, the two institutions combining in a single University on a central campus in 2006. St John's therefore offers more of a city-centre experience situated as it is in Lord Mayor's Walk, close to the city walls. With around 7,000 students it offers a different learning experience with over a hundred different degree options in academic and vocational disciplines available, as well as the thriving post-graduate York Business School.

Both Universities are major sources of employment for the city, in teaching, catering, accommodation and other services with a combined student population of over 26,000. The universities with their well-informed students and staff also provide a huge boost to cultural life and diversity in the city. The best concert hall in York, for example is reputed to be the Jack Lyon Hall at York University, easily accessible for most York people.

The Arts and Culture

York is also a major regional and even nationally important cultural centre for the visual and performing arts.

In 2014 the city was designated by UNESCO as a City of Creative Media Arts, reflecting the richness of its cultural heritage, past and present. One factor is the 250 media arts companies based in the city, employing 3,000 people, more than Nestlés. The city has also become justifiably well known as a major centre for a variety of annual national and regional cultural festivals.

A focal point for the visual arts is York's **Art Gallery** in Exhibition Square. The Gallery has a fine collection and representative paintings from over seven centuries to the present time, including some fascinating historic and contemporary paintings, drawings and watercolours of the city. There is also a nationally important collection of British 20th ceramics. It also houses a major collection of the work of York's most famous painter, William Etty (1787–1849). Etty was born in the city and achieved fame through his somewhat voluptuous nudes that escaped Victorian prudery by depicting allegedly mythological subjects. Etty was also a fine portraitist and also a great campaigner for the protection for the city's historic environment, including the Walls. Appropriately his statue now dominates Exhibition Square.

In terms of the performing arts, the city benefits from three major public theatres. The oldest is the **Theatre Royal** in St Leonard's Place, dating back to 1744 but recently carefully refurbished. The theatre's company offers its own productions but also those of touring groups. **The Grand Opera House** in Clifford Street, opened in 1902, is a large traditional Edwardian theatre, the perfect setting for full scale musicals and operas as well as plays and pantomime. Out on the Haxby Road **The Joseph Rowntree Theatre,** another example of the work of the city's great benefactor, is a more community-based theatre offering space for amateur as well as professional groups. **The Barbican Centre** on Paragon Street also offers a venue for large public events, including major touring concerts of popular music, and sporting events such as snooker.

York also has a vibrant literary scene. Though there are no major novels set in the city, nor has it been used in many celebrated films probably because its streets and buildings are too easily recognisable and might seem to distract from the drama, it was the birthplace of one of the greatest English poets of the 20th century, W.H.Auden (1907–1973) even though he wrote little about Yorkshire as such. One of our greatest living actors, Dame Judi Dench, was born in York and has very close links to its theatre. Her father, a physician, was the medical doctor for the Theatre Royal whilst her mother was its wardrobe mistress. The city has an annual **Literary Festival** which draws authors from all over the UK, and includes the prestigious York Poetry Prize. The city also has several small presses and a flourishing York Writers Group.

It is also the national home of Early Music. Early Music can be defined as music written in the Medieval period (500 to 1400), Renaissance (1400–1600) and Baroque (1600–1750) but (crucially) played on period instruments, whether genuine instruments or modern replicas. The York Early Music Foundation, based in the city, sponsors the international **York Early Music Festival** in the summer months, making use of the myriad medieval and renaissance buildings in the city as perfect venues for music of their period.

Of course, York would not be York without its mandatory annual

Viking Festival, a celebration of all that is Viking – events, exhibitions, entertainment and even a Thing – a symposium to which Vikings and those of Viking extraction from the world can gather to celebrate the city and Europe's great Viking heritage.

The challenges ahead

How will York cope with the two immense challenges facing Britain in the post-Pandemic era and in the face of what seems like a very "hard" Brexit?

Whilst it is risky to forecast outcomes, both Brexit and the pandemic could affect a city so heavily dependent on the hospitality industry and invisible earnings of tourism, especially hard. Many York people may be grateful that the almost overwhelming influx of visitors to the old parts of the city, all year, has ceased. This may be especially noticeable in the summer months with a lack of overseas visitors because of travel restriction and fear of coming to the UK with constant worries of new virus variants. This might influence many visitors, most especially those from USA, Canada, Australasia, China and Japan, who could be increasingly nervous about travelling on long haul flights.

For many it might be delightful to get their city back. It will be an unexpected pleasure to shop in the narrow streets, visit attractions or simply be able walk the pavements without the onslaught of chattering groups, or go into a pub on a Friday or Saturday night without the horrors of hen parties and stag nights and drunkenness in the streets.

But there could be a serious downside.

York's estimated 7 million annual visitors provide a huge boost of spending to the local economy, not just the hotels, B&Bs, pubs, shops, cafes, galleries theatres and tourist attractions, but spreading out as a so-called "multiplier" effect in service industries, as these same businesses in turn spend their money in the wider city economy.

Already Britain has seen a dramatic switch to on-line shopping resulting in many once-popular chain stores closing, leaving huge gaps and empty shops in most High Streets. York, with its wonderful range of smaller, independent shops and outlets, including its vibrant street market, may not suffer in the same way. On the other hand, small businesses in a city like York, heavily dependent on the tourist pound, are especially vulnerable. If income doesn't materialise from summer visitors, rents and bills still have to be paid.

The hope, of course that in the short term at least, domestic tourism – staycations – may make up for the temporary but perhaps permanent lack of long-haul visitors from America, Australasia or the Far East, and even from mainland Europe. Many British people, especially if cheap flights and package holidays abroad are no longer as easily available as they were pre-Pandemic, may once again discover the wonderful heritage of cities like York, and the surrounding Yorkshire countryside, that lies on its doorstep. Whether or not they will spend as generously as overseas visitors remains to be seen.

But a further serious threat is to our universities not just in York, but in other cities. If overseas students are denied access through increasingly severe immigration rules, rather than facing hostility, extra expense and paperwork, many students from both within and outside the EU may choose more welcoming countries. This is especially true of many students from neighbouring countries within the EU who can no longer travel and study freely in Britain without a complex and expensive system of visas and permits. The UK no longer supports the Erasmus international student scholarship scheme; the proposed new Turing scheme will only benefit UK students. No longer can Universities join or compete for many major EU-funded research programmes, and other collaboration projects, and it is research that allows universities to achieve all that they do. Loss of student income and research grants could prove seriously damaging for all our British academic institutions, including our Yorkshire universities.

The great scholar, teacher and author Alcuin of York, one of Yorkshire's most influential civilising influences on Britain, Europe and the World, would have been truly appalled.

Notes

1 Speakman Colin 2020: *John Phillips Yorkshire's Traveller through Time* Gritstone Coop Hebden Bridge
2 Phillips John 1854: *Railway Excursions from the York, Leeds and Hull* Goddard & Lancaster Hull and York
3 Peacock A.J., Joy David 1971: *George Hudson of York* Dalesman Clapham
4 Hartley Marie & Ingilby Joan 1961: *Yorkshire Portraits* Dent London

2

The Vale of York and Mowbray

The perfect place to begin to understand the Vale of York and Mowbray is from the famous viewpoint at the top of Sutton Bank, on the edge of the North York Moors, from where you look across the great plain of farmland that extends across to the distant ridges of the Pennines, as far north as the eye can see towards the Swale and Tees valleys, and south towards the foothills of the Peak District and Trent valley power stations, with York Minster as a central feature.

The Vale of York is the generally accepted title for the flatter, southern parts of the area as far south as the Lower Aire valley and Humberhead Levels, with the Pennines to the west and Howardian Hills and Yorkshire Wolds to the east. From the market town of Thirsk northwards, the broad valley is generally accepted as being the Vale of Mowbray, overlooked by the Hambleton Hills to the east and foothills of the Pennines and entrance to Wensleydale to the west. The land is more undulating here than in the Vale of York; there are more areas of grassland, hedgerows and scattered woodland, and smaller fields as you travel north.

Creation of the landscape

Geologically, the area lies above Triassic sandstones and mudstones, with some Lower Jurassic sandstone, all covered with deep layers of glacial till – clay, sand and gravel. Two huge crescent-shaped moraines created by the debris from the retreating glaciers of the Last Ice Age some 15,000 years ago, form low ridges across the Vale at Escrick and at York. They provided prehistoric routes across the marshes of the valley as well as modern transport links. The complex drainage system of rivers, all tributaries of the Ouse, that flow south of the Tees to meet the Humber – the Swale, Ure, Foss, Nidd, Wharfe, Derwent and the Aire – have all brought rich alluvial deposits over the millennia which, after being drained by human cultivation, has produced the rich farmland of the Vale, some of the finest in the north producing intensive crops of wheat, beet, potatoes and oil seed rape.

A small surviving area of the ancient fenland that once covered much of the Vale survives at **Askham Bog Nature Reserve**, just south of York, managed by Yorkshire Wildlife Trust. The 44-hectare Reserve, situated on the site of a former glacial lake close by the York moraine, is noted for its biodiversity – rare royal ferns, gingerbread sedge, water violets, diverse insect life and small mammals. There are also important small areas of heathland and ancient woodland at Strensall, Stockton and Allerthorpe Commons. The recently extended Lower Derwent Valley National Nature Reserve, east of Wheldrake, is also an internationally important Ramsar Wetland and Special Protection Area because of its old, botanically rich, hay meadows and a habitat for a significant number of birds and waders.

Further north in the Vale of Mowbray near Bedale, and of regional ecological importance, is **Thorp Perrow Arboretum**, a 34 hectare collection of rare and exotic conifers. The collections of trees and plants date back to the 16th century but have been developed and expanded over several centuries. With no less than five National Collections of tree species, as well as 51 Champion Trees, Thorp Perrow is widely regarded as one of the most important arboreta in the UK. It is now a popular visitor centre with historic gardens, lakes, birds of prey and mammals.

The other crucially important geological feature along the edge of the Vale which impacts on the landscape is the long, narrow strip of Magnesian Limestone of the Permian era. This is a remarkable geological feature that runs through the north of England, between Nottinghamshire and the coast of County Durham. In the Vale of York, it forms the natural western boundary of both West Yorkshire and the Yorkshire Dales, but is a distinctive landscape feature of its own where it emerges above ground, sweetening the soil and evident in walls, houses and churches.

This lovely pale stone, durable yet easier to carve, has, for centuries, been precious building material. York Minster is just one of the famous buildings created from stone, with quarries at Tadcaster and near Cawood on the Wharfe used for its construction over several centuries. The bed of a narrow, shallow canal survives near Cawood from where cut stone was floated to wharves on the River Ouse for onward transport to the site of the Abbey. It was also used for the building of Selby Abbey. But the stone has also been extensively used for many country houses, churches, public buildings. Even walls in towns and villages in the Vale of York are dominated by this mellow, sometimes slightly creamy-coloured or pale grey stone, giving towns in the Vale like Wetherby, Tadcaster, Knaresborough, Ripon, Aberford, Spofforth, Harewood, a distinctive character, in some ways not unlike the Cotswolds. But the stone was used much more widely in larger Yorkshire towns because of its high quality, especially for public buildings in towns such as Beverley and York.

Early occupants of the Vale to have a major impact on the landscape were farmers of the Neolithic (New Stone Age) period, which began in England around 11,000 years ago after the last Ice Age. Their most impressive monument is the huge Thornborough Henges, near the village of West Tanfield between Ripon and Masham. The monument consists of three massive circular henges 240 metres in diameter, created by deep banks and ditches, connected by a huge Cursus, or avenue, bounded by parallel ditches. One of the greatest henge monuments in the British Isles, it dates from around 2,500–3,500 BC, part of a whole network of remarkable Neolithic monuments in the two Vales. Close to Boroughbridge and only a little younger, are the celebrated Devil's Arrows, three huge gritstone menhirs or standing stones, the largest almost 7 metres high. All were probably dragged on wooden rollers from Plumpton Rocks near Knaresborough. They date from late Neolithic, early Bronze Age times, between 2,500 and 1,000BC, and again probably part of a long-lost sacred landscape.

Along the Great North Road and its branches

The Vale has long been crucial for communication between the south and north of Britain, and across gaps through the Pennines to the east coast. The Great North Road on the south to north axis began as a prehistoric trade route, taking advantage of the higher land above the marsh provided by glacial moraines or limestone outcrops. The ancient road was improved and developed by the Roman Generals to become the main means of communication and military control through the length of their province of Britannia. Known as Rudgate as far as Boroughbridge and Dere Street northwards towards Catterick, it was literally a "highway" raised one or two metres above surrounding fenland to provide people and provision waggons safe, dry passage between London and York and onwards to Scotland.

The metalled Roman highways remained in use throughout medieval times and into the era of coaching and turnpike road improvements, though sections and routes were varied to meet changing travel needs.

In the early days of coaching, York was the principal destination from London and most stagecoach services via Doncaster and Selby terminated there, with connecting services northwards along what is now the A19 to Thirsk and onwards to Northallerton for Darlington and Durham. In later years, as roads improved with faster Mail Coaches, more direct routes to Scotland bypassing York were developed, more or less on the line of the present A1 west of York, making Ferrybridge, Aberford, Wetherby, Boroughbridge, Leeming Bar, Catterick/Scotch Corner, key stagecoach service towns for Anglo-Scottish foot, horse, waggon and coach traffic.

The patterns of small country towns along what is now the A1 and A19 still reflects the influence of the great coaching era between the 17th and mid-19th centuries. Several fine 18th century inns survive, for example in Selby, Aberford, Wetherby and Boroughbridge. Each inn had large stables where horses could be rested and changed, and food and overnight accommodation offered to travellers. Whole teams of farriers, saddlers, blacksmiths, stable hands as well as bakers and butchers were developed to service travellers and their horses. Generally coaching towns are around 15–20 miles apart, to allow tired horses, and not just travellers, to be rested and changed.

Great estates

The Vale of York probably suffered proportionally more than other areas of Yorkshire from the effects of the Harrying of the North, and in later years from Scottish marauders. This may have restricted the growth of towns and villages and settlement during the Middle Ages, compared, for example with similar areas in the south of England. It was perhaps only the coming of the stagecoach and later the railways that displaced stagecoaches that significantly boosted the growth of the Vale of York towns. Many have kept their character even as new suburbs have grown around them.

Many of large estates and manors established in Norman times survive in some form or other in this deeply rural part of Yorkshire, served by fine country houses. One of the most remarkable of these is **Markenfield Hall**, three miles south of Ripon, a nationally important example of a 14th century Gothic crenallated and moated manor house, with a gatehouse and extensive parkland, built by John de Markenfield, a close associate of Piers Gaveston, favourite of Edward II.

Newby Hall, at Skelton on Ouse, close to Ripon, and owned by the Compton family, is another nationally important house and garden. Designed by Sir Christopher Wren in 1690 with important additions by York architect John Carr and the great Robert Adam, who was responsible for much of the internal design, this house is celebrated not only for its furniture including an outstanding Chippendale collection, paintings and tapestries, but a magnificent collection of classical sculpture in the purpose-designed Sculpture Gallery. The 40-acre gardens, both terraced and riverside, with their own miniature railway, are equally impressive, being voted the best Historic Garden in the UK in 2019. Close by is the beautiful Church of Christ the Consoler built in 1870–1 to the designs of the great Victorian architect William Burges, the building paid for with the unused ransom money collected to the pay the ransom of Frederick Vyner, son of the Marquis of Ripon murdered by Greek bandits in 1870. A similar richly decorated church by Burges was erected in the grounds of Studley Royal, at the other side of Ripon.

Closer to York, near Newton-on-Ouse, is **Beningborough,** another fine early Georgian house in Italian style, built close to the site of a Tudor mansion. It is now owned by the National Trust and is noted for its splendid gardens and as well as its permanent collections. The house has developed a special partnership with the National Portrait Gallery to offer changing and varied exhibitions linked to portraiture.

Though **Lotherton Hall** is a Leeds City Museum and Park, it is situated just east of the A1 close to Aberford, it lies firmly within the Vale of York. This mainly Victorian and Edwardian country mansion was the home of Sir Alvary Gascoigne (1893–1970), a member of a well-known local family from the nearby village of Parlington. Sir Alvary was a British diplomat (Britain's first Ambassador to Moscow and to Japan) who gifted the house and its contents to Leeds City Council in 1968. It has been transformed into an exceptionally interesting museum of costume, furniture, paintings (including a collection of miniature portraits), silverware and ceramics, including examples of work by William de Morgan, and the Burmantofts and Leeds Potteries. There is a historic chapel in what are extensive gardens and parkland. Families are especially attracted by the popular Wildlife World, a bird garden with enclosures for small mammals.

Towns of the Vale

Selby, on the Ouse, at the southern end of the Vale, is known for its magnificent **Selby Abbey Church**. The town probably owes its existence at least in part to what is a charming legend. In 1069 a young French monk named Benedict from the monastery in Auxerre in Burgundy, had a vision which made him feel impelled to leave his parent monastery to travel to England to the port of King's Lynn in England. From there he took a boat up the Humber and then the Ouse towards York. When his boat was passing the little Anglo-Viking farming settlement on the river at Selby, he caught sight of three white swans alighting on the river and took these as a sign of the Holy Trinity. So he immediately disembarked, deciding this was the place to build a small hermitage. His vision came to the attention of Hugh, Sheriff of York, immediately following the Harrying of the North. Hugh in turn gained the support of the Conqueror who, perhaps to appease the Pope's anger at the recent Harrying of the North massacres, granted Benedict land at Selby on which to build an abbey. Work began on the new building with limestone brought by small craft along a specially constructed dyke or canal from a suitable quarry near Monk Fryston, to the River Ouse.

The fact that William the Conqueror's son Henry, later Henry I, known as Beauclerc because of his scholarship, was born in Selby in 1070 as the King and his consort were travelling to York, may also have helped secure financial support for the Abbey. The three white swans form part of the Selby's coat of arms to this day. Though most of the Abbey itself has now long vanished, its magnificent Church with its great Norman columns has survived and is regarded as one the best-preserved Abbey Churches in England. It is especially noted for its magnificent 13th and 14th century stonework, including the wonderful east window, much of it with its original 14th century glass, tracing Old Testament stories. One particular piece of this glass in what is now known as the Washington Window is of special interest. It contains the arms of the Washington family. It is probably the earliest surviving representation of the iconography that was to be incorporated into the national flag of the United States – the stars and stripes.

The town of Selby has an attractive central area of narrow winding streets around its fine market place that retains its ancient cross and hosts a busy Monday market. There are old inns and still independent shops, and pleasant pedestrianised areas. The town developed over the centuries both as a small inland port linked with grain storage and flour milling, as well as a local iron works and for a time was a town on the northern edge of the Yorkshire coalfield. The last of the local deep coal mines nearby closed in 2004.

It was also the terminus of Yorkshire's first railway, the Leeds and Selby that opened as early as 1834. Remains of the original 1830s station, Yorkshire's first, is still to be seen on the riverside road beyond the railway bridge across the Ouse. It lies just behind the present attractive Victorian North Eastern Railway station, where a Civic Society plaque explains the history of this unique surviving train shed. Close by, now hidden by trees, were the wharves from where between 1834 and 1840, passengers left their train to embark on a four-hour journey by steamboat down the Humber to Hull. But once the railway was constructed over the historic swing railway bridge over the Ouse and alongside the Humber to Brough and Hull, the journey took a fraction of the time[1].

A small riverside park and walkway now mark the site of these early wharves where Benedict first landed.

About four miles south of Selby is **Carlton Towers**, a magnificent high Victorian neo-Gothic mansion set within a 250 acre parkland estate. It was designed by Sir John Francis Bentley architect of Westminster

Cathedral and Edward Welby Pugin, son of Augustus Pugin, designer of the House of Commons. The ancestral home of the Howard family, it is now a hotel, conference centre and events venue.

Tadcaster, just off the Great North Road but on the River Wharfe, was also a coaching town of some importance on the main westbound turnpike road between York and Leeds. It was also a junction of routes to Wetherby and Harrogate via the little former spa town of Boston Spa. Strangely, Tadcaster partly missed out on the railway age, as the important connection between York and Leeds, eventually opened in 1840 via the junction at Church Fenton on the York & North Midland line. Tadcaster only got its own station on the relatively less important branch route between Church Fenton and Harrogate in 1849, which in turn was an early victim of the Beeching closures in 1966. But a huge, almost never used (apart from carrying a rail siding to a mill for a short period) viaduct still exists at Tadcaster only a short distance above the 18th century road bridge. This was intended to be a new more direct line to Leeds from York. But soon after the bridge was built in 1849, the railway mania boom collapsed, George Hudson was disgraced and flung into gaol. The shorter line between Leeds and York, which would have used this viaduct, was never built, leaving the viaduct as a slightly ghostly reminder of a long forgotten financial disaster.

Tadcaster's claim to fame began well before the railway age, as the home of one of two of Britain's oldest and most famous breweries, Sam Smith's Old Brewery and John Smith's Brewery, both dating from 1758.

Sam Smith's ales can be enjoyed as far away as London, (Dr Samuel Johnson's famous local inn, **The Cheshire Cheese** in Fleet Street is just one of 20 Sam Smith pubs in the city). Springs deep in the magnesian limestone were considered perfect for brewing ale. Sam's Old Brewery Bitter, the only real cask ale the company now produces, is made from water from the original well in Tadcaster, and it has kept its distinctive taste.

But Sam Smith's has a far larger rival in Tadcaster – John Smith's. The split between the two branches of the Smith brewing family originated from a family quarrel in the 19th century over disputed inheritances. Whilst Sam Smith's has remained a deeply traditional, family-owned company, John Smith, through a succession of takeovers, has become part of the Heineken multinational corporation. John Smith's keg bitter was for a time the second most popular beer in the world, and their Tadcaster brewery is still one of the largest in Europe producing a wide range of internationally known brands of beer and lager.

Travelling north from York, the next market town in the Vale of York, now just off the A19 former coach road is Easingwold. This is a lovely compact market town on the edge of the North York Moors, with its partially covered marketplace and handsome late Georgian and Regency houses and cottages surrounding the square and on Long Street.

Wetherby is an attractive market town, the ancient crossing of the River Wharfe on the more direct Great North Road to Scotland, now mercifully bypassed by the A1, with an old bridge and pleasant riverside and pedestrian areas, as well as a choice of local shops and old inns. Its popular Thursday market was granted to the town by Royal Charter in 1240.

Boroughbridge, like Wetherby on the old Great North Road but also now bypassed by the more direct Great North Road to Scotland from Wetherby, is another very charming, largely unspoiled former coaching town, with several old inns, most now in different usage, a Victorian church with an ornate late Norman doorway and a marketplace with an imposing cross. A short walk from the marketplace are the Devil's Arrows, but a somewhat longer walk from the village centre perhaps along the banks of the Ure lead to Aldborough, one of the oldest continuously inhabited places in Yorkshire. Aldborough, or as the Romans knew it, Isurium Brigantum, was a large Romano-British settlement, the capital of Brigantia occupied and developed at a time when the leaders of the Celtic Kingdom had made their peace with their Roman overlords. Evidence of this comes in two magnificent Roman mosaic floors originally from a Roman villa, and now displayed at a small English Heritage **Roman Museum** in the village. Another has been removed to Leeds Museum. Excavations in the village suggests this was once a large and significant Romano-British town, containing what was a sophisticated, probably fully assimilated Roman colonial settlement. There was a Roman fort on Dere Street, close to what is now Boroughbridge. Recent archaeological finds suggest the town even had its own amphitheatre, but there is probably much more yet to be discovered within this once important Romano-British settlement.

Further along the A19 old coach road from York to the north east is another market and former coaching town of some importance – Thirsk. Archaeological evidence suggests that the site of the town alongside Cod Beck was occupied in Iron Age times. The town was recorded in the Domesday book as belonging to two Saxon Lords Orm and Thor, but its name in Old Norse "Threask" meaning lake or fen is of Viking origin. By the 12th century its manor had passed into the hands of a Norman family, the Mowbrays, the great Norman landowners who gave their name to the Vale. The castle and later manor house has long vanished after Scottish raids. The 15th century Parish Church is regarded as an outstanding example of English Gothic Perpendicular style. Its medieval marketplace, with a charter going back to 1245, still hosts popular Saturday and Tuesday markets. The distinctive neo-Gothic market clock erected to commemorate the marriage of the Duke of York to Princess Mary of Teck in 1896, has become a symbol of the town. It remains a country market town of attractive Georgian and Victorian houses, inns, and boutique shops.

Many visitors to the town are drawn by the name of one of Yorkshire's most popular authors of the 20th century – James Herriot. This was the pen name of Thirsk vet Alf Wight (1916–95). His old home and veterinary surgery are now **The World of James Herriot** visitor centre. The famous **All Creatures Great and Small** series of autobiographical novels used the fictional name Darrowby for Thirsk. Sadly for Thirsk, this was appropriated by the film and television series for more picturesque locations in the Yorkshire Dales as Askrigg and more recently Grassington – though Wight's veterinary work with local farmers and horse and pet owners, was based between the Vale of Mowbray, the Moors and the Dales as well as around Thirsk itself. The Museum is filled with Herriot memorabilia and material that recalls his life and career, including his experiences during the Second World War in Thirsk.

Thirsk, along with Malton and Middleham, is also one of the major centres of the racehorse industry with several large stables and exercise areas. Racecourses at Thirsk itself, Catterick, Ripon, Pontefract, Redcar, Wetherby, York, Beverley and Doncaster of St Leger fame, make racing a huge source of income and employment for rural Yorkshire.

Northallerton, eight miles north of Thirsk, must be one of the smallest county towns of England, yet is the administrative capital of England's largest county, North Yorkshire. A high proportion of its modest population of 16,832 are probably local Government employees and their families linked either to North Yorkshire County Council, or to Hambleton District Council whose headquarters are also in the town.

County Hall is the imposing Edwardian building, also former headquarters of the old North Riding, that stands directly opposite the railway station. Like Thirsk, Northallerton has a fine parish church, with much work in the Perpendicular style. Rather than a single marketplace, it has a long, broad High Street along which every Wednesday and Saturday is one of North Yorkshire's largest and most vibrant markets, with a Market Charter that goes back to 1200. It was also an important coaching town, with some surviving coaching inns and handsome Georgian houses, being on an interchange with coach routes from York and the south, branching to the busy port of Stockton on Tees.

The railway also had a significant influence on Northallerton, its station on the East Coast Main line being at its junction to Cleveland via Eaglescliffe (for Stockton) and Middlesbrough. Unfortunately, the link with the Wensleydale Railway heading westwards to Leyburn Leeming, Bedale, and Redmire, though surviving from a station a mile away at so-called Northallerton West, is currently not in use.

Yarm-on-Tees was the most northerly township in the Vale of Mowbray, an exceptionally beautiful little town in a wooded setting that deserves its honoured place in Yorkshire. Until the Tees Barrage was built, Yarm's old bridge was the highest point of the tidal flow up the River Tees. It has an unspoiled High Street, boarded by attractive Georgian and Victorian houses and shops, a handsome free-standing Town Hall. The great railway viaduct over the river now carries frequent TransPennine trains between Leeds and Middlesbrough that call at its recently reopened station.

Farming – and flooding in the Vale

This is deeply rural Yorkshire. The two Vales are both dominated not by towns or urban centres, nor by tourism activity, but by one prime land-use – arable farming. According to Natural England in 2019

(National Character Assessment 2019) there were no less than 1,089 farms in the Vale of York alone in 2019 compared with 1,139 in 2009, making it a major source of employment and income, activity directed from the many traditional, if modernised, farmhouses that dominate the landscape. This is the breadbasket of Yorkshire. The rich alluvial soils of the Vales are predominantly used to grow arable crops of wheat, barley, oilseed rape and increasingly, as demand changes, other vegetables, though in the west of the area, dairy farms and pig rearing become more evident. Yorkshire as a whole actually produces around 37% of England's pork, including much from this part of the region.

Climate change is now making Yorkshire a good wine producing area, with vineyards established in the Vale of York, such as at the Yorkshire Heart winery near Nun Monkton, and also in the Wolds, Ryedale and even the South Pennines.

It is also one of the areas of Yorkshire which could be most at risk from climate change. If as predicted there are more intensely hot summers, crop production yields will decline, as indeed they will after wet, mild winters, if fields in the extensive flood plains down the Vales are flooded or remain saturated into Spring making them impossible to plough or sow.

Flooding has, of course a major impact on the towns and villages in the Vale as much as on agriculture. Most of the towns in the Vale are prone to or at risk from flooding, and in recent years have suffered major incidents. This risk increases the lower down the particular river valley the town or village is situated. Heavy rainstorms or snowmelt rapidly fill moorland streams in the Pennines which in turn causes rivers like the Swale, Ure and Wharfe to fill to burst their banks, forcing the vast mass of water downriver, flooding water meadows, sweeping away walls, fences, bridges with unstoppable force. Thoughtless development in the late 20th century on the flood plains upstream and so-called improvements, straightened rivers or forcing them between high concrete embankments, has acerbated the problem.

Major floods impacted on York in particular in 1947, 1978, 1982, 2000, 2007, 2015, and 2019. So used to flooding York has become that a complex system of hard engineered flood defences along the riverside to protect homes and livelihoods have been constructed. A flood barrier on the River Foss has saved homes and business on several occasions but has had to be enlarged. The city now has an official Flood Map showing areas of the city most likely to be flooded, and those at some, if less, risk. Buildings in all these areas now need to be designed or adapted if not to be flood-proof, then flood resistant or resilient. The iconic 17th century Kings Arms pub on the Staithe in York, just below Ouse Bridge, has been flooded so frequently, the walls and floor of the bar have been completely covered with waterproof tiles, with all electric sockets now re-sited high on walls to be above anticipated water levels.

In Tadcaster the fine old bridge across the Wharfe was totally washed away in the flood caused by Storm Desmond in 2015, leaving the town split in two for several months until a temporary structure could be put in place to allow traffic to cross.

But for the smaller villages and hamlets alongside the rivers or situated in the sunken marshlands along the meandering stretches of the Wharfe, Aire, Ouse and Derwent, villages such as Cawood, Barlby, Snaith or Saltmarshe there are no easy solutions. As in the Calder Valley further west in the Pennines, the impacts of constant flooding have been catastrophic on homes and businesses, with people unable to insure or sell their properties. This is a tragic situation.

The longer term solution lies not in the Vale of York, but fifty or more miles away in the high water catchment areas of the Pennines, where massive work is now taking place to restore resilience in the system, to reverse decades of moorland draining by blocking out ditches and dykes cut to drain the moors in order to slow down water flows, to restore endangered and eroded peatland, to plants trees and woodland and in the steeper valleys, build "leaky Dams" of logs and brushwood to slow down the flash floods which come from ever intensifying rain storms. A further secret weapon of ecologists and flood managers is to bring back a long lost native of Yorkshire, the Beaver – the active little amphibian that gave its name to the town of Beverley. Beavers are energetic builders of dams which in turn create ponds and small areas of wetland that massively increase an area's biodiversity. Critically, by slowing down the flow of water down the rivers which flow into the Vale of York, this reduces the risk and cost of sudden destructive floods at a fraction of the cost of restoration and preventative work. Already active in Cropton Forest on the upper reaches of a tributary of the River Derwent, the cost-effective beaver is likely to make a major comeback in Yorkshire in coming decades.

These and related issues are likely to be among the pre-occupations of the new Yorkshire Climate Commission. But immediate actions are needed to mitigate the now inevitable impacts of climate change and weather extremes, including flooding, heat waves, drought, moorland and forest fires and their impacts on the well-being and economy of the people of Yorkshire.

Agriculture in the Vale after Brexit

Yorkshire farmers are in the front line to deal with that other great challenge of our time – what increasingly appears to be an extremely "hard" Brexit with potentially serious impacts on farming and on the wider rural economy.

Few people will mourn the passing of the EU Common Agricultural Policy in the UK that resulted in the payment of vast subsidies to millionaire landowners and grain barons, but there is still, despite Government promises, high levels of uncertainty about what will replace it and also the complex system of Environmental Stewardship payments, especially important for upland farmers. The various Environmental Stewardship schemes developed over the decades by Natural England and DEFRA both to support hill-farming incomes and help protect the natural environment, now longer apply and are going through a period of radical change. Post Brexit they are being replaced by what is rather grandly called a new Environmental Land Management System in order to deliver the Governments' long-term environmental objectives set out in their 25 Year Environment Plan. Through ELM agreements, from 2024 it is expected that farmers and land managers will be paid for providing environmental benefits. These include:

- Clean air
- Reduction in environmental hazards and pollution
- Thriving plants and wildlife
- Clean Water
- Mitigation and adaptation measures to minimise the impact of climate change.
- Enhanced landscape benefits

What farmers don't perhaps need is yet more complex paperwork, bureaucracy and form filling. But ultimately there could be benefits from making Britain more self-sufficient in food, which would help the industry enormously.

Equally, as many people fear, there could be special trade deals set up with the USA to allow free access to the UK market for American, Australian, Argentinian or other national agribusiness corporations, capable of producing meat and grain on the great wheatbelt prairies or in gigantic factory farms at a fraction of the price it is possible to do so in more environmentally sustainable ways in the United Kingdom by British farmers. This could result in British consumers, especially those on lower incomes, being forced to accept chlorine-washed chicken or hormone boosted beef in supermarkets.

On the other hand, if many foods, particularly salads and vegetables, become more expensive or even scarce because of tariff barriers and border delays for producers in EU countries like Spain and The Netherlands, this could mean that there could be opportunities for Yorkshire farmers to look carefully at their domestic, even local, markets to fill local shops, stalls and restaurants with high quality local products. High quality, organic farm-produced food, free of additives and pesticides, could be attractive options for consumers in the bustling markets and shops in Yorkshire towns, not just in the more specialised Farmers Markets.

There is little doubt that the Yorkshire Agricultural Society, organisers of the annual Yorkshire Show at Harrogate and much more besides, will be in the lead in advising their members how to exploit new opportunities for Yorkshire farmers to meet what could be a growing demand for locally produced seasonal fruit, vegetables and salads. This could mean a revolution in market gardening. For example, new technologies are now being researched in the University of Leeds and elsewhere, to capture unlimited, low-cost geothermal energy available from deep under the North Sea and even inland in old mine workings in Yorkshire. This could, perhaps, be used to heat greenhouses for early crop production, and to reduce our dependency on imported salads, fruit and perhaps even exotic vegetables.

In the Vale of York and Mowbray there could be interesting times ahead.

Notes

1 Bairstow Martin 1990, 2002: *Railways in East Yorkshire Vol 1* pp8–23 Martin Bairstow Farsley, Leeds

3

The North York Moors and Cleveland

Heather moorland is what makes the North York Moors and Cleveland, that part of the old North Riding between the Vale of Pickering and the Tees, unique and special. The open views in late summer across glorious expanses of deep purple heather and ling towards the coast in this part of Yorkshire are justly famous worldwide. The North York Moors National Park contains the largest area of extensive heather moorland – a rare habitat – in England and Wales, covering 44,000 hectares or around a third of the total 554 square miles of 1,436km² of the National Park.

The evolution of the landscape

Heather both defines the National Park and creates that special sense of place, the cultural landscape we all love, so vividly described by the great geologist archaeologist and historian of the Moors, author Frank Elgee (1880–1944) who in his book **The Moorlands of North Eastern Yorkshire** (1912) uses its ancient name *Blackamore*, a reference to its bleak appearance in winter or early spring.

Elgee, who was born on Ormesby near Middlesbrough and was largely self-taught, fought off chronic problems of ill health to become the much-revered curator of the **Dorman Museum** in Middlesbrough. He also published in 1930 perhaps the finest archaeological study of the Moors, **Early Man in North East Yorkshire**. Fittingly, though he died and was buried in Hampshire, Elgee's life and work are commemorated by a simple but appropriated memorial stone on Blakey Ridge, not far from two more ancient memorials – Old Ralph Cross and Fat Betty.

The North York Moors is one of the oldest of Britain's 15 National

Parks being established in 1952, but also geologically speaking, one of the youngest, being formed largely from Lower, Middle and Upper Jurassic sedimentary rocks, mainly sandstones limestones and shales, but with intrusions of ironstone, laid down from ancient seas and estuaries from between 145 and 210 million years ago. The rocks which so determine the character of the landscape are about a third of the age for example of those of Snowdonia or of the Lake District.

The great period of thrusting and folding of the earth's crust which began 145 million years ago, reaching a peak in the great Alpine uplift some 60 million years ago, followed by millennia of glacial and river erosion, created the high, flat topped moorlands we know today. Those that form the southern part of the National Parks above the Vale of Pickering, the site of a great post glacial lake, we now know as the Tabular Hills. The Tabular Hills are intersected by a series of deep valleys caused by fast flowing rivers and springs cutting through middle Jurassic sandstones down to the softer older grey shales of the Lias to create the numerous valleys or dales which are such a feature of the landscape, including Langdale, Newtondale, Rosedale, Farndale, Kirkdale, Bilsdale. Further west lie the great bulk of the Hambleton Hills overlooking the Vale of York, scoured out by glacial ice. An amazing relic of that time is Lake Gormire, clearly visible below Sutton Bank, and one of the few surviving natural glacial lakes in the North of England. As the Hambletons turn north eastwards they form the Cleveland Hills, "Cleve" meaning cliffs, that overlook the Tees Valley. From here, they are penetrated by the Esk Valley and the network of tributary streams each in their own small valley or dale – Kildale, Baydale, Great and Little Fyrupdale, Westerdale, Danby Dale, Glaisdale and the valley along the Murk Esk which contains Goathland.

It is a landscape which has changed constantly, even since the glaciers finally retreated, around 13–12,000BC leaving landscape of heath, wild grasses and sedge. As the climate changed over the following millennia, scrubby woodland, then birch and pine forest succeeded the heath. By Mesolithic times, around 8,500 BC, early hunters were hunting the aurochs (prehistoric cattle), wild boar, red and roe deer in the woodland. By the time Neolithic farmers were clearing the land for crops and for grazing animals, the appearance of the landscape was changing, and the first of the characteristic long barrows – burial mounds – were being built on the hill ridge summits away from the swamp and marshland of the valleys. But as centuries passed, with communities developing the metal-working skills we use to define as characteristic of the Bronze Age, cultivation of the hills was intensified, banks and ditches, and cairns and marker stones on watersheds between the dales, defined tribal boundaries. Large numbers of round barrows were constructed to bury the dead in ritualised urns. The barrows remain a characteristic feature of the Moors.

There is evidence to suggest that by Iron Age times, where trees had been largely cleared from upland areas, the constantly cultivated but not replenished thin soils were suffering from ever greater impoverishment and erosion which was transforming them into the heaths and moorland we see today. The valleys on the other hand benefited from alluvial deposits washed down by fast flowing from mountain streams and remained more fertile, over the centuries creating the patterns of richly fertile farmed valleys contrasting to the bleak and open uplands, which in later centuries, thanks to careful cultivation of the heather on the great estates for sporting interest, have created the vast heather moorland that now so defines the National Park. Thanks to the Countryside Rights of Way Act 2000, most of these magnificent moorlands are fully open to the public for access on foot.

Nature protection is however especially important in the North York Moors National Park. The park is a European Special Protection Area for two bird species – merlin and golden plover, and important for several ground-nesting species. It is the most northerly habitat for the rare Duke of Burgundy butterfly and most southerly for the dwarf conifer. 23% of the National Park is woodland, though much of that is coniferous commercial woodland, managed by the Forestry Commission, planted as strategic timber reserve between the 1920s and 70s. It is now much more sympathetically managed to achieve greater biodiversity and recreational opportunity. The National Park also contains some nationally important ancient woodland and tree specimens. The River Esk is one of only of seven in England that retains the rare freshwater pearl mussel.

But this is not a natural landscape. The iconic heather moors that give the National Park its identity are a carefully cultivated, managed ecosystem, largely developed over the last 200 years, This increased after the coming of the railways in the 1840s, bringing in a certain kind of tourist; tweed-suited Dukes and landed gentry with their retinues and a passion for a certain exclusive sport – grouse shooting. Careful selective cultivation of the heather, with burning of areas of old heather to allow regeneration of the young shoots beloved of grouse, and removal of competing vegetation such as trees and bracken, have created this distinctive monoculture landscape.

Human influence

Within the valleys, and around the edges of the National Park with richer soils, human settlement flourished. The Moors was not a part of Yorkshire of huge interest to the Romans despite an important military camp at what is now Malton, and what is generally assumed to be a training camp at Cawthorne near Cropton. There is also a celebrated stretch of unsurfaced Roman Road known as Wade's Causeway across Wheeldale Moor, almost certainly a military road servicing one or more of the signal stations on the East Coast, possibly including Ravenscar.

In Anglian times, the North York Moors were in the kingdom of Deira which eventually combined with Bernicia, the kingdom north of the Tees to become Northumbria, an important centre of Christianity, whose King Edwin (586–633AD) converted to the faith in 627. It is said that the great stone cross at Lilla Howe, on Fylingdale Moor commemorates an incident when Lilla, one of Edwin's trusted retainers, gave his life to thwart an assassination attempt on his King. The memorial cross was erected on his grave on a Bronze Age round barrow to denote his sacrifice. This is the oldest surviving Christian monument in England but is only one of around 700 scheduled Ancient Monuments in the National Park, about a third of the total recorded in the whole of the Yorkshire & Humber Region.

Such crosses have another defining feature of the National Park. Their original function was thought to have been as preaching crosses in the early years of Christianity, but most date from the medieval period. They were more likely to have been boundary or waymark posts on moorland routes, so frequently covered by snow or mist. Around 30 remains of named crosses survive on the Moors, but only a few in their original form. The striking Young Ralph Cross on Westerdale Moor, close to the Castleton-Hutton-le Hole was an 18th century replacement of a 13th century cross but was later restored and despite a series of recent accidents and vandalism, has been further restored, as indeed it should be, as part of the logo of the North York Moors National Park Authority.

The Moors are also crossed by myriad ancient paths and tracks, most still legal bridleways or footpaths, across dale heads and between valleys. The celebrated Hambleton Drove Road along the line of the Hambleton Hills was a Bronze Age trade route. It enjoyed new life in the 18th century as a major Anglo-Scottish drove road that enabled cattle drovers and their beasts to avoid paying tolls along the Great North Road and other turnpikes. The venerable Saltergate Inn near the Hole of Horcum which was used by packhorsemen carrying sea salt from the coast to markets inland, was only recently demolished. There were also extensive paved ways or "trods" developed in monastic times, connecting monasteries with outlying granges and villages or most notably between Castleton and Whitby along the Esk. Many of these old trading routes remained in use right until the coming of the railways.

Several now form sections of popular walking routes including the Cleveland Way and Wainwright's Coast to Coast Path that crosses the moors between Ingleby Arncliffe, Blakey Top and Robin Hood's Bay on the coast.

Monasteries were to play a major role in the life of the region. Christianity was brought to Yorkshire by 7th century Irish missionaries and saints, who colonised the island of Iona off the Scottish Coast, and Lindisfarne off Northumbria. The first Abbey of Whitby dates from 657AD when Oswy, King of Northumbria gave his niece Hilda land to create a religious community on a wild clifftop above the little port of Whitby. This was to become a celebrated Abbey, centre of culture and learning. One of its monks, Caedmon (657–684), became the first ever named poet in Old English, the tongue of the Anglo-Saxons and the precursor of modern English. Such was the status of Abbess Hilda, that in 664 the Synod of Whitby met at the Abbey to resolve a dispute between the Celtic and Roman Christians over the date of Easter. Happily it was all eventually resolved, and we have used that formula for deciding the varying dates of Easter ever since.

Viking invaders during the middle and later 9th century destroyed

Whitby Abbey, and the other pioneering Anglian monastic settlements at Lastingham and Hackness. Another two centuries had passed, after the end of the Anglo-Viking kingdom of Jorvik and the Normal Conquest, before Whitby Abbey could be rebuilt this time as a Benedictine Monastery. The present Abbey was commenced in 1220 and flourished as a centre of learning and religious activity until the Dissolution in 1540, when it suffered gradual decay into what has been described as the most picturesquely located ruin in Britain It was the inspiration in part for Bram Stroker's gothic tale of **Dracula** published in 1898.

By the 10th century the pagan Vikings had also converted to Christianity. Several simple wooden churches were rebuilt in more durable and imposing stone. One of the most evocative survivors of this era is the little Minster of St Gregory in a beautiful setting of Kirkdale, a mile west of Kirkbymoorside, where over a doorway, now under the porch of the little church, is a stone sundial which explains how Orm the son of Gamel rebuilt the church at the time of Earl Tostig. This is the most extant stone inscription in Old English to have survived anywhere in England. Tostig was the rebellious brother of the English King Harald Godwinson who in 1066 sided and died with the Norwegian King who led the Viking invading army at Stamford Bridge in 1066.

The churchyard of St Gregory's is also the last resting place of one of the most remarkable poets, influential art critics and education-alists of the mid-20th century Sir Herbert Read (1893–1968), born in a farmhouse close by. Read describes the minster and its carvings in an evocative poem. He also used Kirkdale as the setting for his only novel **The Green Child**.

The monastic heritage

The Norman and early Plantagenet period saw a huge development of religious houses in the North York Moors area, in part owing to William and his followers devoting a substantial portion of their land for this purpose, perhaps in atonement for their own individual crimes committed by the Harrying of the North. No less than 25 religious houses were established around the Moors, though by the time of the Dissolution in the 1530s only 15 were known to be active. These included several different monastic orders, such as Benedictines at Whitby, Augustinian canons at Guisborough, Cistercians at Rievaulx and Byland, Carthusians at the little monastery of Mount Grace near Osmotherly. In some cases, little remains of the buildings but at Byland and Rievaulx substantial ruins survive, now in the care of English Heritage.

Rievaulx is particularly interesting. It enjoys a magnificent setting in a sheltered part of Ryedale, below what later became a fine 18th century terrace with Ionic Temples on a hillside above, built purely to add to the picturesque nature of the setting. Founded in 1131, by the end of the 12th century Rievaulx had 140 monks and lay brothers to look after the extensive areas of land, for example in Bilsdale, granted to the Abbey by wealthy landowners in return for prayers to protect their immortal souls. This estate was managed from a system of outlying granges primarily for sheep. It is estimated that Rievaulx owned around 12,000 sheep by the end of the 13th century, creating substantial wealth through their wool exported through York to the continent.

But the monks were also technically adept, building their own small water powered bloomeries or small forges to smelt local ironstone to meet their own needs – for nails, tools and utensils. After the Dissolution, Thomas Manners, Earl of Rutland who bought the estate of the King in 1545, developed the iron working from the site. By the 16th century there were four highly productive forges including one of England's first blast furnaces. A shortage of local timber and therefore charcoal for the furnaces caused the works to close, but it could be said to be the starting point of the great iron founding industry of Rosedale and Cleveland.

Rievaulx was also noteworthy for a nationally celebrated Abbot whose leadership was a major fact in its success – Aelred. Born in Hexham, Northumbria, the son of a priest, Aelred quickly worked his way up the monastic hierarchy to become Abbot in 1147. As well as his stewardship of the Abbey, which included the construction of the great church whose ruins dominate the Abbey buildings we see today, Aelred was also an outstanding scholar, historian and theologian, producing several sermons, treatises and books. An illuminated manuscript of Aelred's life of Edward the Confessor, written in 1161–3, is a treasured possession of the British Museum.

By this time, and despite the slowing of the process resulting from the Black Death, settlements and larger villages, some of which were to develop into important market towns, were growing all around the edge of the moorland – for example along what is now the A170 at Pickering, Kirkbymoorside and Helmsley, or in the west, Kilburn, Coxwold, Osmotherly, Stokesley and Guisborough. Their place names give useful, but far from infallible, clues to their first or early settlers. The suffix "tun", "ton", or "ing" indicates Anglian origin but "by", "holm" "thwaite" "keld" or "thorpe" suggest Viking – Danish or Norwegian. Another important relic of the Vikings are the strange hog-back gravestones to be found in several local churches or churchyards around the Moors.

Similarly, the larger castles built by the Normans to subdue local communities around the Moors and coast, developed garrison villages that grew into larger and more strategic market towns, now important and picturesque tourist destinations. Scarborough Castle's builders used the site of the Roman signal station on the headland. The existence of castles also boosted the growth of the towns of Pickering, Helmsley, Kirkbymoorside and Malton.

Outside the towns and villages, within the dales and lowlands, was a cultivated landscape of open fields and scattered woodlands. After the 18th century Enclosures this evolved to a landscape of carefully managed smaller fields, contained within neat hedges, fences and walls, with scattered farmhouses, barns and workers' cottages in mellow limestone or sandstone, all with typical warm red pantile roofs. This is essentially the landscape of an 18th and 19th century rural economy.

Most farm income in Cleveland, even in the 21st century, is still primarily from sheep and dairy production. Many farmers in the Cleveland dales retain their rights to graze sheep on the nearby moors. In the richer farmland across the southern limestone belt and into the Vale of Pickering and Howardian Hills, there are more arable and mixed farms as well as livestock farms. Main arable crops grown in the lowland areas include barley, wheat, oilseed rape, potatoes, and there is also more intensive production of pigs and poultry.

Two museums within the National Park offer remarkable insight into traditional farming and the vernacular architecture of Moorland communities. The first is the **Ryedale Folk Museum** in the pretty village of Hutton le Hole. The Museum which is almost a Skansen where medieval and later farmhouses, barns, cottages, workshops have been carefully dismantled from various parts of the Moors and restored and rebuilt in a village setting. Equally, the **Beck Hole Museum** in Pickering is a more conventional museum in a fine Regency house, but with restored shops and craft workshops, excellent interpretive displays and a fine costume museum.

One of the best sources of knowledge about the lives of local communities of times past within the North York Moors, comes from the pen of the Reverend John Atkinson (1814–1900), Vicar of Danby in the Esk valley. Atkinson's classic book **Forty Years in a Moorland Parish**[1] published in 1891 offers fascinating insight, often through anecdote, into the natural history, social history and folklore of his own and surrounding villages[2].

A year later, the London based naval historian and topographer John Leyland, (1858–1924) published **The Yorkshire Coast and Cleveland Hills and Dales**, with illustrations by Alfred Dawson and Lancelot Speed[3], a book which despite its slightly flowery Victorian style, is still one of the best general introductions to the North York Moors, including well researched sections on its geology, human settlement and history.

A more focussed, and superbly illustrated and scholarly study of Moors life and culture up to the early 20th century is **Life in the Moorlands of North-east Yorkshire** by Marie Hartley and Joan Ingilby. Published in 1972 this is the classic book of rural life in this part of Yorkshire, reinforced by a remarkable photographic record.

Towns and villages below the Tabular Hills

Even though life for rural communities has changed dramatically since Marie Hartley and Joan Ingilby were recording interviews with older inhabitants in the 1960s, the towns and villages along the A170 and southern edge of the National Park have changed remarkably little in physical appearance, even over the last century. Much of this is due to the fact that many such town and village centres are Conservation Areas, within the National Park and the wider area, many with buildings listed because of their architectural importance.

Pickering, with its Castle and lively, well-preserved main market street, is typical. The Parish Church of St Peter & Paul has some of the finest medieval wall paintings of any church in England, dating from the mid-15th century, and thankfully protected under limewash until rediscovered in 1880. Illustrations from the life of Saint Catherine and the Passion of Christ include a lurid Descent into Hell for sinners but Resurrection for those who repent. The town is also now the southern terminus of the **North York Moors Railway**.

Kirkbymoorside, west of Pickering is another market town with a long and fascinating history, reflected in the many historic buildings along its main street including three fine old coaching inns, one of which the timber-framed George and Dragon, has its origins in the 13th century. Buckingham House in Upper Market Place was where one of the most colourful characters of 17th century England, George Villiers second Duke of Buckingham, poet and statesman, died. Buckingham fought alongside Prince Rupert's Royalists in the Civil War. He helped to achieve Charles II's Restoration before finally falling out of favour during the reign of James II and returning to his Yorkshire manor of Helmsley. He died in the house of one of his tenants from a chill after foxhunting, with what is now the Bilsdale Hunt. But he achieved immortality in ways he might not have wished in John Dryden's blistering satire **Absalom and Achitophel** (1681) in which he was described as being:

> *Stiff in opinions, always in the wrong,*
> *Was everything by starts and nothing long;*
> *But, in the course of one revolving moon*
> *Was chemist, fiddler, statesman and buffoon.*

Helmsley, with its fine marketplace, **Castle**, intriguing **Walled Garden**, and with **Duncombe Park** house and estate close by and choice of independent local shops, cafes and inns, is a deservedly popular visitor destination. It is also the Headquarters of the North York Moors National Park Authority.

Ampleforth, with its Abbey founded in 1802, and now with a community of 55 monks who live by Benedictine Rule, is a direct link with the great monastic foundations of Yorkshire. Ampleforth College, adjacent to the Abbey, is an independent foundation, a co-educational public school with around 600 pupils.

Kilburn was made famous by its **White Horse**, a notable landmark visible across the Vale of York. This was first cut into the hillside above the village in 1857, either by local schoolmaster John Hodgson and his pupils, or according to other accounts a local tradesman Thomas Taylor, using limestone chippings to provide the white stone so visible on the hillside. Because of slippage of stone down the steep hillside, the landmark, the most northerly hill figure of its kind in the British Isles, requires constant maintenance. It is an easy walk from Sutton Bank.

More certain is the story of Robert Thompson (1876–1955) the Kilburn "Mouseman". Son of a local carpenter, Thompson set up his workshop in Kilburn making handmade furniture inspired by the Arts and Craft Movement. After a chance remark about feeling "as poor as a church mouse", on a whim he carved a mouse on one of his furniture pieces. It became a huge marketing idea. Original Thompson pieces now change hands for thousands of pounds. Thompson's furniture making tradition continues at the Kilburn Workshops and there is now a **Mouseman Visitor Centre** at Kilburn.

Coxwold, with its little church with a distinctive octagonal tower, earns a footnote in literary history as being the home for many years of Laurence Sterne (1713–68) author of one of the early masterpieces of the English novel, **Tristram Shandy**, published in 1759 whilst Sterne was living in Shandy Hall, in Coxwold – the house that features in the comic novel. **Shandy Hall** is now a small museum owned by the Laurence Sterne Trust.

Several of the larger dales that penetrate central moorland areas served as key lines of communication, ending in high moorland roads or sometimes ancient tracks that cross to a neighbouring dale. Each dale has its own particular character and sense of isolation from its neighbour – Rosedale, Farndale (justly celebrated for its wild daffodils each spring), Kirkdale, Upper Ryedale, Bilsdale, and to the north the long valley of Eskdale into which Westerdale, Great and Little Fryupdale and other dales feed.

Eskdale and its railway

Eskdale has attractive village settlements along its lower terraces such as Commondale, Castleton, Glaisdale, Lealholm, Danby, (which has the

National Park Moors Centre at Danby Lodge). Egton Bridge, celebrated for its Gooseberry Show, Grosmont with its iron-making and railway history, lie lower down the valley, above the small inland resorts of Staithes and Ruswarp and the river estuary at Whitby.

All are linked by the Esk Valley Railway, the 35-mile long route between Middlesbrough and Whitby, much of its central section being just single track with passing loops.

The line is an amazing Victorian survivor – a perfectly preserved rural railway which provides car-free access to the heart of the National Park. It wasn't initially built as a passenger railway but as the Yorkshire & Cleveland Railway, opened in 1857, to carry ironstone from Stokesley to Picton where it would connect with the main Leeds-Northern line to Teeside. In 1858, now taken over by the North Eastern Railway, it extended eastwards to Battersby where from 1861 the Rosedale railway brought rich iron ores down the Rosedale Incline heading to the iron foundries of Middlesbrough. It continued eastwards to Kildale finally reaching Grosmont on the Whitby-Pickering line in 1865. A freight branch from Battersby to Nunthorpe carried passengers from 1865, though even in 1910 most trains to Stockton continued via Picton. But by 1950 most trains for Middlesbrough were reversing, as now, at Battersby, and the Picton link closed in 1954.

The whole line almost closed in 1930 when a stone bridge near Glaisdale was swept away by floods, its replacement girder bridge suffering the same fate a year later.

But greater challenges were to come in the 1960s when the Beeching Plan proposed closure of all three surviving rail routes into Whitby, including the coastal route from Scarborough via Robin Hood's Bay, the main line to York via Malton (which has survived from Pickering as the North York Moors Railway). The Esk Valley line only survived because a public inquiry suggested there would be "grave hardship" faced by local communities in Esk Valley if the line closed. Before any further attempts to close the line could be made, attitudes to railways in Britain had changed, and the Esk Valley with its amazing 14 intermediate stations survived. Since then, two new stations have been added – for Middlesbrough commuters at Gypsy Lane in 1974 and James Cook to serve the region's hospital in 2014.

The survival of the Esk Valley line provides a remarkable, if perhaps under-appreciated, railway heritage experience. Among the many lovely structures are bridges, viaducts and cuttings as the single-track line meanders through the valley, crossing and recrossing the Esk river and reversing at Battersby Junction. Beautifully preserved North Eastern Railway rural stations date from the 1860s. Thanks to the work of the Esk Valley Railway Development Company these are looked after by a whole network of community volunteers. The EVRDC is a Community Rail Partnership working closely with Northern Rail to help promote the line and secure service improvements.

Mining in the Moors – jet, alum, iron and potash

If the landscape of the National Park owes as much to the human activity of farming as the processes of nature, one particular industrial activity has also shaped the landscape, and that activity is mining.

The conservationist and writer Ian Carstairs has suggested that the North York Moors is possibly the most intensively mined of Britain's 15 National Parks[4]. Historically, this was for three minerals – jet, alum, and ironstone, but in more recent years for two others, potash and polyhalite, both which are used worldwide in the manufacture of inorganic fertilisers.

Jet, a black, hard semi-precious stone, is fossilised wood from a species of ancient tree – araucaria (monkey puzzle). It is found in its fossil form exclusively within Jurassic rocks. It has been mined from coastal outcrops and used for jewellery and ornaments since Bronze Age times. But the popularity of jet reached a peak in the later 19th century, in part because of its use by Queen Victoria in brooches and necklaces whilst mourning her beloved Prince Albert. Demand for this mineral resulted in the development of a huge cottage industry centred on Whitby where trade and some specialised craft activity in jet still exists. The **Whitby Museum** has an amazing display of jewellery and ornaments made from this once fashionable material.

From 1600 onwards, alum, derived from alum shale found along the coast was extensively mined. Alum was for many centuries the only certain way to fix dye in textiles and therefore in huge demand. Parts of the northern part of the coast of the National Park have been affected by the quarrying and processing of alum shale to produce the mineral.

The industry ended quite abruptly with the development of modern synthetic dyes in the 1860s that didn't require alum to fix colours. This ended what had been a major and polluting industrial activity along the coast but has left a fascinating industrial archaeology of its own.

By then an even more significant mineral was being mined and processed – iron ore. During the 18th century iron ore nodules were being collected on the beach or quarried from rocky outcrops around Robin Hoods Bay and were being shipped to County Durham for processing. But in 1835, when the tunnel was being dug at Grosmont for the new railway line to Pickering, seams of ironstone were discovered, and ore was soon transported on the new railway to Whitby.

Within a couple of decades huge quantities of high-quality iron ores were being discovered both inland at Eston and along the coast and in Rosedale where especially rich veins of high-grade magnetic ironstone were located. More than 80 mines were eventually opened across the moors and coast. To reduce costs, the ore was roasted on site in great kilns to remove moisture and impurities to reduce the weight and bulk for transport. In Rosedale an elaborate horseshoe shaped railway was constructed on the edge of the hillsides above the valley to carry waggon loads of the treated ore down a 700-foot incline to Battersby for onward haulage and shipment by rail to the rapidly expanding ironworks of Middlesbrough.

Much of the iron mining remains in Rosedale, Grosmont and along the Esk Valley Railway were conserved, protected and celebrated in the **Land of Iron Project**, a Heritage Lottery Funded project with the North York Moors National Park Authority, with events, publications and an inter-active exhibition in Danby Lodge Moors Centre to tell the story of iron and its impact on the landscape of the North York Moors and its communities.

The story of iron in the North York Moors and the coast of Cleveland is also part of the story of Middlesbrough – a town which grew from a farm and hamlet of just 25 people in 1800 to a bustling industrial centre and County Borough of 100,000 by 1900. It happened because of the vision of a group of Quakers. In 1829 Joseph Pease of Stockton Darlington and his partners purchased land to create a new deep port lower down the mouth of the Tees to serve the growing rail-linked town of Darlington for the export of Durham coal and Yorkshire lead.

At almost the same time, the discoveries of huge quantities of iron ore in the nearby Cleveland hills provided all the impetus and incentive for the little town of Middlesbrough to grow. Within a couple of decades "Ironopolis" as it became known, grew to be on one of the great centres of the North East for iron and later steel making and heavy engineering. Among great enterprises to emerge in Middlesbrough were Dorman and Long, engineers of both Newcastle's Tyne Bridge and the world-famous Sydney Harbour Bridge. **Middlesbrough Transporter Bridge** across the Tees, one of only three transporter bridges surviving in Britain, is an engineering marvel, linking Yorkshire and Durham by a moving, car-carrying cage. It was built by the Cleveland Bridge and Engineering Company. Opened in 1911 and still functioning as intended, it has rightly become a symbol of the town.

In addition to steel, Middlesbrough and the group of industrial towns on each side of the river estuary that became known as Teesside, also became a major UK centre of the chemical industry, with Billingham boasting the great ICI Manufacturing Plant. Much of that industry activity has declined. The eventual collapse of the steel industry resulting from foreign competition, leading to the closure of Redcar steel works in 2015, was rightly regarded a tragedy for the region (though there is now hopeful talk of its reopening). It left Middlesbrough facing serious challenges; yet the town has fought back with vigour, with a redesigned and reinvigorated town centre, a new University, the **Dorman Museum**, the **Museum of Contemporary Art**, the **James Cook Birthplace Museum** in **Stewart Park**, and a vibrant cultural life.

And the town also enjoys some fine green spaces and parklands of its own, including **Stewart** and **Albert Parks, Flatts Lane Country Park** and the RSPB Reserve at **Saltholme**. Pride of place must, however, go to **Ormesby Hall**, the former home of the Pennyman family of Middlesbrough, now managed by the National Trust; this is essentially a magnificent Georgian house with Victorian additions. Paintings, furniture, carving and exhibits including restored kitchens tell the story of the family. The 250 acres of parkland and gardens include a Victorian fernery and miniature railway.

Current plans for new green energy technology and creation of a Free Port in Teesside suggest a bright future.

But even if it is now part of Teesside and the North East Region, historically and "ceremonially" Middlesbrough and other towns south of the Tees remain part of the White Rose country of Yorkshire. The suburbs of the town include Marton where Captain James Cook was born, and areas of attractive parks and green spaces south of the town as far as Guisborough, and including part of the National Park, all lie within the foothills of the Cleveland Hills, and are all therefore essentially part of Yorkshire.

The latest episode of the story of mining in the North York Moors has taken a new twist with the deep mining of two other minerals, potash and polyhalite. The layers of ancient Permian era rocks deep under the North York Moors and into the sea contains some of the richest sources of these compounds known in the Northern hemisphere.

At Boulby near Loftus, the second deepest mine in Europe was sunk in 1968 to capture the valuable minerals. This was not without some controversy, Boulby Potash Mine being just within the boundaries of the National Park. For this reason, surface development was kept to a minimum and most of the ore mined at the site, with a capacity of up to a million tonnes per year, is taken out by rail, utilising a section of the old coastal railway line between Loftus and Saltburn as a freight branch. The mine is over a kilometre deep and contains around a thousand kilometres of underground tunnels, most of them deep under the North Sea. But as well as being a mine for potash and salt, the pure atmosphere and extreme silence of the depth has allowed the mine to become the site of the Boulby Underground Laboratory used for the development of space exploration technology and investigation by astrophysicists into Dark Matter and the origins of the universe.

Even more controversially in 2017 work began at what is now Anglo-American's Woodsmith Mine, at Sneatonthorpe, about 3 miles south of Whitby. Two immense 1,500 metre shafts, almost a mile deep, are being constructed, making this the deepest mine in the world. Its projected production of over 20 million tonnes of polyhalite ore will be extracted from the site by a 23-mile conveyor belt in a tunnel to Teesport for onward shipping to international markets. As a creator of employment for Cleveland it has won the support of the local authorities and most of the local community, but many conservationists are deeply concerned about the huge impacts of building works and lorry traffic on the fragile ecosystems of the National Park and have concerns about the longer term viability of this huge industrial project, the largest in any UK National Park.

The North York Moors area was almost impacted by another extractive industry, fracking. Around four miles south of Pickering is **Flamingo Park**, a popular zoo and pleasure gardens. The nearby village of Kirby Misperton enjoyed brief national fame when a field close to the village became the site of a tented encampment of protesters against fracking. Fracking is the process of forcing liquid compounds at high pressure into fissures of oil-bearing shale rocks to force out pockets of natural gas. Third Energy, an international corporation, sought to do this at a test site at Kirby Misperton. Their attempts were thwarted for almost three years between 2016 and 2018 by the combined efforts of local protesters and outside environmentalists. Eventually investigation into the financial affairs delayed the project sufficiently for the Government's new change of policies towards the extraction of fossil fuels in the light of the 2015 Paris Accord to emerge. Hopefully this has ended the industry in Yorkshire. There is little doubt fracking at Kirby Misperton would have gone ahead without the efforts of the protesters who risked both physical injury and arrest and even imprisonment to prevent the scheme from happening.

But this will not change the fact for very many people living in Middlesbrough and the towns of Teesside, the Moors to the south of where they live are where their heart is; they are Moorsmen and Moorswomen, and they share with their town a common heritage of iron. It is appropriate that the major catchment area for day visitors particularly to the northern parts of the National Park is Teesside, whether people travel to the National Park by car, bike, by train or bus. Frequent bus services link Middlesbrough and Redcar along the coast to Staithes, Whitby and Scarborough. On summer weekends the network of **Moorsbus** services, one of Britain's best coordinated weekend leisure bus networks, run by the volunteers of Moorsbus CIC, brings people from Redcar, Middlesbrough, Guisborough, Stokesley and other Cleveland towns inland to the heart of the National Park. This includes a breathing-takingly beautiful trip to Danby and across Blakey Top ridge to Hutton le Hole and Pickering, or through Bilsdale via Chop Gate to Rievaulx, Helmsley and Sutton Bank.

The National Park – protecting the heritage

Sutton Bank and Danby Lodge Visitor Centres are the public face of the **North York Moors National Park Authority** which has the difficult task of balancing the economic and land use needs of the local community with its duty to protect one of England's finest inland and coastal environments, both in terms of its landscape and biodiversity whilst encouraging appropriate forms of public access and enjoyment. Visitor pressure, especially from car borne visitors, also has to be managed. It is also assisted in its task by an independent voluntary body and charity, the **North York Moors Trust** which helps to bring in additional funding otherwise not available to the public body, as well as providing additional voluntary help to support the Authority's work.

A sister charity, the **North Yorkshire Moors Association**, whilst it normally overwhelmingly supports the work of the Authority, acts as a "critical friend" and occasionally takes the Park Authority to task over planning and visitor management issues, when it feels it needs to strengthen the National Park's decision making over key conservation issues. As an educational charity NYMA also adds value to the work of the Authority, not only in **Voice of the Moors**, its members quarterly magazine, but in a range of events and publications such as **The History Tree**[5], a series of essays based on certain key years in the history of the Moors, stories of both people, places and events, taking their cue from the rings of a stump of a two-hundred-year-old elm tree which once grew in the garden of the National Park Moors Centre at Danby Lodge.

The majority of day visitors to the Moors come from the National Park's main urban catchment communities of Cleveland, in what is now Teesside.

The Cleveland Way

There is no better way of discovering the intimate relationship of Cleveland and the lower Tees valley with the North York Moors National Park than walking all or part of the 100-mile Cleveland Way. This, Britain's second oldest National Trail starts at Helmsley, in Ryedale, and winds its way past Rievaulx Abbey to Sutton Bank, on the edge of the Hambleton Hills, above Kilburn and close to the iconic White

Horse carved in the pale limestone cliff side. The Way then follows the line of the ancient Hambleton Drove road, before taking the ridge of the Cleveland Hills that overlook Middlesbrough and Cleveland, reaching Botton Head on Urra Moor at 454 metres or 1492 feet the highest point on the North York Moors.

The Way then heads above Guisborough with its ruins of a 12th century Priory, then to the coast at Saltburn, Middlesbrough's own high Victorian seaside resort with its fine beaches, and amazing cliff railway serving its handsome pier. The Way then follows the coast, past Skinningrove and the remains of old ironstone mines to Boulby.

The Cleveland Coast

Boulby is noteworthy not just for its nearby potash mine, but for having the highest seacoast cliffs in eastern England, a full 203 metres (666 feet) above sea level.

The next 26 miles of the Cleveland Way continue along the coast. This is mainly along clifftop, but with steep descends and climbs into various settlements as far as Scarborough. The coast between Saltburn and Scalby Mills is now designated as the North Yorkshire & Cleveland Heritage Coast, reflecting its national importance for geological and ecological interest. The section of seabed along the coast of North East England between Berwick and Whitley Bay is also now a Marine Conservation Zone to protect its underwater ecology and wildlife.

These constantly eroding cliffs and beaches are especially rich in fossils, most notably the spectacular ammonites and brachiopods, but also for the evidence of larger species in the form of footprints of dinosaurs and fossilised remains of other reptiles including such grand species as ichthyosaurus. Some of the many finds by local geologists and palaeontologists can be seen in the excellent Whitby Museum and also the **William Smith Museum of Geology** in the Rotunda Museum in Scarborough. **Whitby Museum** also tells the story of Louis Hunton, (1814–38) displaying some of his finds on local cliffs. Hunton, who came from the nearby coastal village of Loftus, was a brilliant palaeontologist who died tragically young, but whose published research on the relationship of subspecies of ammonites found in nearby Boulby Cliff is regarded as one of the cornerstones of the modern science of biostratigraphy – recognising the age of rocks from types of fossils.

Three miles from Boulby is Staithes. The entrance to this iconic village is down a narrow steep lane leading to a tiny harbour alongside the beck, where traditional coble fishing boats, a design whose principles are said to go back to Viking times, line the banks of the stream. Though the women of the town no longer wear their traditional, elaborate white bonnets, these still make an appearance on special occasions. One attractive, if fanciful, story is that they were brought to this isolated village in the 16th century by refugees from a vessel from the Spanish Armada shipwrecked on the coast. More realistic is the likelihood that the designs evolved to protect the heads and necks of the women of the village when carrying heavy baskets of dripping fish, particularly herring, up to the village for preparation and salting.

During Edwardian times, Staithes hosted a thriving colony of artists, the best known of whom was Dame Laura Knight (1877–1970).

Whitby

Whitby is one of the most fascinating coastal towns in the British Isles. It is the only harbour in England that through a quirk of the estuary of the River Esk, faces north. Its history as a port is as old as England, but its greatest commercial success was to come in the 18th century, when it became, with Hull, one of the two great whaling ports in the North East, whale oil being a hugely important source of energy for light and heat, as well as the many uses for its flesh and indeed its bones, for example for popular whalebone corsets. A massive whale jaw above the west cliff is a stark reminder of this past great industry.

The town was also notable for sail and rope making, and for shipbuilding with several important shipyards in the town, Whitby being second only to Portsmouth in terms of the industry. It was at one of these docks, owned by well-known shipwright Thomas Fishburn that some time in the 1760s, a type of ocean-going sailing vessel known as the *Earl of Pembroke* was built. Known as a bark, its relatively flat bottom made it suitable for use in shallow coastal waters – excellent for marine and coastal exploration. This ship was purchased by the Royal Navy for use by a certain Captain James Cook (1728–79), born in Marton in Cleveland near what is now Middlesbrough. Cook had been apprenticed in both Staithes and in Whitby, and would have been familiar with the type of vessel and its thoroughly reliable makers. The *Earl of Pembroke* was refitted and renamed *The Endeavour* and left Plymouth in August 1769 on its epic voyage which resulted in Cook and his men being the first Europeans to land on the eastern coast of Australia in April 1770. He went on discover, almost losing his ship and his life in the process, Australia's Great Barrier Reef and to discover, circumnavigate and chart New Zealand.

A life size replica of **The Endeavour** is now moored as a visitor attraction in Whitby harbour, and the story of Cook's life and many achievements are explored at the **Captain Cook Memorial Museum** in Grape Lane. This occupies a house where Cook lodged as an apprentice. The Captain Cook Monument, on the highest summit point of Easby Moor, 324 metres or 1,063 feet above sea level, above Great Ayton, looks directly across to that other great icon of the North York Moors, Roseberry Topping. It was erected by local Whitby banker Robert Campion in 1827.

Fortunately for Whitby the decline of whaling coincided with the coming of the railway, in Whitby's case this meant four separate lines. This included the extraordinary pioneering line from Pickering and Whitby opened in 1836 along whose rails initially horse drawn carriages were trundled, with a gravity, later steam-powered, funicular system up the steep incline between Beckhole and Goathland before entering the deep gorge of Newtondale to reach Pickering. After a terrible accident in 1864, this section was later converted to a twin track railway along a new deviation and less steep avoiding route which allowed fast through trains from York and Leeds.

From the south came the cliff top single track line from Scarborough, the stunningly beautiful lost railway which is now the Cinder Track footpath past Robin Hoods Bay. The almost equally attractive scenic line along the Cleveland coast from Saltburn and Loftus closed in 1959. But the meandering single-track route from Middlesbrough through the Esk Valley has survived, as an almost perfectly preserved Victorian rural railway through the heart of the North York Moors.

Ironically, Whitby's most important direct railway line from York via Malton and Pickering was also closed in 1965. Thankfully, the section between Pickering and Grosmont has now become one of the nation's greatest railway heritage success stories. Rescued from closure by a small but determined team of volunteers in the 1970s, it is now the **North Yorkshire Moors Railway** which allows trains to run the full 18 miles from Pickering, Goathland and Grosmont through to Whitby. It is one of Britain's longest and most spectacular preserved Heritage Railways, a major regional tourist attraction with trains hauled by beautifully preserved steam locomotives hauling vintage rolling stock, with regular dining car specials, the highlight of many family celebrations, and stations such as Newtondale Halt and Levisham providing superb access for walkers into the heart of the National Park

The initial Whitby-Pickering line of the 1830s, extended through to Malton in 1845, had already established the village of Goathland, with Mallyan Spout waterfall, and the nearby hamlet of Beckhole, as a popular small inland health resort, offering a choice of fine moorland and riverside walks. The village enjoyed a new surge of popularity when it became the setting of a hugely successful ITV series **Heartbeat,** based on the Constable novels set in the North Riding of the 1960s, by Nicholas Rhea, the penname of Peter J. Walker (1936–2017) born in Glaisdale, and a former Whitby policeman. A remarkable 18 series of programmes were transmitted between 1992 and 2020. The fictional village Aidensfield was based on Goathland and many episodes were filmed in the surrounding area.

The coming of the railway had a huge impact on Whitby. Even before the through line to York was opened in 1845, speculators were buying up property and building new hotels and boarding houses on the cliffs. From late Victorian times onwards, Whitby was establishing itself as a hugely popular seaside resort and holiday destination, one that combined fine beaches, lovely countryside with a rich ecclesiastical and maritime heritage and a fishing tradition that merged into its famed fish and chip restaurants, and kipper smoking.

Whitby continues to appeal to a wide range of holiday tastes. But few Victorian visitors could have imagined how Bram Stoker's take on the Gothic horror tradition would morph into the cult of "Goths" that even in the 21ˢᵗ century is a massive attractor of young visitors who might have less of an interest in James Cook or ammonites.

The **Cleveland Way** between Whitby and Scarborough has few equals in the British Isles for the splendour of its coastal views. A highlight is the old fishing and smuggling port of Robin Hood's Bay where cottages huddle down to a small fishing boat landing area from where contraband was smuggled through a culvert passage underneath the village linked to inns and cottages. Local author and topographer Leo Walmsley (1892–1966) was the son of well-known local painter Ulric Walmsley whose prints are still on sale in the village. Walmsley grew up in Robin Hoods Bay and used the village as the setting for several of his novels.

The Cleveland Way passes the old port and failed resort of Ravenscar before entering Scarborough along its North Bay, continuing along the coats for another eight miles to Filey on the edge of the Wolds, unless of course the walker chooses to close the circuit by taking the 48-mile Tabular Hill Way along the Sea Cut back to Helmsley.

Scarborough

Scarborough, that most iconic of English east coast resorts, dates back to Roman times, not only as a signal station on the headland, but as recent excavations have revealed, a large Roman settlement further inland. Its name Skaraoborg also indicates a Viking settlement, and it may be the ancient town mentioned in Icelandic Sagas. The village appears to have had a fairly stormy existence with frequent attacks and raids by Norse pirates.

Things were more settled by the 12th century, after Henry II built his iconic stone castle on the headland between the two great bays. In the 13th century it was granted a charter for a six week long fair, a market and trading event which attracted merchants from all over Europe, and which flourished well into the 18th century, when it became the subject of the ever popular folk song **Scarborough Fair**.

It continued as a small fishing port and market town until the 17th century. From this time onwards however Scarborough became Britain's, and probably the world's, first seaside resort, as sea bathing even in the icy North Sea from elaborate wheeled bathing huts, was established as a cure for most known ills. What began as a rather specialist spa or health cure for the better off was to change dramatically when George Hudson's railway arrived from York, built in just over a year from its Act of Parliament in 1844 to its opening in 1845.

Like their counterparts in Whitby, Scarborough entrepreneurs saw the opportunity to open up fine new hotels, the most spectacular of all being the magnificent Grand Hotel on a headland overlooking the North Bay. It was opened in 1867 to the design of the Hull architectural genius Cuthbert Brodrick. It was the largest brick-built building in Europe at that time, boasting 4 towers to represent the seasons, 12 floors the months, 52 chimneys the weeks and 365 rooms the days. The little town and its harbour became just a focal point of huge development around the two great bays, with the iconic 12th century castle, both a landmark and viewpoint, in the centre, the handsome spa buildings in the South Bay within extensive hillside gardens, and lovely **Peasholme Park** with its lake and miniature railway in the North. Few resorts in England enjoy a more spectacular setting than Scarborough and the continued success of the town as the place to enjoy every aspect of the traditional British seaside holiday needs no elaboration here.

What is perhaps less well known about Scarborough is that it is now also the home of one of Yorkshire's most exciting and innovative new industries – seaweed farming and processing. A Scarborough company, Seagrown, has established a marine farm for the cultivation, harvesting and processing of various common seaweeds on a site in shallow seas about four miles offshore away from shipping lanes. The seaweed can be used for nutritious food, in cosmetics, pharmaceutical products and most intriguingly of all, in the creation of biodegradable plastics, for example for food packaging. The potential of this green technology to change to fortunes of both Scarborough and the planet is enormous.

Another world beating Scarborough product lies within the creative arts. The modest sized **Stephen Joseph Theatre**, in a former 1930s Odeon Cinema building, is closely associated with the work of one of the world's most performed living playwrights, Alan Ayckbourn. Almost all the playwright's most celebrated works are premiered in Scarborough by the theatre's repertory company before going on to the West End or Broadway. Ayckbourn has written and often directed more than 70 plays which have been performed all over the world including the West End and on Broadway and translated into more than 25 languages. He is probably the world's most widely performed living dramatist. His dark comedies begin deceptively simply but the interplay of characters have an Ibsenesque intensity and often darkness, whilst remaining highly entertaining. His audiences are sometimes left in an emotional situation when they are not sure whether to laugh – or to cry.

Though Ayckbourn cannot be described as a Yorkshire writer as such, as his plays are universal, he works, as indeed William Shakespeare did, with a small team of trusted actors and a theatre which is very firmly based in Yorkshire. The theatre has two stages, the McCarthy studio theatre and The Round which has a "theatre in the round" stage, not a traditional proscenium arch. This gives audience and actors a special intimacy. This close relationship between a master playwright, his actors and his audiences. has produced some of the most remarkable theatre in Britain in the 20th and 21st centuries.

Not far away is another nationally important item – the handsome little neo-classical Rotunda below the Valley Bridge in Scarborough, one of the world's first purpose built museums and hosts the **William Smith Museum of Geology**. As well as celebrating the work of William Smith (1769–1839), it displays John Phillips' remarkable coloured geological sections of the coast, blown up as a diorama with relevant fossils in correct stratigraphical order displayed in the cases below. The section covers the whole Yorkshire coast between Spurn Point and Redcar, based on Phillips' pioneering surveys with his uncle William Smith between 1826 and 1829.

Lake Pickering

South of the National Park the North York Moors blend into the flat low-lying landscape of the Vale of Pickering, created by a former huge post-glacial lake, fed by the River Derwent and its many tributaries. Extraordinarily, the water did not escape into the North Sea eastwards, because of the blocking of any natural passage to the sea by a huge glacial moraine. Lake water, under huge pressure from storms or melting snows, having nowhere else to go, found the weakest point, which was in the south west corner, forcing its way, down towards the Vale of York. In so doing in a few short decades, as the River Derwent, it had gouged out the deep valley we know as the Derwent Gorge before finally joining the Ouse south of Wheldrake.

It was the remarkable Leeds geologist, and President of the Yorkshire Geological Society Percy Kendall (1856–1936), who first unravelled the complex glacial geology and geomorphology of the long vanished ancient Eskdale and Pickering lakes of the North York Moors. The details were published in the great two volume **The Geology of Yorkshire** (1924) written with his colleague Herbert Wroot. The second volume takes readers to explore geological sites all over Yorkshire to be seen from a railway carriage window or reached by walking from now mostly long closed stations [6].

Because the area was so prone to flooding, in 1804 a drainage canal or "Sea Cut" to the coast between Mowthrope and Scalby Mills was constructed by local engineer, aeronautics pioneer and entrepreneur Sir George Cayley (1773–1857) and William Chapman of Whitby.

Well before this time and indeed before Lake Pickering was fully drained, Mesolithic hunter-gatherers were living in the area. At Star Carr, near Seamer, what was probably a lake dwelling or island in shallow fenland was discovered. In it remains were perfectly preserved in the acid peat. Archaeologists have identified what are now regarded as some of the most important finds of Mesolithic culture in the British Isles, artefacts made of red deer, elk and aurach bones and antlers, including spearheads, rare red deer skull ceremonial caps and a unique pendant. The items have been carbon dated to between 8770 and 8460BC.

The Howardian Hills AONB

The narrow Derwent Gorge, now shared by the York-Scarborough railway and the beautiful ruins of the Augustinian Priory of Kirkham, also provides a useful boundary between the Yorkshire Wolds and Yorkshire's smallest Area of Outstanding Natural Beauty – the Howardian Hills, which are also separated from the North York Moors by the valley of the River Rye.

The Howardian Hills Area of Natural Beauty, the only AONB in the British Isles to be named after a stately home – covers 204km or 79 square miles making it one of the smallest of England's AONBs but one of the most distinctive, covering a line of undulating, Jurassic limestone hills, dominated by one great estate, the magnificent **Castle**

Howard. It was designed by Sir John Vanbrugh (1664–1726), noted playwright and architect of genius, with the help of leading architect Nicholas Hawksmoor (1661–1736). Many people regard Castle Howard as Vanbrugh's masterpiece, even excelling that even grander Blenheim Palace in Oxfordshire. As a stunning example of English Baroque, its imposing central cupola has neo-classical Palladian features. However part of the design had varied from Vanbrugh's vision during the century or so it took to complete the palace, from initial concept to final completion with its lavish interior decor.

Castle Howard was built for the Earls of Carlisle, a branch of the great English catholic Howard family of which the Dukes of Norfolk were part. The house and estate are both still in the ownership of a branch of the family that gave the House and AONB their name. The House is now managed by a company on behalf of the family. It is now an internationally important tourist destination noted for its great collections of sculpture, paintings, fabrics, furniture and its remarkable cultural landscape setting. It is hardly surprising that it attracts more than a quarter of a million visitors each year.

This landscape setting is every bit as great a work of art as the House itself. It is a picturesque pleasure garden on a truly epic scale, with long tree lined vistas, with carefully placed obelisks, lakes, bridges, palisades, statues concealed in woods. Two of the buildings are, in their own right, regarded as nationally important masterpieces of their period – Vanbrugh's elegant **Temple of the Four** Winds and Nicholas Hawksmoor's stunning **Mausoleum**. This is a neo-classical fantasy landscape recreated in reality, as if almost stolen from a painting by one of the 17th century Italian or French masters such as Claude Lorraine.

This great estate is surrounded by other carefully managed and cultivated landscapes – including most notably the Hovingham Estate.

A line of attractive villages follows the line of springs along the Malton to Hovingham road. The pretty estate village of Hovingham is dominated by Hovingham Hall, ancestral home of the Worsley family. In the days of the long-closed railway between Malton and Pilling (for Thirsk), Hovingham had a short life as a rural spa based on the allegedly efficacious effects of drinking the local mineral-rich spring waters. The village station, which closed in 1930, was known as Hovingham Spa.

A network of footpaths and bridleways make this a perfect

landscape to explore on foot, by cycle or on horseback. Fertile limestone soils and traditional husbandry give that landscape a rich biodiversity, making this a quintessential, deeply English, almost Georgian, area of countryside, and a very special part of Yorkshire.

Notes

1 Atkinson J.C. 1891: *Forty Years in a Moorland Parish* Macmillan
2 Burns Tom, Scott 1986: *Canon Atkinson and his Country* M.T.D. Rigg, Guiseley
3 Leyland John 1892: *The Yorkshire Coast and Cleveland Hill and Dales* Seeley, London
4 Carstairs, Ian 1987: *The North York Moors National Park* Webb& Bower/Michael Joseph London p20
5 Cochrane Janet (ed) 2018: *The History Tree: Moments in the Life of a Memorable Tree* North Yorkshire Moors Association Whitby
6 Kendall P.F & Wroot H.R. 1924 *The Geology of Yorkshire* authors, Leeds

4

The Yorkshire Wolds, Holderness
and Hull

Immediately to the south of the Vale of Pickering and the Derwent, the land once again rises steeply to another range, this time of more gentle hills and green dales. These are the Yorkshire Wolds. This is one of the least well known, but most distinctive areas of Yorkshire.

The name "Wold" comes from old Teutonic, meaning a wooded forest – hence the modern German word "Wald" – but which in Anglian and in later medieval and modern English, came to mean an area of rolling hills, open down land. But the name "Wolds" for such hills as opposed to "Downs" are found almost exclusively in the eastern side of the country, including Lincolnshire and the East Riding of Yorkshire.

The chalk landscape

The Wolds form a landscape which is totally different in character to any other part of Yorkshire. It is more like a piece of southern England that has found its way north and east into Yorkshire. The people, the traditions, culture and economy may be very different compared with the south, but the landscape is surprisingly similar. This is because of its underlying geology – Chalk.

If you look at a geological map of Britain you will see a great curving band of chalk running along the south coast, starting from the famous white cliffs and rolling Downs of Kent and Sussex, and running through Hampshire, Dorset, Isle of Wight, Wiltshire, Berkshire, Buckinghamshire, the Chiltern Hills, Oxfordshire, Northamptonshire. In Norfolk the chalk is largely hidden under layers of clay, (exposed near Brandon, around Grimes Graves, at those amazing Neolithic flint mines) before sinking underneath shallow waters of The Wash then remerging as the narrow but beautiful line of rolling chalk hills and scars that form the Lincolnshire Wolds. These Wolds are then sliced through by the huge expanse of the Humber Estuary – the Humber Gap – before continuing as a long, narrow crescent of chalk hills some 60 miles long, rising up to 246 metres or 807 feet at Garrowby Hill on the edge of Bishop Wilton Wold.

In Yorkshire these chalkland Yorkshire Wolds cover an extensive area of something like 13,000 square kilometres of what is now the East Riding of Yorkshire and North Yorkshire.

Chalk differs totally in character to the harder, far older Carboniferous rocks, sandstones and limestones of the Pennines to the west or the layers of Jurassic shales, mudstones and thinner limestones of the North York Moors. These are younger rocks, dating from the Cretaceous period, some 142–65 million years ago. During this period what is now the British Isles were covered by warm, shallow seas – the Chalk Sea – with trillions of shells and skeletal remains of sea creatures being compressed into pale, porous, alkaline rock of varying degrees of hardness. Ancient earth movement forced up the underlying chalk to the surface, which over millions of years as a result of glaciation, river erosion and constant weathering, has eroded to smooth flat-topped hills. To the north and west of the Wolds this has created steep escarpments overlooking the Vale of York to the west, and Vale of Pickering to the north, with gentler slopes that reach southwards and eastwards down into and under the alluvial clays of Holderness and the Humber Estuary. Depending on where it is quarried, even though it is porous, chalk can be a surprisingly hard rock. For many centuries it was used as a tough and durable building stone. Chunks of silica in the chalk rock metamorphosed over millions of years into the hard chert or flint nodules. In later ages these provided material to be fashioned into valuable hunting tools for early humans. But you can still see cottages and barns built from chalk in villages such as Hunmanby, Fridaythorpe and Helperthorpe, whilst Flamborough has a magnificent seventeenth century disused chalk lighthouse.

At Flamborough Head and Bempton Cliffs the chalk produces some of the most spectacular cliff scenery in England. Further inland this is a landscape of curious, dry valleys whose streams, if they appear at all, are only to be seen after heavy rain, as rainwater seeps through the rocks underground to deep aquifers on the underlying Jurassic clays, to emerge in wells or springs around the edges of the high chalkland. In several farms and villages in the high Wolds, man-made clay-lined ponds or blocked drainage channels also retain precious rainwater.

To the east and south, the chalk slopes down to gently slip underneath the clay that forms the fertile plain of Holderness. West of Driffield for example, there are not only frequent springs but after wet weather you can actually see water oozing from under the chalk hillside into low lying fields, heading for the many small chalk streams that feed into the Driffield Canal and River Hull. These are the most northerly chalk streams in the British Isles and are noted for their aquatic life.

The need for water has had a massive influence on the settlement patterns in the Wolds. From the days of the earliest occupants, villages and later towns have developed close to the spring lines around the edge of the chalk hills of the Wolds, or close to rivers, springs and streams. Villages within the Wolds have invariably had to depend on dew ponds and wells sunk to locate deep underground aquifers. This has restricted their growth as communities. Huggate, for example in the central part of the Wolds, in days before mains water had to depend on what was reputed to be the deepest well in Britain, 339 feet or 108 metres deep. It is reported that it could take up to 15 minutes to haul up a single bucket of water. Most Wolds villages also had their man-made clay-lined village ponds, reservoirs to capture and retain precious rainwater. There are even records of feuds between villages at times of drought to secure use of precious supplies.

One remarkable geological feature is known as The Great Wold Valley, a long shallow valley cutting some 30 miles across the north of the Wolds, from just east of Wharram–le-Street to the sea at Bridlington. A tiny dip in the valley bottom, close to the main road down the valley, follows the course of the extraordinary Gypsey Race. It is thought this stream, which often vanishes underground in the porous chalk, gets its name because it wanders above and over ground, being little more than dry or damp ditch for much of the year.

This valley was also known to be an important place of worship during Neolithic times, perhaps because water on the surface or underground was regarded as so precious and sacred. There are a number of scheduled ancient monuments in the valley including Duggleby Howe, one of Britain's largest Neolithic burial mounds, Willie Howe and the great Rudston monolith, the tallest standing stone in Britain at 25 feet or 7.6 metres high. It is of late Neolithic or early Bronze Age origin, and probably erected 2,500–2,000BC and is made of Jurassic gritstone, almost certainly transported on great planks and rollers to Rudston from Cayton Bay on the coast, some 12 miles away.

Human settlement still reflects this lack of surface water. The rock breaks down to thin, chalky soils, that quickly dry out, and which for centuries resisted cultivation, resulting in small, scattered villages such as Thixendale or Huggate serving huge sheep walks and rabbit warrens, or the series of villages along the spring line of the Gypsey Race.

Human settlement

This same sparsity of vegetation attracted early human settlement at a time when the lowlands were dense scrub forest and impenetrable bog. The well drained slopes and ridges of the Wolds could be more easily cleared, and grazed, homesteads built, and livestock protected against hostile predators. For these reasons the Wolds are especially rich in evidence of human occupation – settlement and defensive sites, earthworks, burial sites, tumuli and ancient trading routes and trackways of Neolithic, Bronze Age and Iron Age farmers, including the warlike La Tene and Parisii tribes from Northern France. **The Hull and East Riding Museum** in Hull and also the **Treasure House Museum** in Beverley contain a wealth of archaeological finds from these periods of Wolds' prehistory, making this area one of the richest areas in England for evidence of early settlement.

The Romans developed their main road Ermine Street from London and Lincoln towards York and Malton, with a major crossing of the Humber at Peturia (Brough). The fine road from York to Bridlington – appropriately known as Woldgate – can still be traced. In part it is now the busy A166 to Fridaythorpe and Fimber, but in places it is still an ancient sunken greenway along the ridge of the high Wolds.

The Romans also brought improved farming methods to their colonised Iron Age communities. Several handsome villa-farms were built in Romano-British times, indicating a long period of relative peace and prosperity. Mosaic pavements, pottery, jewellery and other artefacts from this period are now exhibited in the Hull and East Riding Museum.

Anglian settlers coming in the sixth century first settled in the Wolds in what was to become the Kingdom of Deira based at York, but with important settlements on the coast and inland close to water supplies. It was at one of these small settlements, at Goodmanham, near Market Weighton, that in 627 AD, soon after his own conversion to Christianity, King Edwin, ruler of what was now Northumbria, instructed his priest Coifi to hurl his battle axe into the pagan temple dedicated to Wotan to the horror of the congregation. As no retribution ensued, Coifi then instructed his followers to burn down the whole temple. This was later replaced with a small wooden Christian church. The little Norman church that replaced it on the same site today is dedicated to All Hallows; All Hallows or All Saints is often an indication of a Christian site of pagan origin.

St John and Beverley

Even before the Norman Conquest, several of the settlements had developed into important small market towns, none more significant than Beverley, on the foothills of the edge of the Holderness plain, its name suggesting a settlement close to the habitat of beavers in what would have be a largely marshy, scrubby wooded area, easily drained by settlers into the Beverley Beck, a tributary of the River Hull.

But it was one man in particular that gave Beverley its pre-eminence – St John. Born in the first half of the 7th century in Harham, a village near Driffield, John became part of the Abbey community at Whitby before becoming Bishop of Hexham, and a pupil of Bede, then Bishop of York and returning to a simple life of meditation and solitude in the "woods of Deira". He became well known for his teaching and various miracles. After his death and canonisation his tomb and shrine became a place of pilgrimage. Amongst the pilgrims to John's shrine was King Aethelstan, the first king of a united England, who had a vision before the battle of Brunanburh in 937AD against a combined army of Vikings and Scots. As a result of this great victory Aethelstan granted land and various powers to enable the modest monastery to become a Collegiate Church of Canons. The town that grew around it known as Bevreli, flourished to become a major regional centre of pilgrimage.

Bevreli was even spared destruction from the Harrying of the North because of its status as a centre of holy worship and pilgrimage. Its access to the Humber estuary down the deepened and enlarged Beverley Beck into the River, from the 14th century onwards linking it with the port of Kingston-Upon-Hull. This ensured its future both as a centre both of wool exports from what becomes the great sheep walks of the Wilds, but also for a cloth production, leatherwork, boat building, and even an iron foundry and brick works. North Bar, one of the few relics of the medieval town wall, dates from the 15th century, being built of local Beverley brick.

The magnificent **Beverley Minster**, the original shrine and sanctuary of St John, was built in three main phases between the thirteenth and fifteenth centuries. It is one of the great ecclesiastical buildings of Yorkshire. Yet at the other end of town, it had a rival – the splendid **St Mary's Church** dating from the 12th and 13th centuries but with a rebuilt Tower to replace the one that collapsed in the 16th century. The beauty and rich decoration of both churches reflect the prosperity of the town, second only to York in terms of its prosperity in medieval times.

Today Beverley remains one of the most beautiful and fascinating small towns in the North of England, with its Wednesday and Saturday Market Places, houses and shops dating from the 15th century along a long pedestrianised street that separates the two marketplaces. The Youth Hostel is in the former Friary Guest House where Edward I stayed in between 1299 and 1309.

Beverley was also the former County Town of historic East Riding, the name for the present Unitary Authority the area still proudly shares. It is also a vibrant cultural centre, with several art film and music festivals, fascinating pubs and busy weekly street markets.

Beverley enjoys an incomparably beautiful rural setting in the form of the three great areas of green space – ancient, grazed commons that surround the town known as the **Beverley Pastures. Westwood** as its name suggests occupies the western edge of the town looking towards the Wolds, with the tall Black Tower ruined windmill its highest point. Across the main York Road is the Racecourse, whilst to the immediate east of the town are **Swinemoor** and **Figham**, both bordering the River Hull and noted sanctuaries for wildlife, most notable for native and migrant species of birds and a wide variety of insect and plant life including rare grasses, sedges, orchids.

Just four miles south of Beverley, on a low chalk ridge above **Skidby** village, is another example of a tower windmill, this time a working example of a once typical East Riding windmill, dating back to 1821 and beautifully restored. It is now the focal point of a small museum of rural life.

Driffield

The other old town of the eastern Wolds with a remarkable heritage is Driffield. There is an almost forgotten mound of a Norman motte and bailey castle behind quiet streets on the upper town, where there is some evidence that the town's park may once have been the site of a Royal Palace, that of King Aeldreth of Northumbria, who reigned between 685–705AD and is reputed to be buried close to what is now St Mary's church in Little Driffield. The town prospered over the centuries but received an important boost in the late 18th century when the Driffield Canal was opened. The old canal basin in the area behind the railway station has been well preserved, at least one of the old warehouses still being used for agricultural stores until 2016. Driffield remains as an unspoiled, typically Yorkshire market town, with its long main street and a fine Parish church of the 15th century.

The pretty village of Wetwang, some five miles from Driffield was the home of a remarkable local geologist-clergyman, the Reverend Edward Maule Cole (1833–1911). He produced some remarkable papers interpreting local geology and history, including **Geological Rambles in Yorkshire** in 1886, that encouraged young men and women of the Wolds area to use the new rail network to explore the rich geological heritage of the Region.

Burton Agnes Hall a few miles to the north of the town is not only a magnificently preserved Jacobean house in a splendid garden setting, but in the grounds the original Norman Manor House is still to be seen, an extremely rare survivor from its period.

The High Wolds

The landscape of the High Wolds was to change dramatically in the late 18th century, primarily thanks to the vision of one man, Sir Christopher Sykes (1749–1801) a member of a family of West Riding merchants who had moved their activities to Hull in the 17th century and acquired a huge estate of grazing land used for sheep farming around the village of Sledmere. Sykes realised that the light, alkaline, chalky soils of the Wolds and relatively dry climate were perfect for the production of wheat and other arable crops, if enriched with fertiliser and irrigated. The new Parliamentary powers of Enclosure allowed him to do this on his estate.

Within a couple of decades, other landowners were to follow his example and the landscape of the Wolds changed from grassy downland to its present pattern of undulating, enclosed arable fields and scattered farms. A tall memorial tower erected in memory of a later member of the family, the charismatic and philanthropic Sir Tatton Sykes (1772–1863), stands as a landmark on the ridge some 2 miles away, erected in 1865 by his grateful tenants. A third member of this remarkable family, also known as Sir Tatton (1826–1913) left his mark on the landscape with a series of 17 new churches for the villages around Sledmere, all designed by leading architects of the time and planned to become "Centres of Christian Arts and Worship".

The home of the Sykes family, **Sledmere House**, a fine Georgian house, restored in 1911 after a disastrous fire, is one of the splendours of the central Wolds. Its richly decorated rooms, collections of fine paintings and ceramics, exquisite furniture and superb gardens, make it one of the leading attractions of the Wolds region.

Despite some inevitable loss of access to what had been the open Wolds, this landscape pioneered by the Sykes family of geometric fields, hedgerows, scattered woods and copses, has a character and beauty of its own, which change with the seasons. The ploughed fields curving over the Wolds in winter and spring has been described as like "corduroy" fabric, colours that change to green and gold as crops germinate, grow and ripen towards harvest, with in recent times, the addition of acid yellows of rape oilseed flowers in late Spring.

Unlike the Moors and Dales where valleys are cultivated and the tops are heather or open grass and peat moorland, with public access, the reverse applies in the Wolds. The tops are enclosed and heavily cultivated, with the only access paths and tracks largely around the edge of fields. But the far less well known numerous and smaller Dales have dry, grassy valley bottoms, their steep, smooth sides, dappled with wildflowers and butterflies in Spring. Since the 2000 CROW Act many have become public access land, making them wonderful places to walk, the alkaline soils attractive for wildflowers, and other wildlife. A mile from the pretty village of Millington in Lilydale, is **Millington Wood Nature Reserve**, a rare ash woodland rich in chalk loving flowers, and grasses.

Despite the obvious natural and man-made beauty of the Yorkshire Wolds, unlike the equally fine Lincolnshire Wolds south of the Humber, the Yorkshire Wolds has never received the protection that designation as an Area of Outstanding Natural Beauty that the area so clearly merits, However, Natural England announced in 2021 that this special area is now shortlisted for full AONB status, though this could take some time to be achieved. In addition, the Yorkshire Wolds and Holderness are now being proposed as a UNESCO Global Geopark. Geoparks are defined as *"single, unified geographical areas where sites and landscapes of international geological significance are managed with a holistic concept of protection, education and sustainable development"*. Given the remarkable and unique nature of the chalk valleys, hills and coastal cliffs of the Wolds, the Yorkshire Wolds qualifies in every way for celebration and protection as a landscape of both national and perhaps international importance.

Few people have captured the distinctive, cultivated landscape of the Yorkshire Wolds better than Bradford born David Hockney, whose water colours, and oil paintings such as **Big Trees at Warter** and even iPhone and iPad images such as **The Arrival of Spring at Woldgate**, have created a world-wide awareness of this very special part of Yorkshire.

Thixendale, another favourite place for Hockney is a linear village close to the meeting of a reputed sixteen dry dales, is perhaps the archetypical Wolds village. Close by is the studio of another well-known Wolds artist and naturalist **Robert Fuller** whose painting and prints of local wildlife, especially birdlife and small mammals on which he is an authority, enjoy a growing reputation.

Thixendale is only three miles walk from the strange, deserted village of **Wharram Percy**, of which only a ruined church millpond – together with some more modern farm buildings survive. This carefully excavated site, now managed by English Heritage has given rare insight into medieval life. The reasons that this and other villages in the Wolds were abandoned are put down to the Black Death of the 14th century but also deliberate clearance of villages in Tudor times by landowners to create larger sheep walks, the prime land use at that time.

The Yorkshire Wolds Way

Welton, High Hunsley, Goodmanham, Huggate, Millington, Thixendale, Wharram-le-Street, Winteringham, Hunmanby and several other iconic villages in the Wolds are also linked by what is perhaps the best introduction to the Wolds – the **Yorkshire Wolds Way**. This is one of England's National Trails, perhaps undeservedly less well known. The 79-mile (127km) walking route starts at Hessle on the Humber, an attractive small town close to the Humber Bridge, and ends at Filey Brigg. The route follows the great west and northern escarpments of the Wolds, with views across the Vales of York and Pickering to the North York Moors, before finally reaching the coast at Filey.

Filey is small fishing community. You'll still see traditional cobles beached at the end of the promenade, and a fine bronze statue of a Filey Fisherman also on the promenade. After the coming of the railways in the 1840s, the little town developed into the prettiest of seaside resorts. It enjoys almost perfect level sands which extend along the huge sweep of Filey Bay, ending with the dramatic long rocky spur that forms Filey Brigg – site of a Roman signal station. It also is where the Yorkshire Wolds Way and the Cleveland Way both start and finish. There is a small country park close by. **Filey Museum**, in two 17th century farm cottages in Queen Street, an old part of the town, is regarded as being one of the best small museums in Yorkshire, with excellent collections and exhibits relating to the Filey fishing industry as well as farming, natural and local history, including the town's evolution as a seaside resort, with a special feature on the coastal lifeboat service.

Winifred Holtby

But the Wolds are as much about the people who created this landscape as the landscape itself. Few writers have ever understood the communities of the Wolds, better than Winifred Holtby 1898–1935, in her novels, journalism and poetry. Born on a farm in Rudston, and sadly buried only 37 years later in Rudston's little Norman churchyard, Holtby's mother was the first female Alderman of the East Riding. Her daughter became a leading feminist and socialist, passionate about social reform and women's rights. Her final novel, **South Riding** tragically published posthumously and written as she fought her terminal liver disease, is simply one the great English novels of the 20th century, a portrayal of provincial England and local Government on a scale unequalled in English literature since George Eliot's Middlemarch. Too often naively dismissed as a love story, this totally misses the significance of the conflict between the reforming head teacher and heroine Sarah Burton, with a passion for social change and the rights of the girls in her care, pushing against the conservative forces in South Riding society that are preventing social justice and change. These qualities are embodied by the man who in spite of herself she admires, and finally loves, because of his personal qualities, landowner Robert Carne. Ultimately the relationship is doomed. But the novel is about far more than that. The processes of local Government and society are analysed in forensic detail with powerful characterisation. Appropriately Carne meets his end in a riding accident as the treacherous cliffs on the Holderness Coast crumble under his horse in a storm, and his corpse is washed away, as cliff debris often is, into the Humber estuary where it was discovered by children playing on the foreshore.

South Riding is thinly disguised East Riding, with its landscapes reflecting Holderness. Flintonbridge the county town of South Riding is Beverley, the town on the sea where much of the action take place is called Kiplington in the novel but is based on Withernsea, whilst the town of Hardrascliffe that also appears in the novel is Bridlington.

Bridlington and Flamborough

Bridlington, as Holtby would have been well aware, is far older than the popular seaside resort which grew around the busy little harbour and sandy beaches in Victorian times. A far more ancient settlement about a mile inland has origins that go back to Anglo-Viking times. This small settlement sheltered by the rolling chalk Wolds and cliffs to the north, dates from 1113 after Walter de Gant, a powerful Norman baron received permission from Henry I to establish what was a Priory of the first Augustinian Order of Canons.

The Priory flourished and its lay brothers were soon cultivating their lands and creating sheep walks to export wool from Bridlington's little harbour and later via the River Hull to the port of Kingston on Hull. By the 14th century, a huge Priory was built, but only the great Priory Church and elaborate Bayle or Gateway to the Priory complex survives. The Bayle Gate now contains a small but remarkable museum of Bridlington's early history and Priory life.

What really created the fame and therefore the wealth of the Priory was the career of a young local youth known as John of Thwing – Thwing is a village some nine miles from Bridlington.

A brilliant scholar, Thwing studied at Oxford before returning to Bridlington to become its Prior and enjoying a reputation that was to soon spread over England for his learning and scholarship and his ability to perform miracles, including reputedly saving the lives of five local sailors in a terrible storm through the medium of a vision. Some twenty years after his death in 1379 he was canonised, and pilgrims came from all over England to pray at St. John of Bridlington's shrine including, in 1407 King Henry IV, and in 1421 his son Henry V of Agincourt fame. Regrettably most of the Priory was destroyed at the Reformation. Only a modern white stone in the churchyard now marks the location of St John's shrine.

The small town that grew around the Priory prospered in later centuries. Now known as Bridlington's Old Town it has a virtually unspoiled main street of Georgian, Regency and Victorian shops.

Bridlington's growth as a seaside resort was entirely due to the coming of the railway in 1846 which brought visitors in their tens of thousands. This was not to the old town by the Priory but to the rapidly developed area around the harbour over a mile away, and also alongside the superb sandy beach. Within a few decades it became one of the most busy and popular seaside resorts on the East Coast. Its harbour remained a focal point of the coastal fishing trade, as well as a popular marina for leisure sailing. Visitors came most especially from the West Riding and Leeds. For much of the 20th century Bridlington was a favourite place for Leeds people to retire, as house and even street names testify.

Only a short way along the coast is a very different world, a spectacular part of the Yorkshire Heritage coast, with chalk cliffs as fine as anywhere in England. Just past the end of the long promenade, is **Sewerby Hall** – a beautiful park and gardens, with a handsome, early 18th century house, now run as a museum by East Riding Council. One highlight is a room devoted to the life of the celebrated aviatrix Amy Johnson, (1903–41) who was born in Hull. Among her many achievements was the first solo flight by a woman from England to Australia in 1936, as well as long distance flights records established alone or with her husband Jim Mollison. Johnson died in the War serving her country, in an accident over the Thames estuary whilst delivering aircraft to the front line. Her memorial room contains photographs and memorabilia of Amy's short but eventful life.

An hour or so's walk from Sewerby past the Iron Age fortification of Danes Dyke is **Flamborough Head**, one of the geological wonders of the British Isles – a series of magnificent sea-carved chalk cliffs which extend around a huge headland. The whole site is now a protected Site of Special Scientific Interest

A tall Gothic Memorial in the centre of the village of Flamborough recalls the tragic events of 1909 when two fishing cobles from the village were overturned, six men losing their lives.

Bempton Cliffs four miles to the north is one of Britain's most important maritime bird reserves. An estimated quarter of a million sea birds – gannets, puffins kittiwakes, razorbills, shags, fulmar nest and breed on the narrow crevices on the cliff face. For years, the eggs of sea birds were consumed by local people, hanging from ropes dangling down the cliff face, an activity known as "Climming". It was another member of the Sykes family, local MP Christopher Sykes who in 1869 introduced the Sea Bird Bird Preservation Act, one of Britain's first pieces of conservation legislation. An RSPB visitor centre and trails to key viewing points now provide safer ways of enjoying now protected bird life.

The west and northern Wolds

The western side of the Wolds has an equally rich cultural heritage. Market Weighton for many centuries, as its name implies, hosted regular weekly sheep and cattle markets and annual fairs for a huge area of the Wolds. It was an important coaching town between the key centres of Hull, Beverley and York.

It was also the birthplace and home of William Bradley (1787–1820) at seven feet nine inches England's tallest man; a fine oak statue in the town centre recalls his presence. The town benefited from the opening of the nine mile long Market Weighton Canal in 1782 that connected the town with the River Humber. It was vital for the export of agricultural produce and import of manufactured goods and raw material. But this in turn was overtaken by George's Hudson's railway between Hull and York in 1847. The opening of the line to Selby in 1848 and eventually through to Driffield in 1890 meant for a time Market Weighton was an important local railway junction. There is little evidence of any railway in the town now, though the old track bed to Beverley is now the Hudson Way, a walking and cycling route to the outskirts of Beverley. It passes through Kiplingcotes, site of England's oldest racecourse.

About three miles from Market Weighton is Londesborough, once the site and estate of a great house owned by the Dukes of Devonshire. It was demolished in 1839 by the sixth Duke to recycle material and help pay for Chatsworth House in Derbyshire, retaining only a hunting lodge. This was bought in 1845 by George Hudson. Hudson built himself a private station on the York-Beverley line but by 1849 he was bankrupt, and the property had to be sold. Now even his railway has vanished. Only the trees planted alongside the proposed grand drive to the station survive, an eerie ghost of vainglorious dreams long extinguished.

Pocklington is another exceptionally attractive unspoiled small market town nestling under the Wolds escarpment. It has a busy (Tuesday) marketplace, an old coaching inn and medieval Parish Church by Pocklington Beck on a site of an Anglian church which in turn dated back to the time when St Paulinus is reputed to have baptised people in the Beck. Like Market Weighton it had its own canal, this time linking to the navigable River Derwent, opened in 1818, which flourished in the pre-railway age. **Burnby Hall Gardens**, just outside the town centre, is an exceptionally interesting public garden and ornamental lake owned by East Riding Council. It contains the UK's national collection of nymphaea, Water Lilies, a spectacular and colourful sight every July.

Further into the Wolds, close by are the villages of Nunburnholme and Warter. Nunburnholme Church contains an ornately carved Anglo-Viking cross, discovered in 1839 as part of the present church wall. Suitably rescued and restored, its combination of pagan animal and Christian carving is one of the finest examples of its kind to have survived.

Warter is an estate village developed by the hugely successful Wilson ship owning family, who made their fortune through the Baltic trade importing vast quantities of Swedish iron ore to Hull. At the height of its success at the turn of the 20th century, the company had a fleet of 98 ships operating as far as southern Europe, America and India. The most celebrated member of the family was Charles Wilson, 1833–1907, MP for Hull who became the first Lord Nunburnholme. But the Wilson family also suffered from horrific misfortune. Stained glass windows or lunettes, rescued a now demolished memorial to two younger members of the family who both died in tragic circumstances, are now kept as fascinating pieces of ecclesiastical art in the **Wolds Heritage Centre**, in the disused church of St. James. The Centre has collections, exhibitions and local trails illustrating many aspects of Wolds culture and history. The 12,000-acre Warter estate, now owned by the Healey family, is about to see a new Warter Priory in the shape of a proposed massive neoclassical mansion to be built on the site.

A perhaps even more impressive example of high Victorian ecclesiastical architecture is to be found in the exceptionally pretty village of Bishop Wilton, north of Pocklington. This is the exquisite church of St Edith's, one of the 17 Sykes churches. It is noted for its 120 foot high spire, fine carvings rescued from the original Norman church, beautiful stained glass and amazing Italian mosaic floor.

Malton on the northern edge of the Yorkshire Wolds is not usually seen as a Wolds town but, separated from its twin Norton by the River

Derwent, it is a natural northern gateway to the Wolds close to the first foothills of the chalk hills at Langton and Settrington. It is also a town of real character. The Roman fort and castle at Old Malton may have long vanished, though the fine church of the Gilbertian Priory remains. The town was also once a small inland port, the highest navigable point on the River Derwent for quite large sized boats such as Humber Keels, which had to be roped-hauled upriver, using mainly human effort. Several old warehouses on the riverside testify to the role of the town as a port. It was also an important staging post on the turnpike road between York and Scarborough. Fine 18th and early 19th inns still grace the town around its extended marketplace and attractive former town hall. Malton now markets itself as Yorkshire's food capital, with a cluster of small shops and restaurants offering local food specialities. There are also two very successful microbreweries in the town. Thankfully, the by-pass carrying the A64 has removed most, but not all, the through traffic in the town centre.

Holderness

Sheep and wool production dominated the Wolds for many centuries. However, the heavy water-retaining soils of Holderness, mainly diluvial glacial till or beds of ancient glacial lakes lying over the deeply buried chalk, were long understood to transform to prime agricultural land once drained, for example into the little River Hull[1]. The name Holderness is that of the old Anglo-Viking Wapentake and comes directly from Scandinavian – you will see "ness" still used for a narrow strip of land or promontory in Norway or Denmark to this day. Holderness extends right down to the narrow Spurn headland in the Humber estuary.

It is also one of the most rapidly retreating shorelines in Europe, the soft clay cliffs eroding at a rate of between one to two metres a year, accelerating as winter storms gain ferocity, often with serious damage to homes, roads or businesses. Since Roman times it is estimated no less than 5km or 3 miles or so of the coast has disappeared into the North Sea, as well as 23 towns or villages. The most celebrated was Ravenser Odd, once a thriving and important seaport. In more recent times whole sections of roads and rows of once idyllic houses have been lost, the village of Skipsea now being at some risk. Longer term even the larger resorts of Withernsea and Hornsea may have cause for concern, with expensive remedial measures needed to protect the townships. Fascinating **Spurn Point**, at the very tip of Holderness, with its famous lighthouse, is now a National Nature Reserve. This is an ever-changing spit of land, the tip of which has now become an island, the road and standard gauge military railway line having been breached by tides in 2013, the access road now being termed a "wash-over" only accessible at low tide.

Another major natural feature of Holderness is **Hornsea Mere**, close to Hornsea town. At 3.2km in length and 1.2k at its widest point, this is Yorkshire's largest natural freshwater late, and an important bird sanctuary, being a Site of Special Scientific Interest and Special Protection Area.

Inland from Hornsea, and only 9 miles from Hull, is **Burton Constable**, one of the most magnificent and best-preserved Elizabethan mansions in England. It was converted from a medieval Pele tower by the Constable family in the 1560s and remained their home for 400 years. With 300 acres of parkland landscaped by the great Capability Brown, it is one of East Riding's most popular visitor attractions.

South west of Withernsea is the village of Arlington in Holderness whose 14th century Parish Church of St Patrick with its tall and elegant spire, visible for miles across Holderness, has been described as one of the most beautiful in England.

Regrettably, the two Holderness rail lines from Hull, to Hornsea and Withernsea were early victims of the Beeching closures in the late 1960s. The line to Hornsea has been converted into a new greener travel use as a popular Sustrans walking riding and cycling trail. Sections of the Withernsea line are also open for walking and cycling, with some parts now nature trails.

Fortunately, the same fate did not affect the Yorkshire Coast Railway which links Hull and Scarborough, edging between the coast and the Wolds between Beverley, Bridlington and Filey and through Hunmanby Dale onwards to Seamer and Scarborough.

Hull

Kingston upon Hull, to give the city its proper title, historically has deep and close economic and social ties with the Wolds and Holderness. Its enterprise and energy from the 18th century onwards, created the wealth of the great families with their fine mansions and estates. By the 19th and 20th centuries and the coming of the railways, its pretty surrounding villages became places where those who could afford to would live in or retire to, some like Hessle or Cottingham eventually expanding into large dormitory suburbs.

Hull in history

If its official and proper name is Kingston upon Hull, nationally and internationally on maps, railway timetables and in popular parlance, Hull is the name most people know and recognise. But Hull actually refers to the modest river on which the city stands, a curious origin of a now familiar city name.

The Hull is a small, meandering river that makes it way down from the edge of the Wolds, fed by water from fast flowing springs that emerge from underneath the chalk hills, close to Driffield and Beverley. It was this river, and its ability to allow sea-going boats to access and embark along its deeper banks, that was the main reason why a great city and port grew where it did, alongside the narrow, deeper river channel rather than the shallow Humber foreshore. This allowed much larger boats to berth in the safe haven formed by the river mouth.

A wharf near the mouth of the river was created by the Cistercian monks based at Meaux Abbey not far from Beverley in the 13th century, in order to bring their wool down the River Hull to load onto larger vessels to cross the North Sea to Continental ports. The hamlet that grew around it was originally known as Wyke.

Edward I, one the most far-sighted if militant of Plantagenet Kings, sometimes known as the Hammer of the Scots, needed a strategic, sheltered harbour on the east coast of northern England to service his navy and his troops for his long Scottish campaigns. So, the King did an exchange deal to acquire the land at Wyke from the monks in 1293, to build in essence a small military port to service his armies heading for

Scotland. By 1299 the little town was given a Royal Charter and named King's Town upon Hull. The Charter granted privileges to the citizens or burgesses, including the rights to hold regular markets and an annual fair, and to trade. The rapidly growing town soon became known as Kingston upon Hull and finally, as the centuries rolled past, this was shortened for most people to become just Hull.

After Edward's time, the port's strategic location enabled it to develop into a major trading port with Continental Europe with steady growth through medieval and Tudor times. Hull soon became a member and later a rival of the German-based Hanseatic League, a group of highly prosperous and influential cities and ports with access to the North Sea who shared free trade rights and royal protection – a kind of prototype European Union. Member cities included Cologne, Hamburg, Lübeck, Amsterdam, Bruges, Riga, Stockholm and in England London, Norwich, King's Lynn, Boston and York. But Hull traders soon also opened up their own new direct links with Baltic ports for the import of timber and iron, or exporting North Sea cod and wool and in later years woven Yorkshire cloth to Spain and Portugal in exchange for sherry and port wine.

Among goods imported from Baltic, German and Scandinavian ports into Hull were timber, furs, resin, flax, honey, wine, herring, wheat, and rye, metal ore (copper and iron) with exported wool and woollen cloth and increasingly, manufactured goods. New deeper docks and harbours were built to accommodate larger sea-going ships. Its strategic location on the Humber also made it the perfect transhipment centre, unloading goods from larger sea-going boats onto smaller sail powered keels and sloops, capable of transporting goods to and from the centre of towns and cities not only along the Humber but along its many tributaries – the Ouse as far as Selby, Goole and York, the Trent as far as Nottingham and Newark, the Don to Doncaster and Sheffield, the Aire and Calder as far as Wakefield and Leeds. The Aire and Calder Navigation gave Hull direct access for steam powered barges and cargo vessels to the growing towns and cities of Leeds, Castleford, Doncaster and Wakefield, exporting huge quantities of coal for domestic and industrial use from the West Riding coalfield. Newly improved Navigations such as the Derwent and the Hull also linked towns such as Market Weighton, Pocklington, Malton, Beverley and

Driffield with Hull, allowing agricultural produce to be exported to the growing industrial cities of the West Riding and coal, raw materials and manufactured goods to be imported. Hull soon became the commercial and industrial heart of East Riding, where fortunes were made often to be reinvested in the great farms, estates and country houses of the hinterland, especially the Yorkshire Wolds.

Kingston upon Hull became a city in 1897, a time when the city was probably at the height of its economic success in the decades just before the First World War, when deep sea fishing and whaling were major businesses for the city, and manufacturing was also hugely important. Around this time the city, now a major port for passenger as well as freight traffic, became a transhipment point for many thousands of refugees coming from Continental Europe fleeing persecution or financial hardship, and heading for the New World, using England as a land bridge. Boat loads of refugees or economic migrants, arrived at Hull, crossed to Liverpool by train and then headed across the Atlantic in great liners to the United States or Canada.

The challenge of the post war years – and present

World War Two was a tragic period in the city's history. In 1941 massive enemy carpet bombing destroyed not only dockland areas, but much of the central parts of the city. Over 95% of homes in the city were destroyed or damaged in some way, and 1,200 people killed and a further 3,000 injured. The miracle is how much of the old town has survived or has been carefully restored in the years since.

In the later years of the 20th century, political, technological and economic change were not kind to Hull. The so-called Cod Wars with Iceland during the 1960s and 70s severely damaged the economic viability of deep-sea trawler fishing from both Hull and Grimsby. The long decline of Britain as the world's leading industrial nation and exporter of manufactured goods, led to a loss employment of manufacturing jobs in the city, but also goods and supplies through the ports,

A bitter dispute with dock workers doing the 1980s accelerated the decline of Hull as a port, together with a rapid growth in container shipping that enabled conventional docks and docker to be bypassed. Much of this new container traffic was based on south coast ports such as Felixstowe, or even Immingham with its easier access for large ships at the mouth of the Humber. The growth of the motorway network also made fast road access to and from the southern ports cheaper, quicker and easier. Declining North Sea fishing stocks of the two "Cod Wars" between Britain and Iceland during the 1950s and 1970s also hastened Hull's decline as a fishing port.

All these factors caused serious hardship for the people of Hull in the latter part of the 20th century, which actions by Governments in the 21st century has only worsened, as indicated by the National indicators of poverty for the city. Recent reports have also indicated that the pandemic has also hit the city especially hard. This may be because of its dependence on manufacturing industries, light engineering and food processing in factories, all activities where people cannot easily work from the safety of home.

But it isn't all bad news. Hull University, established in 1927, is now one of the leading research institutes in the North, with a student population of over 16,000. Recent new development has transformed the city centre, with many of the old docks being filled in and transformed to public gardens, a marina, retail and other development. King George Dock, three miles out of the city on the Hedon Road, built in 1914 for larger steam passenger and cargo shipping, now is the roll-on-roll-off port for P&Os nightly ferries to Rotterdam, carrying thousands of cars, trucks and lorries destined for the cities of the North of England and Scotland. Despite the hopefully temporary impact of Brexit, Hull is still a major port. Associated British Ports now deal with significant, mainly container freight traffic to and from the port which now has a new rail freight siding and employs over 5,000 people at what is a major gateway to and from Western Europe.

The Government's announcement of the creation of a new Humber Free Port, in which goods can be imported and exported without tariffs and red tape kept to a minimum, could give a new economic boost to Hull, Grimsby and Immingham.

Modern industry, mainly in chemical, pharmaceutical and health care, but also light industry and manufacturing, for example with Hull being a centre for the manufacture of caravans, is also hugely important to the city, which now has a population of over a quarter of a million. Hull is also a major UK player in the battle to combat the Climate Crisis. New green technologies include the massive Siemens Gamesa wind turbines for use in a huge new wind farm development in the shallow North Sea off Hornsea are bringing new employment and wealth to the city. Alexandra Dock has a new role for transhipment of turbine blades from the huge new manufacturing base into their off-shore North Sea seabed locations. New recycling plants designed to create energy from waste, plus the creation of an enterprise zone and a new digital science centre in the old fruit market are just some of the other indications of the industrial regeneration taking place in Hull.

The former Blackburn Aircraft factory a few miles outside the city at Brough is the site where pioneering flying boat technology was developed, using the Humber Estuary and East Riding beaches for research flights. In more recent years when owned by British Aerospace, Buccaneer and Typhoon military aircraft and Hawk training aircraft were manufactured at the site. From 2021 Brough has a new future as a major engineering technical research and development centre for, amongst other things, the new Dreadnought submarine.

The city of culture

In 2017 the city was declared the **UK Capital of Culture**. This attracted huge media attention, and brought artists, writers, craftsmen and musicians to celebrate various aspects of the city's heritage. It also encouraged investment in the city, with central streets becoming pedestrianised, buildings restored, and an artistic centre quarter established near the waterfront.

Even before its year as UK Capital of Culture, tourism had already become a major contributor to the city's economy. Since 2017 this has grown significantly. The city attracted, pre-pandemic, an estimated 5 million visitors from UK and abroad. These visitors contributed an estimated £210 million per year to the local economy. Hopefully these levels will soon return, post-pandemic especially if domestic tourism is given a boost by international travel restrictions.

It is a city easy to access directly from the continent with overnight P&O ferries from Rotterdam, even if sadly the Zeebrugge ferry, a probable victim of Brexit uncertainty, has been lost. There are fast road and rail connections from almost everywhere in Southern and Northern England and the Midlands.

If you arrive by rail at Paragon Station you are immediately greeted by a life-sized bronze statue of Phillip Larkin, (1922 –1985) one of England's greatest 20th century poets. Larkin was librarian at Hull University Library for 30 years, a well-known jazz critic as well as a poet, whose dry humour, ironic observations of life in England and mastery of language make him one of the most loved and widely read poets of our time.

Larkin isn't the only poetic voice of note with close links to Hull. The great 17th century Metaphysical poet Andrew Marvell (1621–1678) was born in Winestead in Holderness and came to Hull with his family when he was three, later to be educated in Hull Grammar School. He became both a politician and poet, but kept his links with Hull, being its Member of Parliament in 1659. His statue is to be seen outside the old Grammar School in Trinity Square. A more recent Hull poet was Stevie Smith (1902–71) a fine, often wryly humorous writer the title of whose poem "Not waving but drowning" has become a phrase in the English language.

The **Hull Truck Theatre**, close to the Paragon Transport Interchange is one of the most interesting and exciting modern theatres in the North of England, noted for its willingness to put on contemporary drama which both reflects and questions the world in which we live. A former Artistic Director is the well-known northern playwright John Godber who as well as many television scripts wrote such popular hits as **Odd Squad** and **Bouncers**. Another Hull playwright with links to the theatre was Alan Plater (1935–2010), whose television hits included **Trinity Tales** and **The Beiderbecke Trilogy**, and that witty but radical tribute to Britain's coal miners, **Close the Coalhouse Door**. The city's other theatre, **Hull New Theatre**, in Kingston Place, is in the elegant neoclassical former Assembly Rooms and has a more mainstream touring company repertoire. Celebrated actors of stage and screen who come from Hull include Tom Courtenay, Ian Carmichael, Maureen Lipman and Barry Rutter.

Ferens Art Gallery, recently refurbished, is Hull's major art and sculpture gallery and its permanent collection with work by several Old Masters including Frans Hals and Canaletto, as well as portraiture, marine paintings, and examples of modern and contemporary British art, represented by Stanley Spencer, David Hockney, Helen Chadwick and others.

At the other side of the Square is the **Maritime Museum**. Housed in the handsome former Dock Offices, this is a nationally important collection of artefacts and photographs of people and equipment from the whaling and deep-sea fishing industries of Hull and East Yorkshire, from fishing boats such as the little coastal cobles still in use in Filey and Bridlington for lobsters, to Arctic trawlers and passenger liners.

Behind the Maritime Museum is the Queens Gardens, the former Queen's Dock filled in and transformed to formal gardens and green space, culminating at the far end in the impressive Wilberforce Monument. William Wilberforce, (1759–1833), the great early 19th century politician, reformer and philanthropist, was born in Hull but educated in Pocklington. Wilberforce spearheaded the campaign against the Slave trade at that time supported by huge establishment business and trade interests in Britain. His crowning achievement, the Abolition of Slavery Act 1833 was passed a few days after he died, but he was aware of its imminent passage through Parliament. His former 17th century house, now the **Wilberforce Museum** in the High Street, in the Museum Quarter, offers a fascinating insight into not only Wilberforce's life but the utter, degrading horrors of slavery, including disturbing accounts of how the barbaric practice survives in many parts of the world today.

Hull's waterfront has been transformed with the evocative black Spurn Point lightship at the head of what is now the busy Hull Marina, filled with dinghies and yachts.

Victoria Pier offers fine views across the Humber. This is where the paddle steamers used to cross to New Holland in Lincolnshire. Because of the shallowness of the river, paddle steamers continued to operate the last ferries between Hull and New Holland almost until the opening of the Humber Bridge in 1981. The last coal fired paddle steamer in regular service in UK waters, the celebrated PS Lincoln Castle, continued to chug across the Humber until 1978. The grand ticket offices remain as does perhaps the most elegant public loos in the North of England. Close by to the east is the mouth of the River Hull. A pedestrian bridge across the River Hull leads to The Deeps, and immediately upstream, the Hull tidal barrier. This is a reminder that the city is extremely low lying, being mostly just 2 to 4 metres above sea level and subject to regular floods. During exceptional high tides the barrier is lowered to protect the city from flood risk, but the problem will be increasingly exacerbated in the years ahead by the combined impacts of global warming and rising sea levels.

The Deeps is a spectacular building overlooking the Humber estuary which contains one of Britain's largest aquariums, with over 3,500 fish from every available species, from sharks to small crustaceans, not to mention a colony of penguins. Known as a "submarium" well-lit glass tunnels allow visitors to see species such as huge sting rays from underneath as they swim overhead through huge glass tanks.

The revival of the Old Town with its many narrow streets is a huge tribute to Hull even before becoming the UK City of Culture. You can follow the quayside path past old wharfs and staithes, where the city first developed as a trading port, into the **Museum Quarter**.

The **Hull and East Riding Museum** offers superb insight not only into the story of Hull itself, but the whole of the Wolds and East Riding. It is the perfect place to come to before setting out to explore Hull's Wolds hinterland. It is especially rich on interpreting the geology, archaeology and prehistory of the Wolds, as well as Roman history, including many artefacts from town and village sites within the Wolds. Among highlights are the 3,000-year-old Hasholme Boat found buried in a side stream of the Humber. This was discovered at Hasholme on a small tributary stream of the river. It held a crew of 18 men plus two steersmen, or a crew of five and five tons of cargo. Also to be seen are the curious Roos Carr carved Bronze Age warrior figures, a reconstructed Iron Age village and Roman bathhouse, wonderful Roman mosaics from Brough, Rudston, Welton and elsewhere, the Grimston Sword, Saxon and Viking finds, plus countless other treasures from later periods. Just behind the Museum, on the River Hull, is the Arctic Corsaire, a sidewinder trawler built in Beverley in 1960 and one of the last of the great Hull trawler fleet, now kept as a somewhat sad reminder of a once great fishing industry.

The **Street Life Museum** is Hull's transport museum. It has an amazing, superbly presented collection of original vehicles – carts, stagecoaches, charabancs, buses, trams, cars, and bicycles including a rare proto-cycle hobbyhorse. It also features a carefully restored 1940s high street scene complete with shops and a 1930s railway goods shed.

Hull Minster dates back to 1306 when it was established by Edward I's Queen, Margaret of France. As the city prospered with substantial gifts from the city's wealthy merchant families, the building was extended in the Perpendicular Gothic style. It is one of the earliest great churches in England to make extensive use of brick in the lower crossing towers, and though restored in Victorian times, much fine original work remains. In 2017 in a gesture linked to the City of Culture, it became the city's Minster.

In the Market Place close by, is the fine gilded statue of King William III erected in 1734. Known as William of Orange, he was seen by the people of Hull as protecting their Parliamentary rights and the Protestant succession. He was celebrated, more equivocally perhaps, for the introduction of gin from his native Holland to England. The 16th century Grammar School nearby was where poet Andrew Marvell went to school; the upper floor was, until the mid-18th century, the Meeting Hall of Hull merchants.

The Old Town has specialist shops, wine bars, and several fascinating old pubs in and around the city centre. The George Inn in the evocatively named little street known as Land of Green Ginger, has allegedly the smallest window to be found in England in its façade, whilst the Olde Black Boy, in the High Street, full of atmosphere, dates from 1729. Most fascinating of all perhaps is The White Hart, a 17th century inn reached by narrow alleyway between Silver Street and Bowling Alley Lane. Upstairs is what is known as The Plotting Room, where according to legend, in 1642, Sir John Hotham and his Parliamentary supporters took the decision to deny the forces of King Charles I access into the town. This then led to a siege of Hull by the King's Army, which in turn precipitated the English Civil War, ultimately won by the Parliamentarians, leading to the execution of the King.

The Humber

Hull's relationship with both the North Sea and its great river the Humber is close and intimate. Hull is one of the cities in England in which rising sea levels pose a serious threat and may need further engineering measures over and above the present Tidal Barrier to protect its communities and city centre. Ironically for a city that supported

Brexit, itself a reflection of decades of under investment and poverty, its salvation is quite likely to be Dutch flood management specialists in the tradition of the 17th century engineer Cornelius Vermuyden, with the know-how and skills to keep the North Sea at bay.

You can experience the power and beauty of the River Humber on a direct walk or cycle ride out of Hull along the **Trans Pennine Trail**, a 185-mile green travel route that links Hull with Leeds and Liverpool. The River Humber carries no less than a fifth of all England's river water. It has long been a both a barrier, it divided the ancient Kingdom of Northumbria with that of Mercia, and a means of communication. Evidence of the importance of the latter are the sewn-plank boats of the Bronze Age found near North Ferriby and dating from 2030–1680 BC, now in the National Maritime Museum at Greenwich, and the Iron Age boat from Hasholme now in the Hull & East Riding Museum. At low tides and when river flows are also low, at Brough, near what was probably the Roman barge or a raft crossing from Wintringham Lincolnshire, the river is almost shallow enough to be walked across, a feat performed in 2005 by Graham Boanas of Hull in just four hours.

The river is also a nationally important nature reserve, being both a Special Area for Conservation and Special Protection Area because of the rich biodiversity of its reed beds and mudflats. It is estimated that around 150 species of birds have been recorded in the area of the river.

But the river's crowning glory is surely that magnificent piece of engineering and elegant architecture, **The Humber Bridge**. The bridge joins Yorkshire with Lincolnshire, carrying the A15 from Hull to Immingham and Grimsby, but also a footpath and cycleway linking Hessle and Barton on Humber. Its long central span of 1,410 metres and total length of 2,220 metres made it, for a short period between 1981 and 1997, the world's longest suspension bridge. It remains one of the civil engineering marvels of England, a fitting symbol both of Yorkshire's independence, and connectivity, across the great River Humber, with the rest of England.

Notes

1 River Hull Drainage Group 1983 *Becks, Banks, Brains and Drains* Hull

5

The Yorkshire Dales

The Yorkshire Dales extends across the central Pennines, between the Vale of York and the Lune valley on the edge of the Lake District, a line roughly that of the M6 and West Coast mainland railway; to the south defined by the Aire Gap (roughly marked by the A65 and the Skipton to Lancaster railway) and to the north the Stainmore gap, again roughly the line of the A66. This doesn't quite follow the old North Riding boundary, which followed the southern bank of the river Tees as far as Upper Teesdale and Mickle Fell, at 2,585 feet or 776 metres above sea level the highest point in historic Yorkshire, but generally now considered to be part of the North Pennines.

The Yorkshire Dales National Park

The Yorkshire Dales National Park covers most, but by no means all, of this area. It was designated in 1954, covers 2,769 km^2 or 841 square miles. It is now the UK's third largest National Park after the Cairngorms and the Lake District. This includes the significant 2016 extension of the National Park into Cumbria to include the northern Howgills and the fine area of limestone country around Kirkby Stephen and the Orton Fells, which, as a thoughtful regard to local identity issues, are now known as the Westmorland Dales.

The Yorkshire Dales National Park Authority has the difficult job of managing the competing demands of conserving one of Britain's most iconic landscapes with its rich biodiversity with that of the enjoyment of that landscape by up to 4.7 million visitors annually – including 4.2 million day visitors – 93% of whom arrive by car – and 700,000 staying visitors (Source YDNPA 2020). In addition, the Authority, as local planning authority, though without any direct responsibility for housing or transport, has to look after the needs of around 24,000 local residents. However, it is worth noting that tourism in the National Park is worth around £374 million annually creating the equivalent of 4,400 full time jobs, mainly in the hospitality and retail industries.

The Park Authority is also supported in its work by the **Yorkshire Dales Society**, now branded **The Friends of the Dales**. This is an educational charity, established in 1981, of around 1,300 members who work closely with the Authority to help increase understanding and respect for this unique environment, by means of regular talks, site visits, website features and the quarterly **Yorkshire Dales Review**. However, as a conservation body, it is also prepared at times to act as a "critical friend" to take issue on those few occasions where it feels the Authority is not doing enough to protect the National Park. For example the Friends have been critical of the Authority's over-generous policy of allowing isolated roadside barns to be converted for residential usage, arguing that such conversions invariably come with changes to windows and other features that alter the character of the building, often used as holiday lets or second homes, and the addition of large parking space or ports for at least two parked cars, all of which adds to traffic pressures on narrow roads.

In 2007 having felt the Authority was not doing enough to retain access to the Park for urban communities without their own transport, the Society set up a pioneering volunteer-led Community Interest Company, the Dales & Bowland CIC which now manages most of the popular DalesBus Sunday bus network between the cities of West and North Yorkshire and the heartlands of the National Park.

A recent (2020) visitor survey by Trip Advisor confirmed that for many people in Britain and elsewhere, the Yorkshire Dales is the most-loved National Park in Europe[1], receiving more votes even than the Lake District which has over twice as many visitors.

And indeed, you don't have to spend much time searching television channels or bookshops to see the almost endless publications, programmes and films which celebrate the landscape of the Yorkshire Dales. For many people from outside Yorkshire, the Yorkshire Dales has become almost synonymous with Yorkshire itself.

Evolution of a landscape

What makes the landscape of the Dales so very special is the almost perfect balance in that landscape between the green, intimate pastoral Dales, with their complex patterns of drystone walls, scattered barns, farms and idyllic stone villages and the barren, brown, semi-wilderness of the open fells. The higher summits have the appearance at least of true mountains even if they rise to only around 700 metres or 2,300 feet. Well into the middle of the 18th century it was assumed that the mighty craggy outline of Ingleborough rising above the Lune and Ribble valleys and visible from the coast was England's highest mountain, despite being dwarfed by Scar Fell or Helvellyn only a few miles further west.

As always, it's all about the underlying rock structure. The best way of understanding the rock structure of the Dales is to imagine a huge cake consisting of endless layers of sedimentary rocks from primeval seas and river deltas massively thrust upwards between 50 and 60 million years ago by titanic movements of the earth's crust and continents. The giant cake was thrust upwards at an angle, sloping from east up to west, bursting from under the newer Triassic and Permian rock underlying the Vale of York. Add to the process an endless, weathering, scouring and erosion by glaciers, deserts, winds, and rivers to eventually expose the older underlying layers of Carboniferous gritstones, shales and limestones. Dating back 300–360 million years, their name signifies coal bearing rocks, though coal has only been found in quantity worth mining in the Ingleton area and in thin seams for local use in the higher Yoredale limestones above Wensleydale, Wharfedale and Garsdale.

Over the next huge spans of geological times, sequences of glaciers and rivers over aeons gradually gouged out the long, narrow dales, leaving the huge ridge ridges exposed, like fingers of a gigantic hand. In the west, in the centre of the hand rise the great flat-topped summits of the Three Peaks and neighbouring fells, capped by weather resistant millstone grit. Beyond the great Pennine Fault in the north west of the National Park, where the geology is more typical of the Lake District than the Dales, lies the huge, rounded summits of the Howgill Fells, consisting of even older, smoothly eroded sedimentary Silurian and even Ordovician rocks dating back 485 million years.

Carboniferous Limestone, especially the Great Scar Limestones exposed by the line of the Craven Faults to the south of what is now the National Park, creates the most spectacular scenery of the National Park – Malham Cove, Gordale Scar, Warrendale Knotts, and other craggy outcrops, as well as the miles of frost, rain and wind eroded limestone pavements. Further north and east, the thinner layers of Yoredale limestones deposited between softer shales have created those distinctive step-shaped fell summits of dales, and on lower slopes, countless shimmeringly beautiful waterfalls.

This should potentially be a very rich area of biodiversity. Because of centuries of overgrazing by sheep in particular and use of the much of the upland for mining or grouse rearing, away from a relatively few sheltered gills, protected limestone woods and crags, there are less wildflowers and variety of species than might be imagined. However things are changing. National Nature Reserves on Ingleborough and at Ling Gill in Upper Ribblesdale, and the nature reserve at Malham Tarn on a unique raised peat bog served by lime-rich springs, illustrate what happens when areas can be protected from intense grazing. The National Park's **Limestone Country Project** of the 1990s pioneered the encouragement given to Dales farmers to reintroduce older breeds of cattle such as Shorthorns or Galloways, whilst reducing the number of sheep to allow wildflowers to regenerate. **The Yorkshire Dales Millennium Trust**, an independent charity set up by the National Park Authority in 1997 to deliver conservation work and education in the Dales, passed its target for planting of a million trees some time ago with the support of hundreds of willing landowners. Likewise, the **Woodland Trust** has created many hectares of new woodland. These are almost entirely native broadleaved trees. In some coniferous plantations, the red squirrel has made an impressive comeback. Peregrines now nest on Malham Cove and hen harriers and osprey are seen on the higher moors, whilst the once rare red kite is now regularly to be seen over the moor edge or house roof tops in areas like lower Wharfedale.

But geological and natural history interest is not confined to areas of land above ground. Acid rain acting on the limestone has created an extraordinary underground world underneath the Yorkshire Dales. Surface streams penetrating and enlarging cracks or fissures into the limestone gradually erode deep potholes and labyrinths of underground caves and passages. Some of these are justly celebrated – Gaping Gill above Clapham leads to an immense cavern 340 feet (103 metres) deep, famously capable of holding St. Paul's Cathedral and hosting England's highest unbroken waterfall. The stream eventually emerges within Ingleborough Cave three miles away.

Many of the caves such as Ingleborough Cave, Weathercote, Hunt Pot, Alum Pot, became well known to intrepid cave hunters, used to tying a candle to a hard hat to guide their way through the pitch blackness. Particular caverns, formations or individual stalactites and stalagmites attracted fanciful, sometimes literary names, a tradition that continues within the Show Caves of modern times. Published in 1780s, topographer John Hutton's book **A Tour to the Caves in the environs of Ingleborough and Settle** became an instant best seller and started a tradition of speleological literature that continues to this day. With an estimated 2,500 known caves, including Britain's longest proven continuous system of passageways known as The Three Counties (Yorkshire, Lancashire and Cumbria), the Dales is now one of Britain's premium areas for caving and caving diving, an activity that needs to be undertaken with one of the region's top caving clubs. Fortunately, there are also no less than three beautifully lit Show Caves open to visitors all year – Ingleborough Cave at Clapham, White Scar Cave at Ingleborough (England's longest show cave) and the intriguing Stump Cross Caverns, near Greenhow above Nidderdale, first discovered in the 1820s by local lead miners.

At Victoria Cave, near Settle there is also a link with early human civilisation, with the recently discovered reindeer antler bone tools, carbon dated to between 12,521 and 12,433BC and the oldest human artefact so far found in Yorkshire, an Upper Palaeolithic bone harpoon from around 10,800BC.

But it was Bronze Age farmers rather than the earlier hunter gatherers who were to have a profound impact on the landscape we see today. There are stone circles to be traced in Langstrothdale and above Grassington and still visible signs of Bronze and Iron Age fields and settlements in areas around Malham and in Upper Wharfedale. The hut circles on the summit of Ingleborough also suggest an Iron Age seasonal camp, defensive or religious settlement.

These early farmers began the constant process of land clearance and removal of tree and scrub cover and as on the North York Moors, eventually produce the bare, treeless fell and ridge summits we see today. But evidence suggests that late Neolithic, Bronze and Iron Age farmers were already learning to manage their woodland by coppicing trees to provide a constantly renewable supply of poles and staves for tools, and for building, fencing and charcoal production.

The Romans, in their efforts to subdue the warlike Celtic Brigantes, left lines of campaigning roads still visible on the landscape. The most impressive of these, built by General Julius Agricola towards the end of the first century, connected their fortresses in Ilkley in Wharfedale and Bainbridge in Wensleydale. It is visible between Buckden and Bainbridge, as the stony track over what is now known as the Stake Pass. Another is the ancient Cam Road linking Ribblesdale with Bainbridge. Mastiles Lane above Malham was another campaigning road and also the site of a small Roman military fort.

The lack of larger civilian settlements and the occasional Iron Age hill fort and defensive fortifications as in Grass Wood, at Park Rash above Kettlewell, and above Grinton in Swaledale, suggests that the Romans may have regarded this isolated and relatively impoverished region was not worth the effort of full pacification, though there is evidence they were mining lead in Upper Nidderdale.

It was the Anglian and later Viking settlers, both Danes from the east and Norwegians from the west, that left the strongest evidence of human activity along the Yorkshire Dales. This is evidenced in patterns of scattered farmsteads and more centralised farms from within villages, bearing names of Anglian or Norse origin we use today. Wharfedale is a perfect example of a valley settled by Anglians with its string of villages from Ilkley and Addingham up to Buckden, (with a Norse intrusion at Burnsall and Appletreewick). Norse settlements such as Dent and Garsdale have their typical, more isolated and independent "statesmen's" farms and narrow land holdings up the hillsides and are more typical of the Lake District. You can also see the shallow grassy terraces on many hillsides, evidence of ploughing strips known as lynchets or raines where grain – mainly oats and some hardy species of wheat – was grown for many centuries.

The Northern word "Dale", a word which probably came from old Norse "darl" and similar to the modern German word "Tal", can also mean apportionment of land. Even to this day older inhabitants of the Dales still have almost tribal links with families in their own dale, with people in neighbouring dales perceived as being very different, even though, as the crow flies, people "over the hill" may live closer to them than their neighbours living at the top end, or further down the valley. Accents and customs, for example the way dry stone walls are constructed, can vary even between adjacent dales.

For the great Norman Barons, who after the Conquest had been awarded grants of land as spoils of war, and their Plantagenet successors, the attraction of the Dales was as much for a leisure activity – hunting – as for economic activity. In particular hunting of red and later roe deer, and wild boar was popular, using hounds or even falcons. The system of Foresting, creating large game reserves on poorer areas of upland but subject to stringent forest laws, had a huge impact on the evolving landscape we see today. There were several huge hunting Forests or Chases, extending from the well-established towns around the Dales such as Knaresborough with a defensive castle, or others extending to the dale heads. Examples where evidence can still be seen include Barden Forest, once the hunting estates of the Cliffords, whose hunting lodge at Barden Tower still survives. Langstrothdale Chase had a lodge probably close to where the Buck Inn now stands at Buckden. Wensleydale Forest survives in folk memory through the tradition of the Bainbridge Hornblower who sounds his ancient horn to guide benighted travellers off the hills. Knaresborough Forest covered much of the eastern Dales and part of the Washburn Valley. Deer Parks, land enclosed by walls, ditches or fences and to protect deer, were also another major land use which have survived in areas such as around Castle Bolton, and on the Studley Royal estate.

Many of these landscapes evolved through careful management into the great heather grouse moors of Victorian times, in effect shooting reserves, in the eastern side of the Dales, for example around Barden in Wharfedale, and above Gunnerside in Upper Swaledale, Wensleydale and Nidderdale. These moorlands are now precious areas open for public access; all are a spectacularly beautiful purple in late summer.

Grants of land to the emerging religious houses of Norman times were also to have an enduring impact on the Dales landscape we see today. It was the monks and lay brothers of the great Abbeys of Fountains,

Jervaulx and Sawley (Cistercian) Bolton (Augustinian Canons), and Eastby (Premonstratensian) that laid the foundations of what was to become Yorkshire's and for a time England's greatest industry – wool production. The immense sheep walks of the Yorkshire Dales managed from outlying granges, for example as at Kilnsey owned by Fountains. A little carefully reconstructed 15th century ling thatched barn alongside Grimwith Reservoir was part of the Grange at Grimwith owned by the Bolton Canons.

After the Dissolution, when monastic land was sold by the Crown to private owners, the production of wool from the farms and granges continued, only diversifying in the lower dales into beef and dairy farming as demand changed in later centuries.

Many of the abbeys were demolished; but others were left to become picturesque ruins in the centre of grand country estates. In most cases they have also developed a leisure use which continues into the 21st century. Wharfedale between Bolton Priory and Barden Tower for example has long been one of Yorkshire's great artificial leisure landscapes. In the early 19th century, the Priory and its picturesque riverside were painted by Girtin, Turner, Ruskin and Landseer, but further upriver carefully arranged woodland views were developed by the heirs of the Cliffords, the Dukes of Devonshire. The Reverend William Carr, the enterprising vicar of Bolton Priory's magnificent church, now the village of Bolton Abbey's Parish Church, was largely responsible for designing the network of walkways with spectacular views above the notorious Strid, often enjoyed from strategically placed benches.

Carr's other claim to fame was as the breeder of the largest cow ever to be publicly shown in England, the Craven Heifer, born in 1807 at Bolton Abbey and eventually weighing a massive 2,496 pounds (1,132 kg). The beast remains a popular image for inn signs and for a time was depicted on bank notes of the Craven Bank. Bolton Abbey and Strid Woods are now one of the most popular visitor attractions in the North of England, carefully managed by the Chatsworth Estate at Bolton Abbey, an unofficial Country Park within the National Park that attracts hundreds of thousands of visitors annually.

2nd Edition - January 2014

The Association of British Counties map of

Yorkshire

This unique map shows the historic County of Yorkshire and its three Ridings, together with the current (2014) areas for administration within its borders. While these areas are subject to periodic reorganisation, the historic County remains unchanging.

About this map:

Successive reorganisations of boundaries have brought counties for Local Government, the post and for the ceremonial purposes of the Lieutenancies - to name a few.

Through all of this change, the boundaries of the historic county of Yorkshire and its Ridings have never changed, been disbanded nor faded into oblivion.

Ceremonial Counties:

NY - North Yorkshire
SY - South Yorkshire
EY - East Riding of Yorkshire
WY - West Yorkshire

Local Authority Areas:

1 - Redcar and Cleveland Borough
2 - Middlesbrough Borough
3 - North Yorkshire
4 - City of York Council area
5 - East Riding of Yorkshire District
6 - Kingston-upon-Hull City Council area
7 - City of Bradford Metropolitan District
8 - City of Leeds Metropolitan District
9 - Calderdale Metropolitan Borough
10 - City of Wakefield Metropolitan District
11 - Kirklees Metropolitan Borough
12 - Barnsley Metropolitan Borough
13 - Doncaster Metropolitan Borough
14 - Rotherham Metropolitan Borough
15 - City of Sheffield Metropolitan Borough

Administrations mainly outside Yorkshire, but serving parts of it:

D - County Durham
C - Cumbria
L - Lancashire
O - Oldham Metropolitan Borough
S - Stockton-on-Tees Borough

Key to the Borders:

Historic Counties
Ridings of Yorkshire
Ceremonial Counties
Local Authority Areas

North Sea

NORTH RIDING
EAST RIDING
WEST RIDING

COUNTY DURHAM
WESTMORLAND
LANCASHIRE
CHESHIRE
DERBYSHIRE
NOTTINGHAMSHIRE
LINCOLNSHIRE

NY
EY
WY
SY

Redcar
Middlesbrough
Guisborough
Whitby
Scarborough
Filey
Bridlington
Driffield
Beverley
HULL
Stamford Bridge
Norton
Malton
Northallerton
Leyburn
Richmond
Ronaldkirk
Mickleton
Sedbergh
Ingleton
Settle
Slaidburn
Barnoldswick
Skipton
RIPON
Harrogate
YORK
Selby
Goole
Doncaster
Rotherham
SHEFFIELD
Saddleworth
Halifax
Huddersfield
Dewsbury
BRADFORD
Keighley
Ilkley
Otley
LEEDS
Wakefield
Barnsley

River Tees
River Ouse
River Derwent
River Humber
Wharfedale
Wensleydale
North York Moors
Yorkshire Wolds

Map & text courtesy Association of British Counties ©

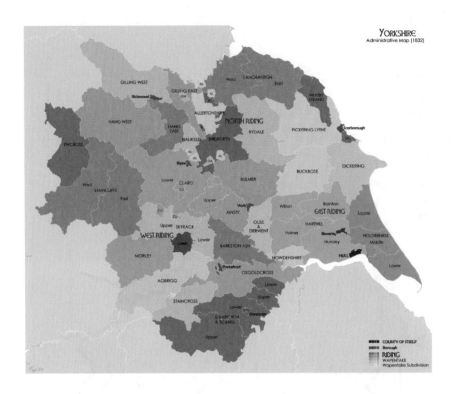

The Yorkshire White Rose flag on Ilkley Moor – the spiritual heart of Yorkshire. The town of Ilkley extends below, with Wharfedale and Beamsley Beacon in the background (*Phil Bell*)

York
Multangular Tower section Roman Wall, Museum Gardens
(lower levels Roman, upper layers medieval)

"Anglian Tower" late
Roman/early Anglian
addition to Roman Wall

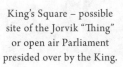

Clifford's Tower –
constructed by order
of Henry III in the 13th
century, replacing an earlier
structure, to a design
unique in England.
(*Dorian Speakman*)

King's Square – possible
site of the Jorvik "Thing"
or open air Parliament
presided over by the King.

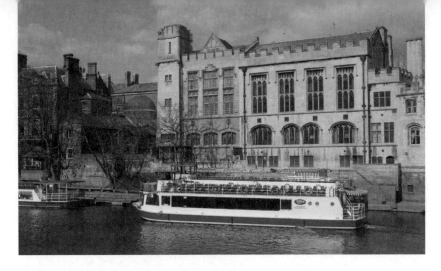

The Guildhall – site of York's Roman bridge across the Ouse (*Dorian Speakman*)

Merchant Adventurer's Hall (left) Rowntree Park (right)
The Millennium Bridge – walking and cycling route across the River Ouse

Vale of York
View of Vale of York and Mowbray
from Sutton Bank. Note glacial
Lake Gormire in the right
foreground (*Tim Barber*)
Thornborough Henges from the
air (*Tony Newbould – Wikipedia
Commons*)
Thirsk Square and Clock
Gothic Folly, Hackfall Woods
Selby Abbey

North York Moors & Cleveland

View across Rosedale from the old ironstone railway line

Kirkdale Minster – Anglo-Viking church with the most extant Anglo-Saxon stone inscription engraved on a sundial inside the porch.

Staithes on the Cleveland Coast

(*Tim Barber*)

North York Moors
Walker on the Cleveland Way near Sandsend (*Tim Barber*)

Byland Abbey
(*Tim Barber*)
Vanburgh's Temple of
the Four Winds, Castle
Howard
Wild daffodils growing
on the banks of the River
Dove, Farndale in
early Spring
(*Dorian Speakman*)

Yorkshire Wolds
Horsedale, near Huggate
North Landing, Flamborough Head
(*Dorian Speakman*)
Hull Victoria Square and Maritime Museum
(*Tim Barber*)
Beverley Saturday Market

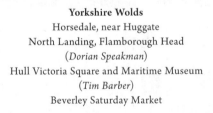

Yorkshire Dales
Classic barns, walls and herb-rich meadow
landscape, Upper Swaledale
Sedgwick Memorial, Dent village centre
Thorns Gill – 17th century packhorse bridge
carrying the Craven Way over Gayle Beck
(source of the Ribble) Upper Ribblesdale

Thornton Force, on the Ingleton Waterfalls.
Ribblehead Viaduct (*Tim Barber*)

Yorkshire Dales
Scar House Dam, Upper Nidderdale
Muck spreading, Walden, near West Burton
Knaresborough – River Nidd and Railway Viaduct (*Fleur Speakman*)
Otley Bramhope Tunnel Railway Memorial (*Tim Barber*)

Forest of Bowland
Dunsop Bridge
Cyclist at Trough of Bowland
Hark to Bounty Inn, Slaidburn
Fox Weathervane – Tosside
(*all images Dorian Speakman*)

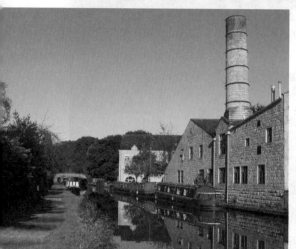

South Pennines
Autumn colours in Colden Clough Woods, Hebden Valley
(*Dorian Speakman*)
Rochdale Canal Wharves, Hebden Bridge (*Dorian Speakman*)
Worth Valley locomotive approaching Oxenhope
Top Withens inspiration for *Wuthering Heights*, Castle Hill, Huddersfield

**West Yorkshire – Wakefield,
Bradford, Kirklees, Calderdale**
Halifax Piece Hall
Shibden Hall Halifax
J.B. Priestley Statue outside Media
Museum, central Bradford
Bradford Wool Exchange
Huddersfield Station and St George's
Square. Statue of Harold Wilson is
visible bottom right
Hepworth Sculptures outside the
Hepworth Museum Wakefield

West Yorkshire – Leeds
Contrasts in Leeds – 18th century Canal Basin and warehouse overlooked by 21st century
Bridgewater Place
Cuthbert Brodrick masterpieces Leeds Town Hall (*Tim Barber*) and in interior of Corn Exchange
Harewood House
Turk's Head Yard – Whitelocks Luncheon Bar

**South Yorkshire –
Barnsley, Doncaster,
Rotherham**
Rotherham Minster
Elsecar Beam Engine –
the world's oldest steam
engine still in its original
engine house
and setting
Conisbrough Castle
Barnsley Town Hall
Doncaster Mansion
House (*photo © doncas-
termansionhouse.co.uk*)

South Yorkshire – Sheffield
The Sheffield's last surviving Cementation Furnace in Doncaster Street
The Bessemer Converter that revolutionised steel making in Sheffield – now on display at
Kelham Island Museum
The stainless steel salmon that forms part of the Cutting Edge water feature outside
Sheffield Station
Entrance to the Winter Gardens

Industry in the Dales

Though it now seems hard to believe, there was a time when the Dales were at the cutting edge of the industrial revolution. Though less apparent than in the more heavily populated valleys of the South Pennines, from the 18th century onwards the fast-flowing rivers and streams were being utilised to power waterwheels for textile mills in many Dales villages and small towns. In the early years these were primarily used for cotton spinning in the west, but also flax in Nidderdale in particular. As the 19th century progressed, wool and fine quality worsted yarns were processed in the larger mills, in locations where coal could be brought in larger quantities along the canals and eventually railway networks, to power steam mill engines. Sometimes old corn mills as at Linton in Craven were adapted or rebuilt, but often these were entirely new multi-storey buildings big enough to hold new power looms. Towns and villages like Skipton, Airton, Settle, Sedbergh, Aysgarth, attracted new workers and industry, though as the 19th century progressed, the smaller mills in outlying settlements soon suffered from competition for the larger mills downstream in the West Riding and many were soon closed, their buildings demolished or put to other uses.

Two particular extractive industries over the last three centres have, however been a greater threat to that special beauty of the Dales.

The first of these was lead mining. Lead and other minerals, most notably zinc and sometimes copper, occur in the Dales in areas of faulting usually between gritstone and limestone deposits, where ancient subterranean action has forced igneous mineral-bearing rocks to the surface in narrow vertical veins containing galena, an ore of lead. Such outcrops were probably being worked from Iron Age times. A huge ingot of lead recently purchased for the Craven Museum in Skipton and stamped "Brig" meaning from Brigantia was discovered in 1731 at Heyshaw in Nidderdale. This suggests sophisticated industry and trade in lead from the area during Roman times. Lead mining and smelting continued sporadically at least in Wharfedale and in Nidderdale during the Middle Ages, but grew rapidly in Tudor and Stuart times as demand and extraction skills – some of it based on German technology – increased. The moorland above Grassington contains lines of deep hollows formed by old bell pits along the lines of veins.

From the 18th century onwards the lead industry grew massively, with mechanisation of the mines. Local landowners such as the Duke of Devonshire in Grassington, the Yorke family in Nidderdale and Lord Wharton in Swaledale, brought in skilled Cornish and Derbyshire mining engineers using the latest mining technology to sink deep shafts to capture the rich veins of ore hidden beneath the surface.

From those last years of 18th and early 19th centuries, the Yorkshire Dales was in the forefront of mining technology. On Grassington Moor horse gins were constructed to haul galena ore from shafts, and a complex network of aqueducts were built from catchment ponds to drive waterwheels to crush the ore and drive pumps to drain shafts. In Hebden Gill a tunnel, the Duke's Level, was driven into the hillside to drain the mines, with an abortive scheme to create an underground canal for small ore-carrying barges. Large smelt mills were built to convert the ores to pigs of lead, powered by locally produced charcoal and as the industry grew, by coal mined from thin seams high on local moors. A new road was built from Grassington to Gargrave to bring lead to the wharves on the new Leeds-Liverpool canal to Leeds, for onward shipment down the Aire and Humber to London where demand was massive.

Workers came to the Dales mines from as far away as Cornwall, Ireland and Derbyshire as well as other parts of Yorkshire. Many Dales village grew rapidly in size with new terraced cottages to house miners and their families in villages such as Grassington, Kettlewell, Grimwith, Pateley Bridge, and the villages of Upper Swaledale.

For over a century lead mining and smelting was a highly productive industry in the Dales. But wages were poor, the work was hard and life expectancy was short. Many young boys in particular were forced to crawl into the flues of the smelt mills to collect highly toxic lead residues; many suffered poisoning. Disease was rife.

The growth of Methodism in the newly expanded mining villages brought an attempt to reduce drunken and licentious behaviour. The building of Mechanics and Literary Institutes were also an attempt to increase literacy and to improve both education and morals.

After surviving periods of boom and bust, the industry came to a sudden end 1870s when imports of lead by the new steamships from mainland Europe, most especially from Spain, led to declining prices from increasingly thin and hard-to-work veins. The industry struggled on for a few years but soon all the mines were closed. For many years communities had survived on the fragile twin economies of substance farming in the summer and lead mining in the winter. Poverty and out-migration occurred on a large scale, many families having to leave for the expanding cotton mills of Lancashire or worsted mills of the West Riding, or the foundries of Middlesbrough, or even emigrate to the colonies or USA.

One estimate is that up to 40% of the land in the National Park has to some degree been damaged or contaminated by lead, most of it out of sight, high on the moors above the valleys. Huge areas of moorland are pock-marked with deep, often now dangerous, shafts and entrances to horizontal levels, and remains of old buildings – flues, smelt mills, storehouses which over the last century and a half have gradually crumbled into ruins.

If this scale of environmental damage, and pollution of water supplies were happening now, there would rightly be an outcry. Ironically, the remains of the industry that have survived are now regarded as important relics of a once vanished way of life, precious pieces of industrial archaeology to be carefully stabilised, made safe and interpreted for modern visitors. Such visitors can only be thankful that workers, at least in Britain, do not have to suffer the appalling conditions of previous centuries. Even their cramped and pokey cottages that in larger towns and cities would have been long demolished as slums, now exchange hands for large sums of money for "character" weekend retreats or holiday lets.

The coming of the railways from the 1840s onwards brought with them a second extractive industry, which was to safeguard the subsistence economies of many communities in higher Dales but also threaten the environment. This was quarrying.

The Yorkshire Dales contain some of the finest Carboniferous limestone in the British Isles, an essential ingredient for agriculture, chemical and pharmaceutical industries, cement, steel making, and in later years road building. All these industries were expanding rapidly in the late 19th and early 20th centuries. What had been small local quarries producing limestone to be burned to quicklime for agriculture or mortar production from the scores of little local lime kilns seen throughout the Dales[2], grew to become part of a far more intrusive industry when first the (little) North Western Railway was built between Skipton and Ingleton in the 1840s to be followed by the Settle-Carlisle line in the 1870s, the Wensleydale Railway in the 1880s, and the Yorkshire Dales Railway Grassington branch in 1900. Sidings from all these lines led into local quarries where huge new kilns could be constructed to burn lime, with plenty of coal for this purpose brought from the West Riding coalpits by train. The Springs branch of the Leeds Liverpool Canal behind Skipton Castle serving Skibden Quarry was also a rich source of limestone for use in the industries of the growing towns and cities of the West Riding.

During the 20th century this industry grew in scale, with new or expanded quarries opening with their own sidings from railway lines, or close to railheads in Ribblesdale at Stainforth, Horton, Swinden, Ribblehead, or near Ingleton, Threshfield and Kilnsey in Upper Wharfedale and at Redmire in Wensleydale. There were also quarries opened at Helwith Bridge in Ribblesdale and Ingleton to extract the hard, Silurian slate which provides excellent crushed stone for road surfacing and remains in high demand. By the mid-20th century some of these quarries had grown massively. As transportation switched away from rail to what by that time were more economical lorries, not only were the quarries themselves a major source of noise, smoke and dust, but the heavy road traffic they generated was causing huge problems in Dales town and villages. At Ribblehead, not only were precious limestone pavements at risk, but the foundations of a rare Viking-era farmstead.

Thanks to constant pressure by environmental groups such as the Council for the Protection of Rural England, the Yorkshire Dales Society and Council for National Parks on the Yorkshire Dales National Park Planning Authority, planning and environmental controls eventually became more rigorous. But also, the quarrying industry itself became much more responsive to its wider environmental footprint. Some quarries in very sensitive areas such as at Ribblehead (now a nature reserve), Skythornes, Meal Bank (Ingleton) Giggleswick and Kilnsey have been closed; rail transport has been improved as at Swinden near Threshfield and at Helwith Bridge a new siding constructed. Kilns have been redesigned and screened to reduce noise and loads on road vehicles are better protected to reduce spills. Not only are there tree planting and other amelioration measures in place around the last few (large) working quarries, but all the major quarries now have programmes of restoration and after use in place as nature reserves. So, though there are still some problems remaining from an industry which was once a major blight on the Dales, things have improved massively over the Dales as a result of constant political pressure but also a receptive and more responsible local industry. Not all problems have been solved, such as heavy quarry waggons still causing blight, danger and disturbance through the narrow main street of Settle and along several Dales roads.

Railways and Tourism

The railways that enabled the expansion of quarries in the Dales also brought another more welcome major change to the Dale which was to help compensate for the decline of lead mining – tourism. The first railway to reach the Dales was the line from Darlington to Richmond in 1840. One prime reason for its initial construction was to carry lead from Swaledale to Darlington and onwards to Stockton or the new port at Middlesbrough. But this railway was also soon bringing visitors to the Dales. The topographer John Phillips, writing in the early 1850s, described idyllic walks in Swaledale from Richmond Station[3]. Though the railway was closed by Beeching in the 1960s, the fine station building has been preserved and converted into an important local leisure and visitor centre and retail outlet, even housing a bakery and small brewery.

By the late 1840s the little North Western Railway, eventually taken over by the Midland Railway, opened their line from Skipton to Lancaster and Carnforth, with a branch to Ingleton to connect with the London and North Western line for Sedbergh, Tebay and Scotland. Within a couple of decades Ingleton and its famed waterfalls became a popular inland resort. Clapham Station was over a mile from its village, but horse-drawn chaises would take the better-off directly up to the entrance to Ingleborough Cave three miles away. The summit of Ingleborough itself was now accessible for keen walkers on an easy day trip from Leeds, Lancaster or Bradford. Ingleton soon developed into a popular inland tourist resort catering for this new influx of energetic, initially rail-based visitors.

In 1849 Sir Titus Salt of Salts Mill in Saltaire treated his entire workforce to a day trip to Malham. Passengers alighted at little Bell Busk Station for the five mile walk to the village.

Though Bell Busk station has long closed, the railway from Skipton to Lancaster and Morecambe has survived and has even enjoyed some recent improvements to its service, thanks to Northern Rail and the line's Community Rail Partnership. With stations at Gargrave, Hellifield, Long Preston, Giggleswick, Clapham, Bentham and Wennington, the route, now branded as the Bentham Line, remains an extremely important lifeline for local communities and visitors to the Dales.

The line between Ilkley and Skipton via Bolton Abbey opened in 1865, but a relatively latecomer in 1901 was the Yorkshire Dales Railway between Skipton and Threshfield for Grassington which again increased the popularity of this village as a tourist destination.

The Wensleydale railway from Northallerton to Hawes was opened in 1854 and extended to Garsdale in 1878 where it met the most iconic of all the railways of the Dales – the Settle Carlisle line.

The story of the building of the Settle-Carlisle, part of the Midland Railway's ambitious, independent through route to Scotland, needs no retelling here, nor does the huge and successful popular campaign of the 1980s to prevent its closure. This included the local stations which were reopened in 1975 and 1976, for special Dales Rail charter trains provided for walkers and locals by the Yorkshire Dales National Park Committee. Though initially only open for special trains on summer weekends, a full daily service was restored in 1986. This paved the way for the decision in 1989 to retain the line. The prime reason for saving the line was its value to the local economies of the Yorkshire Dales and Eden Valley.

The railway with its great viaducts, tunnels, embankments and cuttings is a major landscape feature in its own right in Upper Ribblesdale, Dentdale, Garsdale and Eden Valley, and is now deemed a "linear conservation zone". Nowhere is its cultural significance more evident that at Ribblehead, where the great viaduct has become an icon not just of the Yorkshire Dales but for the whole of Yorkshire.

It has even been suggested that the term "Yorkshire Dales" for this area only came into regular use as a result of the railway age and clever marketing by the LNER of the area in the 1930s as a tourist destination served by their trains, through their striking series of colourful posters. No doubt the term "Yorkshire" only had to be added as a prefix for the benefit of southerners who needed to be told exactly where in England "The Dales" were when booking their train tickets.

Though the term "Yorkshire dales" was used as early as 1789 by Wordsworth in his narrative poem **Peter Bell** *"and he trudged through Yorkshire dales/Among the rocks and winding scars"*, it wasn't in general use in the 19th century, even by such authors as John Phillips. The romantic author Halliwell Sutcliffe (1870–1932) writing in 1929 in his best-selling book **The Striding Dales** refers not to the Yorkshire Dales but the Yorkshire Highlands – though he uses the term "Dale" for individual valleys or dales. Likewise, that doughty Yorkshire topographer and champion of footpaths, fell walking and access to moorland, A.J. Brown (1894–1969) in his **Broad Acres** of 1945 simply refers to the "great dales and moors of the west" of Yorkshire.

Equally interesting, John Dower (1900–1947), the Ilkley-born architect and author of the seminal 1944 Report which set up the conceptual framework of English and Welsh National Parks, surprisingly divided what we now know as the Yorkshire Dales into three distinct if adjacent areas, all possible National Parks – the Craven Pennines, which extended as far as Wensleydale, the Swaledale Pennines and the Howgill Fells.

By the time, via the Hobhouse Committee, these recommendations became part of the 1949 National Park and Access to the Countryside act, Dower's three distinct areas, including just the West Riding half of the Howgill Fells, were melded into what became the Yorkshire Dales National Park, formally designated in 1954. The term Yorkshire Dales has remained in use for the area, nationally and internationally ever since.

Sadly, only a minority of visitors now make their journeys to the Dales by rail, despite it being such a pleasant and relaxing mode of travel. Many people however now travel through the Dales by rail on the Settle-Carlisle line, purely for the scenic views and pleasure of the journey, and on a few days each year by heritage steam services. Other visitors enjoy an experience of vintage travel along not only Settle-Carlisle line, but also at weekends and holidays on the two restored

Heritage lines in the Dales, the **Wensleydale Railway** between Leeming and Redmire, and the **Embsay and Bolton Abbey Steam Railway**. The little restored station at Bolton Abbey, that lost its regular through train services from Leeds and Ilkley in 1965, was once a prime means of access to the Yorkshire Dales, being used by tens of thousands of visitors annually, from royalty to people from the smoke-filled streets of Leeds and Bradford. As well as regular vintage steam hauled trains, the Railway restores and preserves Victorian and Edwardian coaches and saloons for special dining events. There are long term plans to reconnect the line to Skipton to allow services to run through from West Yorkshire once again.

Bus services, despite their huge popularity as a means of access to the Dales between the 1950s and the 1980s, have now declined to relatively marginal usage. At weekends this has been partially reversed by the excellent weekend DalesBus network from many towns in West and North Yorkshire to the heart of the Dales. Cheaper Dales Rover tickets available and valid on different bus companies' services, also reduce the cost of travel. This network, like the Settle-Carlisle railway, offers so many freedoms for walkers that cannot be enjoyed by motorists, for example to enjoy linear walks or to cross on foot from one dale to the next to return by a different, perhaps contrasting route. This is true rambling freedom, the ability to plan a choice of more adventurous hikes, free from the restrictions of having to always return to a parked car.

Despite such opportunities, the private car is now the dominant mode of travel for local people and visitors alike, with inevitable problems of congestion, visual and air pollution, and isolation for those without their own transport. This ease of access has in turn led to overusage of some areas – Malham, Bolton Abbey, and the Three Peaks area in particular. Lack of effective traffic management strategies – there is no park and ride services in the Dales even to the most congested beauty spots – is a continuing issue.

Equally, in the Yorkshire Dales, the familiar approximate 80:20 rule operates – 80% of people invariably choose to go to 20% of the places. The other side of the coin is that the presence of so many visitors offers opportunities for many local businesses to support livelihoods. As the recent pandemic all too cruelly demonstrated, without these concentrations of seasonal visitors, many tourism enterprises and small businesses in the Dales or Moors cannot survive. But for more discerning visitors, there is still the 80% of both National Parks which remain relatively quiet; perfect places to walk, cycle, ride and in the wilder places, enjoy peace, tranquillity and natural beauty.

Wharfedale

Each Dale has its own special character and interest. Wharfedale is the natural boundary between the Yorkshire Dales and urban West Yorkshire but the entire Dale from the old town of Wetherby upriver northwards and westwards, has many characteristic features of a Dales landscape.

Otley under the shadow of the heavily wooded Chevin, may be within the city of Leeds' boundaries, but it is actually an old Dales market town at the crossing of the Wharfe, dating back to Anglian times, with a late Norman church. It has a cobbled marketplace, busy on Fridays and Saturdays, a network of narrow courtyards and ginnels, several old pubs and a pretty riverside area. As well as being a textile centre it was also a centre of the printing industry, in the 19th and 20th centuries noted for the manufacture of printing presses. It is also a prime gateway via Washburndale into Nidderdale AONB whose boundaries border the town. The churchyard contains an evocative stone memorial, in the form of a model of the entrance to Bramhope tunnel, to the 24 men who died during the building of the tunnel between 1845–9.

Ilkley, situated at the next major crossing of the Wharfe, in a magnificent setting between the high moorland summits of the curving Dale, has an even older history. The town dates back to Iron Age times, becoming an important crossroads and ford, defended by a small fort and civil centre known to the Romans as Olicana. A Roman altar dedicated to Verbeia, goddess of the Wharfe, is kept in the medieval **Manor House**, behind the church. The Manor House was built on the remains of the Roman fort, recycling much of the masonry stone. It is now the local community-owned museum, small art gallery and event space. The Parish Church close by contains three remarkable Anglo-Viking crosses, a direct link to the kingdom of Jorvik. The complex carvings combine Christian and pagan iconography in a powerful way.

In the 19th century Ilkley became known as The Heather Spa, with chalybeate (iron rich) springs in the town centre and freshwater springs on the high moors. It was in such icy cold moorland springs that the popular medical practice of hydrotherapy or water cure developed. This began initially in the 18th century at White Wells, a little spring-fed plunge bath high on the edge of Ilkley Moor. But it was properly developed in the mid 19th onwards from two grand hydrotherapic hotels that were built as treatment centres. The treatments offered, including cold baths, douches and special diets, were closely based on the methods of Dr Vincenz Preissnitz (1799–1851) from Austrian Silesia. The hotels were situated on the moor edge – the first in a building, now luxury apartments, designed by the great Cuthbert Brodrick, the second at what became known as Ben Rhydding, long demolished, on the site now covered by the golf course.

The real benefit of the cure for many people was to escape the poisonous polluted air of Victorian cities. Ilkley became what the Germans were later to call a Luft Kurort or fresh air resort. Walks were laid out around the town and onto the moors, with small ornamental lakes created, known as the Ilkley Tarns. Steps and bridges built at nearby Heber's Gill half a mile from the town centre created a romantic, picturesque glade of trees, ferns and waterfalls to lure patients onwards and upwards. This tradition of Ilkley as a centre for healthy walking continues to this day.

Among important guests who came to take the cure was Charles Darwin in 1859 shortly after he had finished his great thesis **On the Origin of Species**. Darwin was a notorious hypochondriac and needed the peace and rest the town offered.

Addingham the next village up the Wharfe has a rich pre-and early industrial revolution heritage, being a centre for hand loom weavers and weaving shops. In the 18th century the village saw the first efforts to combine individual operations under a single roof, creating perhaps the country's first collective "manufactory", for weaving[4]. When mechanisation came to the village, utilising the power of the rivers and local becks for waterwheels, the village thrived. This was not without its problems when in 1820 Low Mill, the mill and industrial hamlet at the south of the village, suffered from some of the worst Luddite Riots.

At Farfield, just north of Addingham, is one of the earliest Quaker

Meeting Houses, built in 1689. A mile further up-river is the great Bolton Abbey estate, as described above.

From Bolton Abbey onwards the Dale gets ever lovelier. It is also followed by one of England's most popular recreational footpath routes – the 81-mile Dales Way, which links Ilkley in Wharfedale with Bowness on Windermere. A mainly riverside route it passes through Barden, Burnsall, Grassington, the former lead mining town now the main tourist village and walking centre of Upper Wharfedale, past Grass Wood Nature Reserve, filled with wildflowers in Spring, including the intensely lovely bird's eye primrose in Bastow Woods. It follows high limestone terraces to the old lead mining village, now busy walking centre, of Kettlewell, where the popular story of the **Calendar Girls** was filmed. The celebrated calendar featured the ladies of Rylstone WI, a hamlet between Grassington and Skipton. The Dales Way continues along the riverside to Buckden, the last village in Upper Wharfedale, then on through Hubberholme with its tiny Norman Church, and into Langstrothdale, eventually to cross Cam Fell, the source of the Wharfe. Once across the watershed The Way descends Dentdale heading for Sedbergh at the base of the Howgill Fells, before making its way up Lunedale to the Crook of Lune at Lowgill, the former boundary of the old West Riding, and only a few miles from the Lake District.

Airedale and Malhamdale

Malhamdale further west has a quite different character. It is actually the northern section of a far larger and more famous Dale – Airedale, the source of the River Aire being Malham Tarn.

The old town of Skipton, with its great Norman Castle guarding the Aire Gap, is the prime gateway not just to Malhamdale, but to all the southern and western Dales from the south. Its handsome medieval church and pattern of courts and burgess plots perfectly preserve the pattern of a medieval market town. It was the coming of the Leeds-Liverpool Canal in 1770 which enabled the town to benefit from the industrial revolution with the cotton mills which dominated the town for nearly two centuries. The combination of a spectacularly well preserved Norman **Castle**, the outstanding **Craven Museum**, a canal basin with woodland walks, a popular High Street with a busy four-days-a week market and choice of local shops, as well as good transport links, has made Skipton the natural service centre and focal point for the whole of Craven.

Airedale becomes Malhamdale north of the small former coaching town on the Keighley-Kendal turnpike road and little canal port of Gargrave. From here the dale and its narrower, winding river heads northwards via Airton to Kirkby Malham. This is the village where invalid John Dower, wrote his great UK National Park report in 1944; it was also American author Bill Bryson's favourite place in England as recorded in his **Notes from a Small Island** (1995); the little Victoria inn, next to the medieval church that gives the village its name, was his much-loved local pub. The dale terminates beyond the village at the magnificent 80 metre high, 300 metre long limestone crescent and primeval waterfall of Malham Cove.

Malham village lies at the centre of some of the finest karst limestone scenery in the British Isles, including the Cove, Janet's Foss and spectacular Gordale Scar and large areas of crag and limestone pavement. It is also a hugely popular visitor centre, starting point for many splendid walks, with a National Park Centre, pubs and cafes to cater for visitor needs.

The Pennine Way climbs past the Cove and Malham Tarn with its Field Centre and its wonderful raised peat bog Nature Reserve, to soon leave crowds behind, crossing Fountains Fell. Busier paths are rejoined once again over Pen y Ghent and into Horton-in-Ribblesdale on the Three Peaks Walk, before the Way heads over Cam Fell and quieter tracks to Hawes and Swaledale.

The Three Peaks and the Western Dales

A particular problem for local residents in Upper Ribblesdale is the huge popularity of The Three Peaks Walk, a 24-mile circuit of Pen y Ghent, Whernside and Ingleborough. What started off as a walkers' cult challenge has now been taken over by the major national and local charities as a highly effective source of money raising for worthy causes, which has brought serious problems of parking congestion in the villages and major footpath erosion. Remedial work on the heavily used paths has had to be largely paid for out of other public sector budgets, not those of the charities.

Ribblesdale to the south and west is primarily a Lancashire river for much of its length, has its own dedicated long distance trail, the Ribble Way, following the river from its estuary in the Lancashire plain, past Clitheroe and edging the Forest of Bowland before reaching the old market town of Settle.

Overlooked by **Castlebergh Scar** (a fine local viewpoint) and the pale crags of the Craven Fault, Settle is the start of the spectacular limestone country of Craven. It is also a former coaching town and still a popular stopping place and centre for visitors, again with fascinating courts with boutique shops to explore. **Victoria Hall** just behind the town centre, dating from 1853, lays claim to be England's oldest surviving music hall, and is now a focal point of cultural life in Upper Ribblesdale. The Folly, a splendid 17th century yeoman's house on the back lane to Upper Settle, houses the excellent **Museum of North Craven Life.**

West of Settle the old turnpike road to Kendal, now the A65, skirts the old village of Giggleswick and heads up the now by-passed Bucker Brow towards another rather special village of the Yorkshire Dales, Clapham. This was the birthplace and home of the remarkable botanist Reginald Farrer (1880–1920) plant collector and botanist, author of several books that established the principles in England of rock gardening. Many of Farrer's plants in the form of trees and shrubs, survive in the Clapham estate, which lies above the pretty village. Clapdale Beck above the village was dammed by the Farrer family to provide both hydroelectricity to the estate and create an ornamental lake. The track through the shallow valley through the Estate leads to the celebrated **Ingleborough Show Cave**. It is also part of one of the most popular hikes in the Dales past Gaping Gill Cave and on to the summit of Ingleborough.

Crummackdale, a steep and dramatic cul de sac valley that cuts into the shoulder of Ingleborough, contains, on a high limestone terrace at Norber, some of the most spectacular glacial erratics to be seen anywhere in the British Isles – huge, lichen-covered boulders of Silurian rocks, perched above much newer limestone pavement, like massive primeval sculptures.

Ingleton, an attractive village with a now forgotten local coal mine history, is the starting point to ascend perhaps the most popular of Yorkshire's Three Peaks, Ingleborough. Ingleton's other major claim to fame is the 7km (4½ mile) **Waterfall Walk**, following specially constructed paths alongside the River Twiss, past a series of picturesque gorges and waterfalls, returning down the River Doe. The walk offers one of the most fascinating geological trails in England with a wide variety of different rock strata revealed by the two cascading streams, from Cambrian, Ordovician and Silurian slates to more typical Carboniferous gritstones, shales and limestones. Because these paths and footbridges are on private land with insurance issues, admission is only by ticket from the main Ingleton entrance.

The extension of the National Park boundary to include the lovely Upper Lune Valley in Lancashire means that the former Westmorland, now Cumbrian, town of Kirkby Lonsdale is now on the edge of the National Park. This compact market town, with several fine Georgian Houses and old inns around its marketplace, is celebrated for the ancient **Devil's Bridge** over the Lune, now part of a small park, but also, just behind the parish church, the viewpoint up the Lune Valley known as **Ruskin's View**. Painted by Turner in 1822, it was revisited by his disciple John Ruskin (1819–1900) painter, philosopher and art critic, in 1875. He later wrote that it was *"one of the loveliest views in England, therefore in the world."*

Despite the popularity of Ruskin's View and Devil's Bridge, the Lune valley above Kirkby Lonsdale, however, is one of the less well known of all the Yorkshire Dales. It rises from several small becks which drain the northern Howgill Fells around Newbiggin-on-Lune and Weasdale, to Tebay, before the little river twists south through the Lune Gorge where it is met by the Dales Way, West of Sedbergh, it is joined by the Rawthey from Garsdale and the Dee from Dentdale. Sedbergh, home of the famous public school and a former Book Town, still with excellent book shops, is the perfect place from which to explore the great open expanse of the Howgill Fells. On the northeastern flank is the spectacular 198-metre-high waterfall of Cautley Spout, the highest linked fall of its kind in the UK. The ancient, slaty Silurian rocks of the Howgills, more typical of the Lake District, create a very contrasting landscape to the Carboniferous limestones, sandstones and gritstones of the southern dales. But the smooth, glaciated, rounded summit domes, described by Wainwright as being *"like velvet curtains in sunlight, like silken drapes at sunset"*[5] are in fact partly a man-made landscape.

Carbon dating and pollen sequence analysis of soils suggested that after the last Ice Age and until around the 10th century, this became a mostly wooded landscape dominated by alder, birch, oak and hazel, trees which rapidly decreased and vanished over a relatively few years, to be replaced by heather and rough grassland[6]. This process was particularly marked around the 10th century, the time immediately following Viking settlement in Dentdale and Garsdale, very probably when trees were felled for fuel, fencing and house building, and sheep, perhaps ancestors of the ubiquitous Herdwick, began to graze saplings, preventing natural regeneration and eventually resulting in impoverished soils. This in turn led to heavy soil erosion and run-off, creating a network of highly unstable side valleys and gullies, especially vulnerable after heavy rainstorms. Such storms have become increasingly frequent in recent years because of global warming. If for no other reason than to reduce flooding in towns lower down valleys such as the Lune and Eden, it may be essential to change grazing regimes and increase tree planting and natural regeneration on the Howgills and other summits of the Dales to slow water flows downriver, to reduce some of the most dramatic impacts of climate change.

Close to Sedbergh, Firbank Fell above the Lune is linked to the worldwide movement of Quakerism. This was where a great meeting, in 1652, of a thousand Friends took place. It was addressed by the charismatic founder of the Quaker movement George Fox. A boulder known as Fox's Pulpit still marks the spot where he preached. This was one of the crucial moments in the birth of the movement. The tiny Friends Meeting House at Brigflatts, on the edge of Sedbergh, dating from 1675 was also the inspiration for one the most admired poems of the late 20th century, Basil Bunting's autobiographical **Brigflatts,** published in 1966.

Dentdale, the only one of the main Yorkshire Dales whose river flows north-westwards, is a dale with a very different character and its own intimate beauty. In normal weather conditions, the River Dee runs mostly underground for much of its length, leaving a dry riverbed or with just the occasional pool. The hedgerows along the twin lanes that run down the valley are white with blackthorn and dotted with primroses in Spring.

Dent Town, as it was then known, with its cobbled streets, the only settlement of any size in the valley, was in the late 18th century approximately three times larger than it is today in terms of population. Families were sustained by farming and hand knitting. Thousands of woollen stockings, gloves and hats were made by the villagers from local grown wool. Knitting was undertaken with cleverly designed knitting sheaths to enable three needless to be utilised at once, usually at remarkable speed. This work was often done whilst walking the fields or doing other work including tending sheep; or with other family members whilst sitting round the household fire during winter evenings, singing songs. Their finished goods were sold at Kendal market. By the end of the 18th century, competition from the huge new water and steam-powered mills of the West Riding and elsewhere wiped out this industry within a couple of decades and the village never recovered.

Dent is also celebrated as being the birthplace of one of England's greatest scientists of the 19th century – Professor Adam Sedgwick (1785–1873) whose geological work unravelling the complex, contorted rocks of the Lake District and Snowdonia, including the Pennine Fault that crosses Dentdale, led to his discovery and analysis of what are known as the Cambrian series of ancient rock strata. Sedgwick's remarkable two slim volumes – the **Memorial by the Trustee of Cowgill Chapel** and its **Supplement** published in 1869 and 71 are a precious record of his boyhood in Dentdale at a time when the Dales and its communities were irrevocably changing as the Industrial Revolution was transforming so many aspects of life in England.

The Settle-Carlisle railway, an astonishing feat of late Victorian railway engineering, climbs Ribblesdale, calls at Horton in Ribblesdale, the popular hiker's village and starting point for the Three Peaks Walk, and continues to Ribblehead, with its welcoming Station inn, and the iconic Ribblehead Viaduct. There are magnificent walks from here, over Ingleborough, or following the becks that form the headwaters of the Ribble or climbing over the shoulder of Whernside along the medieval Craven Way drovers' road into Dentdale.

The railway enters the 2404 metre (just under 1¼ miles) Blea Moor Tunnel, before crossing the daleheads and watersheds of both Dentdale to Dent Station, the highest station on any mainline railway in Britain, and Garsdale where the Wensleydale branch for Hawes and Northallerton once headed east. Both these stations are sited some miles from their respective villages. From Garsdale the railway continues to the summit of the line at Aisgill, 356 metres (1,169 feet) above sea level and close to the sources of both the Yorkshire Ure whose waters eventually enter the North Sea and the Cumbria Eden whose waters head for the Solway Firth, bordering Scotland, for the Irish Sea. The upper Eden Valley's history and heritage lie firmly in Westmorland and what is now modern Cumbria.

Wensleydale

The River Ure, or to use its older name the Yore, forms Wensleydale, a dale with a character totally its own. Broader and grander than its sister valleys, the parts of the Dale seen from the A648 road that most visitors use, may on a first visit seem relatively unprepossessing. However, away from the valley floor, there are some of the most distinctive and special landscapes in the Dales to discover.

The town of Hawes is the natural capital of Upper Wensleydale. With its popular Tuesday Market this is one of the remotest, but fiercely independent small towns in the North. For many years, the town was the home of legendary Kit Calvert, farmer, and archetypical Dalesman, self-taught scholar (Kit was a fine speaker and writer of North Riding dialect – and even translator of parts of the New Testament), who ran a bookshop in the centre of town. If he was not in his shop, there was an honesty box to pay for books. But he also became a hero of the Dales in the 1930s when he led the campaign to prevent the closure of the town's dairy and almost single-handily ensured that the unique Wensleydale Cheese continued to be made in the Dale, using milk from local dairy farms.

History had to be repeated in 1992 when Dairy Crest, the semi-nationalised conglomerate, decided it was more "economical" to produce Wensleydale cheese elsewhere in England even including, it was rumoured, in Lancashire. Invoking the spirit of Kit, local people supported what was in effect a management buyout. The Wensleydale Creamery is now one of the top attractions of the Yorkshire Dales, a proud symbol, like Ribblehead Viaduct, of the indomitable Yorkshire spirit. It has also ensured work for Dales communities including support for local farmers who supply the prime ingredient. By espousing the clear principle of locality and provenance in its production within the community that created that very distinctive brand, Kit Calvert and the Wensleydale Cheese company were ground breakers of their time. **Wensleydale Creamery** as it is now known produces a wide variety of high-quality cheeses and other products and is also a leading tourist attraction as visitors can watch the cheese making process. Hawes also has a traditional **Ropemakers**, where visitors can see ropes being made and an appealing range of locally owned shops. The outstanding **Dales Countryside Museum** in the old station yard, which contains the hugely important collection of Dales farming artefacts collected by the great Dales authors and historians Marie Hartley and Joan Ingleby. There are even hopes and plans of one day restoring the railway line from that station through to Garsdale to re-join the Settle Carlisle line.

Wensleydale has a rich heritage to offer. Bainbridge, a compact village, has the site of a Roman fort, village green and old inn; it was a former hunting lodge of the Forest of Wensleydale. A horn kept in the Rose and Crown is still blown on winter nights at 9pm between the end of September and Easter to guide benighted travellers off the surrounding fells. The village now also hosts the headquarters of the National Park Authority.

Only a short walk away lies the second largest natural glacial lake of the Dales, Semerwater, in the lovely tributary valley of Raygill containing England's shortest river, the Bain. According to ancient legend, recorded in a medieval ballad, the lake was supposedly created by a storm summoned by an angel disguised as a beggar visiting the village that once existed in the valley. Because the beggar was shown no compassion by villagers, in revenge the entire village was flooded apart from the home of an impoverished elderly couple who had offered him meat and drink.

Askrigg, a former small coaching and clockmaking town on the pre-turnpike age Lancaster to Richmond road, enjoyed fame as "Darrowby" in the first James Herriot TV series and films. Aysgarth Falls, the three natural waterfalls along the Ure were painted by Turner. **Bolton Castle** in the village of Castle Bolton, is the best-preserved 14th century castle in the North of England. Mary Queen of Scots was imprisoned here; visitors to the castle enjoy fascinating exhibitions, gardens and falconry displays.

Middleham, lying on a low ridge above the confluence of the little River Cover with the Ure, is still dominated by its magnificent if somewhat ruined **Castle**, now protected by English Heritage, which for a time was the home of young Richard Duke of Gloucester who became Richard III. The village with its cobbled squares and old inns, reflects the days when there was a busy stagecoach route between Skipton and Richmond crossing from Kettlewell across the murderously steep Park Rash pass into Coverdale.

Leyburn, on a terrace above the river valley, is the principal market town of the central part of Wensleydale. It is noted in having not only some excellent local food shops but hosting regular Food Festivals showcasing local produce. Leyburn is linked by the Wensleydale Railway to Redmire and the attractive little market town of Bedale.

Swaledale

From this part of Wensleydale, a choice of tarmac roads and moorland tracks over the fells lead into what many people consider to be the finest of all the Yorkshire Dales – Swaledale. This narrow, intimate valley offers perhaps the perfect barn-and-wall landscape of the Dales, reflecting a form of post-Enclosure farming that flourished in the 18th and 19th centres. Cattle were overwintered in outlying barns where winter fodder was stored, both as a source of insulation and also a ready source of manure for the meadows in early Spring. Much of this nationally important landscape of small fields, drystone walls and scattered barns is now supported by a variety of agri-environment schemes, promoted by the National Park Authority, Natural England, and the Yorkshire Dales Millennium Trust.

The classic view of this landscape from above Thwaite appears in many books and photographs about Yorkshire and the Dales. This is especially appropriate in that Thwaite was the birthplace of Richard (1862–1928) and Cherry (1871–1940) Kearton, two brothers, both celebrated naturalists, who were among the world's first wildlife photographers. Cherry became a close personal friend of US President Roosevelt.

Swaledale around Muker in particular has some of the most wonderful herb and flower-rich ancient meadows in the British Isles, only comparable with upper Teesdale. The colours in early summer are truly spectacular. These meadows are now protected by the National Park and Natural England who work closely with local farmers to ensure the meadows are mown at the exactly the right time of year to enable the natural reseeding of annual flowers.

The head of the dale, around Ravenseat, has acquired a new national fame being the home of the **Yorkshire Shepherdess**, broadcaster and writer Amanda Owen, whose documentary films and books have given audiences vivid insight into the life of farming communities in the Dales as they still are in the twenty first century.

Almost all the villages of Swaledale have at some time or other been affected by lead mining industry, even the tiny hamlet of Keld not far from the nearest mines workings extending into Swinnergill. Villages like Thwaite, Muker, Gunnerside, Low Row and above all Reeth, and the whole of Arkengarthdale survived through the dual economy based on farming and lead mining, which tourism, supporting accommodation providers, cafes and craft shops has only partially compensated for. Swaledale looks more to Darlington and Teesside for the bulk of its day visitors with their less affluent spenders.

An enterprise which demonstrates just how the tourist's pound can be used to support the wider economy is **Swaledale Woollens,** a unique cooperative based around the production and use of wool from local sheep breeds. This includes the ubiquitous and hard wearing Swaledale from local fleeces, as well as the softer Wensleydale. The wool has to be sent out of the Dale, usually to Bradford or even Leicester for processing, but to return as high-quality knitting wool for local people, usually the wives of local farmers, hand craft high quality fashion garments, mainly sweaters but also gloves and scarves, not only for the London market but through their own Muker shop. Usually, the label on the locally made garment will tell you the person who did the knitting and the village they came from. The village also celebrates its farming heritage every Spring with the Muker Show and there is still a Muker Silver Band which has its origins in the great days of lead-mining.

Reeth, the unofficial capital of upper Swaledale, with its fine village green and small National Park Centre, cafes, pubs and shops, is also the home of the delightful **Swaledale Museum** with numerous artefacts, photographs and documents, especially relating to the local lead mining industry but also farming and the social history in the Dales.

The town of Richmond is one of the North's great treasures, both for its great Norman Castle, rightly named the best preserved of its period in England, that dominates the town and the riverside gorge of the River Swale over which is stands; also for the fascinating, mainly Georgian, market town that surrounds it. The construction of the castle was initiated in 1070 by Alan Rufus, one of William's comrades-in-arms at the battle of Hastings, his reward for military prowess a huge grant of land and the right to build this great defensive fortification above the Swale. Now in the ownership of English Heritage, **Richmond Castle** is worth a visit if only to enjoy amazing views of the old town and river gorge from its ramparts. There are also moving exhibits relating to the Conscientious Objectors of World War I who were imprisoned here. Richmond's cobbled semi-circular marketplace with its cross was almost certainly once part of the courtyard of the Castle.

Among the town's particularly interesting buildings is the neo-Gothic Culloden Tower, on a grassy slope west of the town. It was erected by John Yorke, of Gouthwaite Hall in Nidderdale, who was the local Whig MP for Richmond in 1746, to celebrate the ruthless and bloody crushing of the Scottish Jacobites in that year. A building of far happier memories is Richmond's **Georgian Theatre**, opened in 1788 and is Britain's most complete 18th century theatre which still functions as a theatre. The **Richmondshire Museum** collections relate to the archaeology and social history, including farming and lead mining, of the whole District, whilst the **Green Howard Museum** is a major regional military museum based on the history of the illustrious Yorkshire-based regiment.

Richmond's magnificent old **Station**, a beautiful neo-Tudor building designed by the noted railway architect G.T. Andrew was opened in 1845 to serve the branch line from Darlington. The railway closed in 1969, but the station has been imaginatively converted into a facility for the local community and visitors with a cinema, restaurant, café bar, art gallery, heritage centre and a range of artisan shops.

Nidderdale AONB

The south eastern corner of the Dales, however, was not included in the Yorkshire National Park in 1954 mainly because of objections by local Water Boards, fearful of encouraging public access onto water catchment grounds at a time of more limited filtration and purification techniques. Much of this area is protected within the **Nidderdale Area of Outstanding Natural Beauty**, which was established in 1994. Covering 600km^2 or 233 square miles, mainly of Upper Nidderdale, but including also Colsterdale and the Washburn, geographically and culturally this is part of the Yorkshire Dales. Unlike the National Park, the AONB is not managed by a separate authority but comes under the jurisdiction of Harrogate Council under the guidance of its own Joint Advisory Committee.

In terms of landscape quality, Upper Nidderdale is as fine as anything in the adjacent National Park. Villages such as Wath, Ramsgill and Lofthouse have great charm, but Middlesmoor is a rare example of a Pennine hill village. The view from Middlesmoor's little church at the end of the ridge down the Dale beyond Gouthwaite Reservoir is one of the finest in the whole of the Yorkshire Dales. The walk around the two top reservoirs of Scar House and Angram offer some of the wildest and grandest lake landscapes of England outside the Lake District.

Yoredale – Lower Wensleydale

Two important Dales towns mark the division between the hill country of the Dales and the Vale of Mowbray – Masham and Ripon.

Masham in lower Colsterdale has a huge Market Place and fine Parish church which dates back to Norman times. Like Tadcaster it is also the home of two rival Breweries which have become nationally known. Theakstons was established in 1827, having been taken over by the now defunct Scottish and Newcastle Brewery. This is now independent and owned by the Theakston family. Black Sheep Brewery was started by family member Paul Theakston in 1991 when S&N chose to move production elsewhere. The town also hosts a popular Steam Engine and Fairground Organ Rally each July, and a Sheep Fair in September.

South of Masham, near the village of Grewelthorpe, is the remarkable **Hackfall Woods**, an 18th century leisure landscape along a wooded gorge of the River Ure, with carefully constructed paths, picturesque follies, grottoes and waterfalls and a remarkable recently restored hydraulic powered fountain. It was designed in the 1730s and built by eccentric local landowner John Aislabie, disgraced former Chancellor of the Exchequer who also designed the water gardens of Studley Royal. It has recently been fully restored by the Woodland Trust and the Hackfall Trust with the help of a Heritage Lottery Grant. A mile north west of Grewelthorpe is another fascinating, far newer woodland attraction – the 45 acre **Himalayan Garden and Sculpture Park** with its outstanding collections of rhododendrons, azaleas and Himalayan poppies.

Ripon is situated close to where the little Rivers Laver and Skell join the Ure. With a population of 6,702 (2011) it is England's third smallest city. It has a fine Market Place dominated by a huge obelisk designed by Nicholas Hawksmoor capped by a weathervane in the form of a horn. The horn is sounded every evening at 9pm, from the four corners of the Market Place, a tradition which dates back to 866AD. To see this task carried out by the Hornblower was one of the duties of the Ripon Wakeman, a role which combined that of magistrate, constable and mayor. The former Wakeman's House in the Market Place, dating from the 13th century, is now a cafe. The **Ripon Workhouse Museum** nearby, offers extraordinary and moving insight into the lives and often inhumane treatment of so many poorer members of the community well into relatively recent times.

The Cathedral is the focal point of the heritage and history of the city. It has its origins in the early years of Christianity in Northumbria. In 672 St Wilfrid dedicated a small Benedictine monastery on the site, St Cuthbert being based there for a time. In the 10th century the Abbey became a Collegiate Church for the wider region, eventually becoming the Minster and finally the Cathedral for the great Anglican Diocese which covers this huge part of Yorkshire, including most of the Dales. Most of the present magnificent building, the fourth on the site, including the great East Window and towers, dates from between the 13th and 16th centuries. Saint Wilfrid's surviving 7th century Crypt underneath the present Cathedral is a rare example of Anglo-Saxon architecture and of national importance.

To the west of Ripon lies **Fountains Abbey and Studley Royal**. Now owned and managed by the National Trust, (though the Abbey Ruins themselves are managed by English Heritage) this World Heritage Site designation is a cultural landscape of international importance in its magnificent setting in a magnesian limestone gorge along the little

River Skell. The great Cistercian Abbey ruins, including the magnificent abbey church, and the adjoining outbuildings, date largely from the 12th and 13th centuries when the Abbey with its huge land holdings and its network of outlying granges was at its peak. The magnificent gothic arches of the Cellarium where wool from granges across the Dales was stored before being taken to Ripon and by boat along the Ouse to York for onward transhipment to Venice or Flanders, is a symbol of the emerging power and wealth of England in the late Middle Ages. This growing prosperity grew throughout Tudor times, again evidenced by the fine house of Fountains Hall, built by local landowner Sir Stephen Proctor in 1609 from stone robbed from the Abbey.

Equally impressive are John Aislabie's hauntingly beautiful 18th century Water Gardens with their carefully sited crescent pool, waterfalls, statues, walkways, follies and reflections are a masterpiece of landscape design. All is set within the great Studley Royal Deer Park with William Burges' magnificent 1878 church of **St. Mary** on the brow of the hill. The great drive that links the obelisk and church through the parkland to the park gate is aligned exactly to the western façade of Ripon Cathedral. Little wonder that Fountains Abbey and the Studley Royal Estate superbly managed by the National Trust with its excellent Visitor Centre, are now one of Yorkshire's top heritage attractions.

Nidderdale

Brimham Rocks, on a headland above the valley some five miles west of Fountains Abbey is a remarkable natural feature – an outcropping of gritstone and sandstone crags, prominent above the valley, which over millennia have been eroded by wind, rain and frost into a series of fantastic shapes, given fanciful titles such as the Dancing Bear by Victorian topographers. It is now a hugely popular National Trust property enjoyed by many thousands of visitors per year as somewhere to stroll, scramble and admire the views across the Dale.

The little town of Pateley Bridge, now the headquarters of the AONB, is situated at an important crossing of the River Nidd in use from monastic times. The town grew to its present size in the 19th and 20th century as a result of both lead mining and quarrying for fine quality sandstone building stone. This was taken along the now defunct

Nidderdale Railway branch to Harrogate and as far as London for use on many projects. But the railway didn't end at Pateley. During the building of the Scar House and Angram Reservoirs between the 1890s and the 1930s, the little Nidd Valley Light Railway, owned by Bradford Corporation, was built mainly to carry building materials, but also passengers, including site workers. Several of the old village stations, for example in the centre of Lofthouse, can still be seen.

Quarrying for sandstone still continues at Coldstone Quarry high above the town near Greenhow. Just above the quarry, a huge modern outdoor sculpture has been erected. Known as **Coldstone Cut** it consists of two huge spirals and viewing platforms offering superb views across the Vale of York, and now forms a popular local visitor attraction. In the side valley below, Ashgill, extensive remains of the lead mining industry can be explored along the 9-mile Bewerly Industrial Heritage Trail accessible on foot from Pateley Bridge.

Close by is **Stump Cross Caverns**, another of the fine Dales Show Caves. In the 1820s local miners broke into an amazing network of natural caverns. Beautifully lit, dry show caves now reveal the underground beauty of the caves where important discoveries were made of the long-vanished fauna of the Dales when Britain's climate was warmer.

Much of the story of the lead mining, quarrying, and the building of the reservoirs, and the flax industries whose huge mills, now turned to mainly residential use, still dominated the lower part of the valley, is told in the **Nidderdale Museum** which occupies the town's former Victorian workhouse.

But Upper Nidderdale and its adjacent valley of Washburndale – more generally just known as the Washburn Valley – are also sometimes labelled the Reservoir Country, dominated as they are by the massive reservoirs – Angram, Scar House, Gouthwaite on the Nidd and on Thrushcross, Fewston, Swinsty and Lindley on the thickly wooded little Washburn river. Between them, these reservoirs including those in Colsterdale, provide most of the drinking water needs for both Leeds and Bradford, and other towns into Lancashire through Yorkshire Water's complex river and pipeline supply network which also links with the two Barden Moor Reservoirs and with Grimwith.

The reservoirs and their often heavily castellated dams are wonderful pieces of architecture and civil engineering in their own right. They lie within some of the finest open heather and rough grazing moorland of the Dales, areas of peatland, vital for carbon storage and nature conservation. As well as being managed for conservation, especially birdlife, they are also important areas for recreation, carefully maintained for public access by Yorkshire Water with well screened car parks and marked public and permissive paths around each of the reservoirs, including the areas of coniferous woodland that surround several of the reservoirs.

Harrogate and Knaresborough

Outside the AONB boundaries, the outward spread of Harrogate is all too evident in commuter villages such as Dacre, Birstwith and Hampsthwaite which have expanded in recent years, being within easy travel distance of Harrogate.

Harrogate, whilst not superficially part of the Dales, is an important gateway to Nidderdale and beyond. It also has its own fascinating geological interest. Mineral rich springs bubble up through the marshy, high ground on the fault line that forms the edge of the narrow magnesian limestone ridge that divides the Yorkshire Dales from the Vale of York. Some of the springs are high in sulphur content, hence the foul smell, and others, often only a few metres away, are chalybeate, or iron-rich springs. Both were once regarded as excellent for digestive and other problems. The first spring to be discovered was Tewit Well on the Stray which dates back to the late 16th century. The octagonal Royal Pump Room, on the site of the Old Sulphur Well, is now the town's Museum, with exhibits about the historic spa and costumes recalling the days of Regency Harrogate. The nearby Bog Field, contains a total of 36 different wells or mineral springs, out of the 88 recorded in Harrogate, some still marked with small well-head pavilions. It was renamed **The Valley Gardens** in the 19th century to attract rather more visitors to what were to become Harrogate's most attractive public park.

A special feature of the town centre is the magnificent area of open space in the heart, The Stray, 200 acres of open grassland, ancient common land now protected by bye laws, dotted with crocus in spring.

The Victorian spa town of Harrogate soon became the Cheltenham of the North. A popular area of shops and galleries west of the town centre is still known as Montpelier. Several grand hotels in the town centre catered for visitors to the spa. The ornate Royal Baths, which though largely converted to other uses, has kept its unique and beautifully restored **Turkish Baths**. The lovely Edwardian **Harrogate Theatre**, originally known as the Grand Opera House, was opened in 1900, whilst the **Royal Hall** dating from 1904 originally known as the Kur Saal and based on a similar spa hall in Ostende, Belgium, catered for concerts and other major events.

From the middle of the 20th century onwards, the town transformed from being a Victorian spa to becoming a national conference centre, the hotels serving a new clientele. The old Spa Rooms were demolished, to be replaced by a major auditorium and suite of rooms for conferences and conventions, which have since been expanded into what is now the Harrogate Convention Centre.

About a mile from the town centre, the Yorkshire Showground hosts the annual **Yorkshire Show** to showcase of all that is best in Yorkshire farming and agriculture. Many other outdoor events and activities are held there.

The spectacular **RHS Gardens at Harlow Carr** a mile west of Harrogate into Nidderdale have grown to become one of the most important and popular botanic gardens in the North of England. Harlow Hill, the wooded area just at the far side of the Valley Gardens, commands a magnificent view across the Vale of York, with, on clear days, both York Minster and the White Horse of Kilburn on the North York Moors, visible.

The River Nidd enters the Vale of York east of a town that is far older than Harrogate, Knaresborough. The town is situated directly above a steep gorge cut by the river through the limestone, celebrated for the tiny Hermit Cave and Chapel of Saint Robert and also for **Mother Shipton's Cave and Petrifying Well**. This popular Victorian-era attraction includes a spring and waterfall from a limestone spring where objects such as hats or gloves hung under the falls for a few months are "petrified" by a thin covering of tufa or limestone deposit.

The town owes its existence to its Castle, which dates from around 1100. In 1205 it became the important royal residence in Yorkshire for the notorious King John. Other royal residents included Edward II who eventually gave the castle to his infamous favourite Piers Gaveston. John of Gaunt Duke of Lancaster Lord of the Manor of Knaresborough between 1371 and 1399 owned the castle which served as the administrative centre and Hunting Lodge for his nearby estate in the Forest of Knaresborough. In 1644 it was besieged by Parliamentary forces in the Civil War at the time of the decisive battle of nearby Marston Moor. The keep and fortifications were largely destroyed by the Roundheads in 1648 just in case they ever got into Royalist hands again. The **Castle and Courtyard Museum** now contain exhibits relating to the history of the castle and town.

The most photographed image of Knaresborough is not its Castle, despite its illustrious history, but the great railway viaduct on the line which was opened in 1851 as a branch off the Leeds-Thirsk railway towards York. It had a difficult birth. The first attempt to build a bridge in 1848 collapsed into the swollen river thankfully before it could be used. It took a further three years and much legal and financial wrangling to get the replacement built, its pillars castellated to fit in with the dramatic gorge and Castle. It is now the centrepiece of one of the most popular views in Yorkshire, with or without a train crossing.

Artists and writers of the Yorkshire Dales

Over the last 250 years the Yorkshire Dales, like the Lake District, has become an embodiment of our love of the "picturesque" so perfectly captured in that famous view at Knaresborough, but in all the other many popular tourist centres of the Yorkshire Dales. This is most notably in Wharfedale Wensleydale, Malhamdale, Ribblesdale, Swaledale where particular vistas, especially of hill summits, castles, abbeys or waterfalls, have been captured and recaptured by generations of artists and photographers until they have become imbedded into our consciousness. This began in the late 18th and early 19th centuries, from the time of Thomas Girtin, John Sell Cotman, James Ward, Julius Caesar Ibbetson. Most influential of all was J.M.W. Turner (1775–1851) whose exquisite water colours of Semerwater, Aysgarth Force and Richmond Castle were turned to engravings, widely reproduced, but first used to illustrate Thomas Whitaker's **History of Richmondshire** published in 1823. This work inspired many other writers, and later photographers, to come to the Yorkshire Dales.

This involvement with the visual arts continued with the work of Edwin Landseer, John Ruskin and many others. But the embryonic tourist industry of the Dales was given a major boost by the energy of one man – the extraordinarily energetic writer and promoter both of art and of an idealised view of pre-industrial England, Edmund Bogg (1851–1931). Bogg was born in the Yorkshire Wolds and came to Leeds to open a picture framing shop and studio in Woodhouse Lane. In the 1890s Bogg set up a walking, outdoor art club known as the Leeds Savage Club. Bogg's escapist vision of a dreamy pre-industrialised romantic rural past was an uncannily precursor of certain aspects of James Herriot films. His book **A Thousand Miles in Wharfedale** of 1892 was an immense success. For this and subsequent publications he used engravings and drawings by several Savage Club members such as Percy Robinson, Gilbert Foster, Albert Hazelgrave and Owen Bowen as well as his own photographs.

Arthur Reginald Smith (1873–1943) was another very fine water colourist encouraged by the example of Edmund Bogg's publications. He earned extra cash by illustrating books such as Halliwell Sutcliffe's **Striding Dales**. Smith tragically lost his life by drowning in the River Wharfe.

Over the decades several other artists of note were attracted to the Dales, including such well-known names as Constance Pearson, Fred Lawson, Reginald Brundrit and in more recent times, Janet Rawlins, Judith Bromley, Piers Browne and Katherine Holmes of Malham whose powerful, atmospheric semi-abstract paintings of Dales hillscapes have earned her a national reputation[7].

The artist Marie Hartley (1905–2006) combined a love of the Dales and her artistic skills and powers of observation to produce a unique and special contribution to the Yorkshire Dales. With her partner Ella Pontefract (1896–1945) and later after Ella's untimely and tragic death, with Joan Ingilby (1911–2000), she produced a series of classic books about each of the main Yorkshire Dales, including, in 1968 with Joan Ingilby, that important piece of social history **Life and Tradition in the Yorkshire Dales**. Writing at a time of huge change in the Yorkshire Dales, when traditional methods of husbandry on Dales farms, particularly with horses, which had remained in use from the middle ages onwards, were rapidly disappearing with post-war mechanisation. The interviews with Dales people provide a vital record in their books;

the artefacts that they also gathered are now in pride of place in the Dales Countryside Museum.

If the more sentimental writers like Bogg and Sutcliffe were creating a new market for the landscape of the Dales, more serious authors, scientists and historians, were beginning to create an understanding of the huge educational resource represented by the natural and human cultural landscape of the Dales.

The greatest of these, and also of the North York Moors and Coast, was undoubtedly the pioneering geologist and topographer John Phillips (1800–74), whose masterly book **Rivers, Mountains and Sea Coast of Yorkshire** (1854) is still one of the best books about Yorkshire ever written. But other serious authors were to follow. Harry Speight (1855–1915), of Bingley was a noted historian and author. His **Romantic Richmondshire** of 1897 or **Upper Wharfedale** published in 1900 are still sought-after classics for their wealth of detail, superb illustrations and accuracy of information.

The Dalesman, founded in 1939, is one of Britain's longest and most loved regional magazines and regional publishers. It has done much to establish, over three generations, through a series of scholarly, well informed but often light-hearted articles and books by some of the region's top writers, much of the identity of the Yorkshire Dales. However, in a very gentle way, the magazine has gradually extended its coverage to the whole of the county of Yorkshire. It has in a very real sense become a voice of Yorkshire, not just the Dales.

But 20th century Dales scholarship owes much to the life's work of one individual who was also a regular contributor to the Dalesman over many decades – Arthur Raistrick (1896–1991). Raistrick was a geologist and mining engineer, a Quaker and conscientious objector, who in World War II gave up his academic teaching post because of his university's links to the armaments trade. He came to live in Linton, near Grassington in 1940. Over the next 40 years he and his wife Elizabeth sustained themselves by research, teaching and writing, especially about the social and industrial history of the Dales, including its lead mining, producing such classic books as **The Pennine Dales** (1968) and **The West Riding of Yorkshire** (1970). It has been suggested that Raistrick almost single handedly created the discipline of **Industrial Archaeology**, with his book on the subject published in 1972.

Challenges for the 21ˢᵗ century

Arthur Raistrick, the Yorkshire Dales Society Dalesman of the Millennium, was one of the founding fathers of the Yorkshire Dales National Park. He served, as an often-dissenting voice, on its first West Riding Committee. He would have fully recognised the Park's many later successes in terms of protecting the environment and even, working with farmers, its rural economy. He would have welcomed its expansion into Westmorland in 2016 but regretted the constantly reducing budgets, the restricted public transport. He would have hated the severe pressures of visitor traffic and parked cars at busy tourist honeypots, including his own village of Linton.

He would also have worried deeply about the subtle social cleansing of the Yorkshire Dales area, as rising house costs continue to price out young people in favour of the elderly retired from affluent parts of England, resulting in all the familiar problems of youth out-migration and an ageing population. With closure of local schools, pubs, and loss of regular and affordable local buses services, young people continue to leave the area to seek better reimbursed employment elsewhere. The danger is that the Yorkshire Dales could develop into one vast retirement home, based entirely around the mobility offered by the private car, but denied to those who cannot afford to own a car, or through age or infirmity can no longer drive.

These trends are also now fuelled by new pressure from the South East, turbocharged by both the move to the digital economy and the recent pandemic. This means people, with jobs even based in London, now can buy a first or even second property in the Yorkshire Dales and work from home. This could price even a small Dales cottage, or even former council house, out of the range of all but high earners. This also comes at the very time when the promotion of Yorkshire and the Yorkshire Dales, through nightly popular television programme about the outdoors, country walking, and idyllic life on farms, is ever increasing. This can only increase pressure on limited availability of housing, especially on more affordable homes or social housing in the larger villages and market towns of the Yorlshire Dales and North York Moors.

The other major challenge and opportunity for the Yorkshire Dales, as well as elsewhere in the Pennines and the North York Moors, is the key role its moorlands offer to help mitigate the impacts of climate change. The Yorkshire Peat Partnership, managed by Yorkshire Wildlife Trust, are currently carrying out major work on Fleet Moss, and above Oughtershaw, headwaters of the Wharfe, to restore and encourage the growth of sphagnum moss on eroded areas of moorland to stimulate peat regeneration. This work is supported by such agencies as the National Park Authority, the Environment Agency, Natural England, Yorkshire Water and the new Yorkshire Climate Commission. This also accords with a number of significant tree planting and river management schemes by the National Trust on Malham Moor and in Upper Wharfedale and with similar projects in Swaledale.

Perhaps this is just the kind of urgent, skilled work that might encourage and enable young people born in the Dales to return; or maybe in their later years to run an on-line business, or to work in yet to be imagined forms of agritourism or sustainable food production initiatives. This might include making more productive use of marginal uplands for fruit and vegetable cultivation, linked to climate change mitigation schemes and new land management initiatives. These initiatives would also need to be linked to imaginative rural skills training or apprenticeship schemes which the National Park Authorities and Nidderdale JAC are pursuing. Many such schemes are being developed and supported by the inspirational Yorkshire Dales Millennium Trust.

However, the twin challenges of affordable housing and public transport networks, accessible and available to all, will need to be tackled before any such revival of rural communities can, in the longer term, fully succeed. These are key themes of an important new report (2021) by the **North Yorkshire Rural Commission** *Rural North Yorkshire the Way Forward* which offers a vision for a prosperous future for North Yorkshire's most rural areas.

Notes

1 Drury Colin: God's Own Country: Yorkshire Dales named best national park in Europe: in The Independent 27th January 2021
2 Johnson David 2002: *Limestone Industries of the Yorkshire Dales* Tempus, Stroud
3 Speakman Colin 2020: *John Phillips Yorkshire's Traveller through Time* Gritstone, Hebden Bridge
4 Mason Kate 1989: *Woolcombers, Worsteds and Watermills* Addingham Civic Society
5 Wainwright Alfred 1972: *Walks on the Howgill Fells* Westmorland Gazette Kendal
6 Harvey Adrian 2017: *Excursion Guide to the Geomorphology of the Howgill Fells* Dunedin Edinburgh p25
7 Joy David 1997: *Painters of the Dales* CPRE Craven Settle

6

The Forest of Bowland

If you were to name the wildest, loneliest place in Yorkshire, this might be in somewhere that most people believe is in Lancashire – the Forest of Bowland.

Only about 10% of this magnificent Area of Outstanding Nature Beauty, covering 803 square kilometres of what is a western outlier of the central Pennines, lies in what is now North Yorkshire.

The AONB covers a massive expanse of heather moorland, gritstone crags and peatland bog that forms a huge crest of fells, rising to 561 metres (1841 feet) to the immediate south of the Yorkshire Dales, separated to the east and south, by central Ribblesdale and by the Wenning/Lune watershed to the north.

This is a land dominated by the higher Carboniferous era sedimentary rocks – millstone grit, sandstone and shales, with only one small exposure of limestone in the Hodder valley around Whitewell.

Across the Ribble lies the AONB Pendle Outlier, dominated by a single feature, one of the great landmarks of the Pennines, Pendle Hill, with its surrounding villages.

Since 1974 around 90% of the AONB has been in present-day Lancashire, with only a narrow strip of land east of the ridge formed by Tatham, Catlow and Tatham Fells in North Yorkshire. Yet before local Government reorganisation – and ignoring the thoroughly Lancashire Witch Country around Pendle Hill – around 50% of the AONB, including the whole of the Hodder Valley almost as far as Clitheroe, was within the West Riding of Yorkshire. These cultural links remain.

The southern and western flanks of the Bowland Fells overlooking the Wyre Valley, including Longridge Fell and the Abbeystead Moors have always been thoroughly Lancastrian, but it may be a surprise to know that even the celebrated Trough of Bowland was, for over a thousand years, within the old West Riding. A boundary stone dividing historic West Riding from ancient Lancashire survives at the summit of the pass.

The name "Forest" does not mean in this context extensive woodland but refers to the fact that so much of this area was formerly medieval hunting reserve. There were in fact no less than five such areas protected from Norman and Plantagenet times for their wild game, especially deer, where enclosure of the land and hunting of game by local people was prohibited – this included the main Royal Forest of Bowland itself, but also the Forests of Quernmore, Bleasdale, Wyresdale and Pendle, all initially under the jurisdiction of the powerful de Lacy family, then later various Dukes of Lancaster.

There was also a small Cistercian Monastery, **Sawley Abbey**, close to the old Forest boundary village of Bolton by Bowland. The Abbey owned land locally at Rimington and as far away as Gargrave, Ilkley and Tadcaster but suffered from rivalry with its close and more prosperous neighbour at Whalley. After the Dissolution in 1537, the buildings were robbed for the ready-dressed stone and only small sections of wall and foundations remain, under the care of English Heritage.

To some extent the Forest Laws and aristocratic ownership explain why so much of Bowland has been left as wild, open countryside, which at least on the tops has lost most of its tree cover. Villages have also remained small and undeveloped. Land ownership patterns have not changed fundamentally over the centuries – much of Bowland is still owned by great families, including the Duchy of Lancaster, Lord Clitheroe and the Duke of Westminster, but also the main regional water company United Utilities. There are also several estate villages under the ownership of aristocratic families, which at least means most are free from modern ribbon development.

The Abbeystead Moors used to enjoy a certain notoriety being one of the largest areas of open countryside in England where ramblers were forbidden to walk, crossed as the moors were by few rights of way; a flashpoint even after the creation of the AONB in 1964. The situation, aggravated by threatening notices, lead to angry trespass and protest, only finally resolved in 2000 with the passing of the Countryside and Rights of Way Act.

Now the opposite is true – the moors throughout Bowland offer a magnificent, open wilderness where walkers can enjoy a sense of space, light and grandeur. The uplands are also precious areas for wildlife – about 13% to the AONB is Special Protection Area. Bird life to enjoy includes the legendary, and rare, hen harrier – the logo of the AONB – but also peregrine, merlin, buzzard, golden plover, snipe, ring ouzels and much more besides including even the occasional osprey.

Sadly, the protection of birds is not without its controversy on occasions with for example even hen harriers being found trapped or poisoned and failing to breed by loss of chicks, though gamekeepers deny any knowledge of such practices. The water company United Utilities who own 25,000 acres of moorland including main water catchment areas around Stocks Reservoir and the headwaters of the Hodder work particularly closely with the RSPB, the AONB and Natural England and local farmers and gamekeepers to protect these iconic bird species and the precious moor and peatland habitat. Much of this work has been achieved through a scheme known as the Sustainable Catchment Management Programme.

The landscape of Bowland has more in common with the Scottish Highlands than the Pennines, in terms of the scale and openness of the landscape and, in the moorlands, lack of obvious signs of human occupation. The two narrow, winding moorland roads northwards from Slaidburn to High Bentham via Cross of Greet or to Clapham via Stocks Reservoir and Grisedale Forest both have the character of mountain passes, offering spectacular views of The Three Peaks, are thrilling for both the motorist and the cyclist. Equally impressive, is the Trough of Bowland that emerges over Abbeystead Moors past the Jubilee Tower before descending to the southern outskirts of Lancaster beyond the M6.

Stocks Reservoir was built between 1926 in 1933 to provide water for the towns of the Fylde coast. This required the flooding of a small hamlet known as Stocks in Bowland. The hamlet's little church of St James was removed stone by stone and carefully rebuilt at Dalehead a mile away just above the Reservoir.

The lack of tree cover on the Bowland fells is contrasted by the dense conifer woods around and above Stocks Reservoir that form Gisburn Forest. Now managed by Forest England, these 1,200 hectares of mainly commercial spruce woodland have become a major recreational centre, the trees providing the perfect screening for a wide range of outdoor recreational activities. The most significant of these is mountain biking, with over 16km of waymarked trails of various grades, together with a choice of walking routes that include the land around Stocks Reservoir. There is a large central car park at **Gisburn Forest Hub** next to the 15th century farmhouse at Stephen Park. Visitors can enjoy a café, bike hire, a small exhibition centre, as well as a range of seasonal events including music, cloud spotting and dark sky festivals.

The little village of Tosside just above and within easy walking distance of Gisburn Forest, now has the distinction of being divided in the village centre by what is now the Lancashire-North Yorkshire boundary. Unbelievably the buses supported by the County Councils that used to run through from Settle to Slaidburn and Clitheroe, now turn round at Tosside rather running into the "foreign" territory of Lancashire. A weathervane above the Jubilee Memorial exactly on the county boundary boasts a fox rather than the usual cockerel, to indicate into which county the wind is blowing, possibly reflecting the popularity of foxhunting in the area. Tosside now celebrates an annual Fox Festival where people in the village, instead of hunting foxes, dress up in fox costumes, the best costume winning a prize, a tribute to one of the most charming if sometimes destructive wild creature of the Forest.

The Hodder Valley which extends west of Slaidburn is the most beautiful in Bowland, its meandering river which bends so significantly at Dunsop Bridge is probably the meaning of "Bow" – that is the wide bend in the river and the dale that gives its name to the area. The fertile pastures, scattered woodland and comfortable farms are a sharp contrast to the bleaker, rugged uplands.

The valley is also an area of traditional herb-rich, flower filled meadows, especially beautiful in early summer. One of these at Bell Sykes farm, near Slaidburn was chosen by HRH Prince of Wales in 2013 to be Lancashire's Coronation Meadow to celebrate the 60th anniversary of the Coronation. Say it quietly, but when our Queen was crowned, the meadow was in Yorkshire.

The valleys of Bowland as well as the fells, offer perfect walking country, with a choice of paths connecting unspoiled farms, hamlets and villages.

Most notably of these is Slaidburn, the focal point of the former West Riding part of Bowland. With its café on the open riverside green below the old stone Hodder Bridge, it has long been a popular visitor destination. The village has a fine old 18th century former grammar school, a medieval church and the historic **Hark to Bounty Inn**. This inn is reputed to date back to the 13th century, though the present building dates from the 17th. An upstairs room also served as the local manorial court, where local miscreants were dealt with, a usage that continued until the mid-1930s.

The pub's name has a delightful history. For centuries it was known rather prosaically as The Dog. In 1875 the local squire, who was also the local Rector, and a keen huntsman, was a regular. During the local fox hunt, he came into the inn with his fellow huntsmen for refreshment. Hearing the hound pack baying excitedly outside the door, he recognised the bark of his favourite hound above the rest and came out with the phrase "Hark to Bounty" which so amused the gathered assembly that the pub's name was promptly changed.

The ancient track over the pass between Croasdale and Salter Fells known as the Hornby Road or Salter Fell Track can be followed by the strong walker or mountain biker between Slaidburn and Wray. This is one of the great walks of the Pennines. Part of it utilises a section of what was a former Roman road heading from Ribchester towards Cumbria and Scotland.

The other villages along the Hodder, Newton, Whitewell and Cow Ark and Bashall Eves retain their charm and a reputation for hospitality, with award winning gastropubs at both Newton-in-Bowland and Whitewell.

Browsholme Hall, the magnificent ancestral home of the Parker family, near Cow Ark, dates from the early 16th century. It is one of the oldest continuously occupied family homes in the ownership of the same family in the North of England. Especially notable for its gardens, oak panelled rooms and relics of the Yorkshire Jacobites, it is now open to the public on certain days in the summer months and is also a popular conference centre and wedding venue.

Bashall Eaves close by was the original home of the Bowland Brewery, in a small farmhouse. This is now the **Bashall Barn Food Visitor Centre**. The Bowland Brewery, whose ales are highly regarded for their excellence, is now based in a former textile mill in Clitheroe. Bowland is also known for its farmhouse cheeses.

Dunsop Bridge, named after the crossing of the little river Dunsop, is a charming village near the confluence of three rivers– the Hodder, the Dunsop and Langdon Brook. It lies within in a beautiful basin of high surrounding fells at a crossroads where roads lead northwards to Lancaster or south to Clitheroe. The village is now, fittingly, the headquarters of the Forest of Bowland AONB.

It is also reputed to be at the exact centre of the British Isles. This is not as sometimes imagined in the village phone box, but around 4 miles away near to Whitendale Hanging Stones. This lies on the hillside above a deep hollow in the fells where the narrow and beautiful Dunsop valley splits into the secret Whitendale and Brennand valleys.

Appropriate to perhaps claim that the centre of Britain is indeed in the historic West Riding of Yorkshire.

7

The South Pennines

In essence, the South Pennines is that extensive area of the Pennines between the Yorkshire Dales National Park and the Peak District, notable as being the only part of the Pennine Chain between Derbyshire and the Scottish border not to have received any national landscape protection designation. Its boundaries to the east might be roughly defined by the urban areas of West Yorkshire, and of Greater Manchester and East Lancashire to the west.

This is a bleaker, tougher landscape than the Dales to the north, dominated by the hard, darker gritstone, sandstones and shales of the Carboniferous era, punctuated by only occasional scatterings of limestone boulders carried down as far south as Airedale in glacial drift. But it is an area with a beauty and grandeur of its own.

Exactly where the divisions lie between the Yorkshire Dales and the South Pennines is open to debate. Natural England bizarrely assume the River Wharfe to be a division, but that makes no sense. Stand on the summit of Burley Moor or follow the ancient packhorse way over the peat moorland and crags from Dick Hudson's to cross the watershed of Rombalds and Ilkley Moor, to the point where the whole soft and beautiful green valley opens out below you to the north and west, and you know you are in the Yorkshire Dales. But look southwards from the watershed into central Airedale and the landscape is much browner, bleaker, and dominated by dark millstone grit crags and the peri-urban fringes of West Yorkshire, though with fewer mill chimneys than in the recent past. That is the South Pennines.

The contrast is stark.

Yet in both landscape and cultural terms, this sub-region contains some of the most characteristic features that define Yorkshire worldwide, celebrated by some its greatest writers and in more recent times film makers.

If you walk up to that rather special, iconic building on Ilkley Moor, White Wells, the 18th century white painted building, containing moorland spring-fed plunge baths and the little cafe and its terrace where in the summer months the white and blue flag of Yorkshire is invariably flying, you look down and across the heather and scrubby woodland hillside into and along Wharfedale, as the great valley swings around to Bolton Abbey. But behind you the moorland rises sharply up to the same watershed that divides two contrasting aspects of the Yorkshire Pennines.

Ilkley itself, immediately below the Moor, whose rooftops are visible from the terrace, is also, with its busy electrified commuter railway and dense housing, a dormitory suburb once of Bradford, now primarily of Leeds. The ever-expanding suburbs from Otley through Menston, Burley, Ben Rhydding to Ilkley and onwards to Addingham threaten to eventually merge, as a result of ever weaker Green Belt protection, to become one long suburban outlier of urban West Yorkshire.

So, three aspects of Yorkshire's cultural identity, are intermingled at White Wells.

It is no coincidence perhaps, that Victorian popular pseudo folk-song in Yorkshire dialect – *On Ilkla Moor Baht 'At*[1] has become the unofficial national anthem of Yorkshire.

The South Pennines truly start south of the crags and millstone grit outliers of Ilkley Moor along the moorland edges above White Wells, along Burley, Ilkley and Addingham High Moor and over that area of bleak and eroded moorland into that most typical of Yorkshire valleys of Airedale. These uplands, as in the Moors and Dales to the north and east, attracted early settlers. Both Baildon and Ilkley Moors are of national importance for their mainly Bronze Age rock art, complex designs and patterns including the mysterious cup and ring markings. Some of the designs may have been a way of marking boundaries, religious rituals or even communicating with the imagined deities of the moon and stars.

You are never far from the sight of industry in the South Pennines. In the higher valleys are hamlets of weavers' cottages, with their narrow second floor windows, wherever possible built north facing for even light, where hand loom weavers earned their living before the powered looms took their trade away.

The smaller waterwheel powered mills along becks in the gills and narrower valleys, were in turn largely replaced by the larger steam powered mills in the valley bottoms, each with their distinctive chimneys, more easily and cheaply supplied by the canal and railway with coal and raw material and from which their products could be exported towards Halifax, Bradford and onwards to Hull or Liverpool.

Typical stone villages of the South Pennines have groups of 17th or 18th century weavers' cottages clustered around a church (if medieval, usually heavily restored in Victorian times). But there is also usually a large Nonconformist, probably Methodist or Baptist Chapel, and a late 18th or early 19th century mill, that may or may not have kept its chimney before being converted in more recent times to apartments or offices. There will usually be a fine mill manager's house, a vicarage or manse, rows of workers' terraced cottages. Other buildings might have at one time included a smithy, a school, a village shop and post office, a telephone box.

These were self-sufficient economic units, linked not only by what are now a network of lanes and minor roads, but also more direct footpaths, some stone flagged, and tracks between the hamlets and villages, most especially packhorse tracks. The tracks and trails of trade still exist throughout the South Pennines, often as narrow enclosed ways between Enclosure-era drystone walls, sometimes climbing hillsides at ferociously steep gradients.

Many paths and tracks linked with the main, eventually turnpiked roads along the valleys, others, like the paved path from Dick Hudson's to Ilkley, cross over the moortops to access adjacent valleys. Upper Calderdale, for example contains some of the densest networks of public rights of way in the United Kingdom. Many of these are 17th and 18th century former packhorse routes.

Up until the coming of the railways in the mid-19th century, these old ways would be busy with packhorse traffic, trains of well laden packhorses – sturdy Dales ponies – carrying sacks of cloth and other material, some with woven pannier baskets, taking finished pieces of cloth to market as far as Halifax or Leeds and bringing goods and supplies from the towns to outlying settlements on return journeys.

Farms and hamlets would receive their supplies from regular travelling tradesmen and pedlars. The recent changes in shopping habits in the internet age may have, in a curious way, turned behaviour in a full circle for the many commuters and retirees who now occupy many of the farms and weavers' cottages of the high Pennines, with supplies arriving by Amazon or Tesco, modern equivalent of the old pedlars or badgers, to save the inhabitants from the physical need to travel to shop.

The Brontë heritage

Yet perhaps the most iconic shared images of the South Pennines, which most readily capture the idea of Yorkshire in popular imagination worldwide, are to be found around and above the Worth Valley, a little tributary valley of the Aire, above the little mill village of Haworth, an area that is often referred to slightly confusingly as "the Yorkshire Moors". This is an area of bleak, largely treeless and windswept, overgrazed, upland pasture or heather moorland with scatterings of sheep, crossed by lines of straight drystone walls, punctuated by outcropping crags of weather-worn millstone grit, stone farmhouses or ruined barns, penetrated by rocky gills containing fast-flowing becks, with perhaps a small waterfall and isolated rowan tree. There are also large, artificial expanses of water in the larger hollows and side valleys, municipal reservoirs with their elaborate stonework and access roads. Often to be seen along the hillsides are the half-buried aqueducts that carry their outflow along the contours to distant purification works in the cities.

A clue to explain the powerful resonance of this part of the South Pennines lies in its other popular name – "Brontë Country". The literary masterpieces of the three gifted sisters, living in the Parsonage of what was the highly polluted mill village of Haworth, have, over the last two centuries, changed the way people perceive the area. The term Brontë Country is now a standard term of tourist literature.

This happened above all because of the work of Emily, poet, keen walker and extraordinary novelist, whose single novel **Wuthering Heights** (1848) is rightly regarded as one of the greatest novels in the English language. Yet this is a novel firmly based in one place and at one particular time in history, in Yorkshire's South Pennines.

It has been correctly suggested that the moorland landscape became almost a character of the novel, representing both spiritual, emotional and perhaps even sexual freedom for the characters of Heathcliff and Cathy Earnshaw. It is also a powerful social novel of the early years of the 19th century, with the "new money" earned from manufacturing by the Linton Family contrasting with the relative poverty of the old yeoman farming family, the Earnshaws; both families being massively disrupted by the intrusion of Heathcliff. Heathcliff is a dark-skinned waif brought back by Mr Earnshaw, significantly from what the author would have thoroughly known and understood as being the slave-trade port of Liverpool. The beautiful and sensitive landscapes so perfectly captured by all three sisters, but most especially Emily in her prose and poetry, has profoundly affected the way we look at the landscape. This has become imprinted within our own collective imagination. Emily even brings Yorkshire dialect into her novel, superbly and accurately recorded in the person of the old servant Joseph[2].

Other writers, such as Glyn Hughes in his fascinating study of the essence of the South Pennines, **Millstone Grit**[3], painters such as Ashley Jackson, and photographers such as Simon Warner of Stanbury have also tried to recapture that essential magic. The famous walking route to the ruined farm and isolated tree on the ridge above Stanbury Moor known as Top Withens, one of the locations that may well have been the inspiration for the Earnshaws' farm of Wuthering Heights, is not only well walked by Brontë aficionados, but is now signposted in Japanese, a delightful touch for the many Japanese admirers of Emily's work.

Little wonder that tourists by their thousands come to Haworth, mainly by car and by coach, but not all to the literary shrine of the old Parsonage now **The Brontë Museum** with its manuscripts and memorabilia of the celebrated literary family. For many, the cobbled main street, period houses, cafes, pubs and tourist shops have created a place to soak up an atmosphere of sentimental nostalgia for an imagined Victorian world, with little relationship to the tragically short lives of the Brontë family, the toughness and realism of their greatest novels, and spiritual intensity of their poetry.

Many people also arrive by the **Worth Valley Railway**, that perfectly restored heritage railway line. The branch line from Keighley to the mill communities of Ingrow, Oakworth, Haworth and Oxenhope only opened 1867 long after the deaths of the sisters – though Charlotte and Anne did actually used the newly opened railway from Keighley to Leeds for Anne's last tragic journey to Scarborough in 1848.

The 4½ mile branch line closed in 1961 but reopened in 1968 as a heritage steam railway to Oxenhope thanks to the efforts of a group of local enthusiasts led by the vision of a Keighley man who later became the local MP, Bob Cryer. This railway is now perhaps the most filmed railway line in the British Isles. Its beautifully preserved Victorian stations, most especially that at Oakworth, have featured in innumerable television and film period dramas. None were more memorable than the hugely popular 1970 film of Edith Nesbit's book **The Railway Children,** which was very much centred in the landscape of the Worth Valley, not just the railway.

The Worth Valley is a tributary valley off that broader, glaciated dale, Airedale where there are many more weaving hamlets and mill villages so very typical of the whole of the South Pennines.

Keighley in the centre of Airedale is a former textile town, also a noted centre for the manufacture of textile machinery that has kept its Victorian character. Like Bradford, Keighley now has with a significant Muslim community. **Cliffe Castle Museum,** in its fine park at the edge of the town, in the grand neo-Gothic Victorian mansion of local mill owners the Butterfields, is now the town's museum. Exhibits on the geology, archaeology, natural and local history of Airedale include a reconstruction of Timothy Feather's handloom workshop, and a carefully restored parlour of the Castle showing how it would have been furnished at the time of the Butterfields.

Keighley is also at the edge of some attractive South Pennines countryside, including the Worth Valley. But there is attractive countryside around such villages as Laycock and the fascinating hamlet of Goose Eye, named after a local mill. Newsholme Dean was once an extremely popular beauty spot where millworkers from the town would come on foot to enjoy precious open space at weekends and public holidays.

East Riddlesden Hall, south of Keighley is a fine example of a prosperous South Pennine Yeoman's house, dating from the first great wave of prosperity in the textile industry of the 17th century with its fine plaster ceilings, oak panelling, fireplaces, and a wonderful Rose window. It was built by a wealthy Halifax clothier, Richard Murgatroyd, a Royalist sympathiser in the 1640s. After a series of different owners, it is now under the protection of the National Trust. There is a magnificent medieval tythe barn in the grounds.

During the 18th century, the Yorkshire woollen industry boomed. The fast-flowing rivers and streams were excellent for the washing and fulling of raw wool. They also provided the power for early mechanisation, in what are now often little more than ruined shells of former mills in narrow side valleys and wooded gills. Improved turnpike roads and canals also enabled wool to be brought in from areas as far away as the East Riding for processing into fine quality worsted cloth. This included the process of beating fabric with hammers or "fulling" to secure an even texture, usually at a communal water powered fulling mill. At the start of the 18th century Yorkshire was producing around 20[%] of the nation's woollen cloth. By 1900 this had leaped to 60%, 80% of which was exported abroad via Leeds and Hull. Yorkshire became synonymous internationally with high quality wool and worsted cloth production.

The steep tributary valleys and valley sides, and in places even valley bottoms, still contain small but precious areas of ancient woodland, predominantly of oak, birch, holly, beech, and sycamore that thrive in the thin, acid soils. As the Calderdale cartographer and writer Christopher Goddard has pointed out[4], this former "wildwood" has over the centuries provided a huge range of human needs: being pollarded for naturally regenerating timbers for building, fencing, charcoal for early bloomeries (small outdoor forges) for the smelting of lead, copper and iron, bark for tanning, its acorns and beech mast for pannage, even young holly shoots cut in "hollins" for animal feed. Despite constant reduction in size and abuse over the centuries, but also husbandry and much natural regeneration in more recent years as industries have declined, these woodlands have survived, as a part of our history and rich source of biodiversity. Areas such as Shipley Glen above Saltaire, or parts of the St Ives Estate and around Druid's Rock above Harden and Bingley still contain remnants of ancient Pennine woodland.

Trans-Pennine Transport

The Aire Gap had long been a major communication route through the South Pennines, the early medieval roads being replaced by the mid 18thcentury by better surfaced and well-engineered Turnpikes such as the Leeds-Keighley, Otley-Skipton and Keighley-Kendal roads.

But it also had a waterway which provided the first direct route by barge from the North Sea at Hull via the Humber, the Aire-Calder and Leeds, to Liverpool on the Irish Sea – the Leeds-Liverpool Canal.

Constructed in stages between 1770 and 1778 through Airedale, but only reaching Liverpool in 1812, this is a classic contour "Broad" canal, engineered to follow the natural curves through the valley in order to reduce the need for lock and consequent high-water consumption, but at a cost of extending distance. At Bingley in central Airedale the building of locks to ascend the higher parts of the Dale could not be avoided and the result was a "staircase" – a still hugely impressive feat of early canal engineering. The Five Rise and nearby Three Rise Locks in Bingley are a popular regional tourist attraction. The towpath of the Leeds-Liverpool Canal from Leeds through the dale to Keighley (with a branch into Bradford) has now been upgraded and improved for cycling and walking, known as the Airedale Greenway. From Silsden it merges with National Cycle Route 696 onwards across the Pennines towards Liverpool.

But cross-Pennine travel was revolutionised from the late 1840s onwards with the opening of the steam railway through Airedale. The Leeds & Bradford Railway extended to Keighley and Skipton in 1847 and later as the North Western and finally the Midland Railway through the Aire Gap towards Lancaster and eventually Scotland.

Trans-Pennine transport in all its forms, including packhorse ways, turnpike roads, canal, railways and 20th century motorways, and even unsightly bypasses, have had a major impact on the South Pennine landscape.

None more so perhaps than M62 The Trans-Pennine Motorway. The summit section of the M62 between Outlane and Milnrow is considered one of the most spectacular sections of motorway in the British Isles, a magnificent piece of engineering, at one point dramatically combined with the Scammonden Dam. It is also one of the most exposed, and frequently struggles to remain open at times of heavy snowfall.

The motorway, opened between 1971 and 1976, has also spared the older cross-Pennine former turnpike trunk roads, such as the A58 through Calderdale and the A62 through the Calder Valley, from the overwhelming pressure of heavy traffic which would have otherwise destroyed the local communities that had developed along them.

The Colne Valley

The impact of transport is equally evident in the southern part of the South Pennines within Yorkshire, namely the Colne Valley, a major Pennine valley which is not the given the accolade of being a "Dale". But the little River Colne flows through yet another typical Pennine dale of small towns such as Golcar, Slaithwaite and Marsden and numerous scattered mill villages and hamlets, connected by turnpike road, the Huddersfield Narrow Canal, and mainline railway, all modes built to connecting the growing industrial towns and cities on both sides of the Pennines.

The **Colne Valley Museum** at Golcar occupies four traditional Pennine weavers' cottages, one of which has been restored to recapture what it would have looked like when occupied by a family of hand-loom weavers. There is a model of a spinning jenny and a recreated clog-makers' workshop, as well as much other material relating to life in the valley in the early industrial age.

Slaithwaite was for years the butt of jokes aimed at its local inhabitants as being so foolish or inebriated as to try to pull the image of the moon as a piece of silver out of the canal with a rake, hence being known as "moonrakers", a jest turned to its advantage with an annual Moonrakers Festival made with lanterns every February.

Unlike Airedale or Calderdale, the Colne Valley does not follow a natural gap through the Pennines but is a cul-de-sac valley, terminating at a variety of steep moorland passes over the Pennine watershed. Marsden, no doubt in retaliation by the inhabitants of Slaithwaite for the Moonraker jibes, was reputed to be the last place in Yorkshire to discover the wheel. In truth most of its trade until the coming of the turnpike roads and building of the Huddersfield Narrow Canal through the valley, came by packhorse, including one of the most famous of all trans-Pennine trade routes, Rapes Highway, which crosses a natural pass through the Pennines to the cotton town of Milnrow in Lancashire and on to Rochdale. The site of a packhorse inn still survives at Eastergate Bridge, a beautifully preserved packhorse bridge, close to the town. When a local landowner tried to close this ancient route in the early 20th century, he was defeated by local protesters after a famous court case. Stone pillars were then erected by the local council to mark the way of the old trade route across the moor, most of which still survive.

Wheels most certainly came to Marsden in the form of waggons and coaches after the building of the first turnpike road in 1759, which led from Wakefield to Austerlands on the outskirts of Oldham. It was surveyed by the great road engineer John Metcalf, known as Blind Jack of Knaresborough, (1717–1810) who, despite being blind from childhood owing to smallpox, became one of the greatest road engineers of his age. Metcalf pioneered his technique of floating the new road on bundles of heather across the deep bogs on Pule Hill, a device later used by George Stephenson when building the railway between Liverpool and Manchester over Chat Moss. Even though later roads were constructed in the 19th century to reduce the gradients of Metcalf's pioneering route, much of the route is still in use but you can trace part of the original road no longer in use as it crosses the watershed at Pule Hill.

Equally impressive was the great tunnel under Standedge to carry the Huddersfield Narrow Canal between Marsden and Diggle. This was a magnificent feature of engineering, using pick and shovel but also early use of dynamite, with vertical shafts sunk from the surface from where material was extracted. The tunnel, which was started in 1794 and opened in 1811, took 17 years to build, requiring the services of two celebrated engineers, Benjamin Outram and Thomas Telford. At 5675 yards (5,189 metres), it is the oldest, highest and deepest canal tunnel in the British Isles. It was finally closed in 1944. After many years of campaigning and a £5 million scheme for the restoration of both the full length of the canal and the tunnel, the tunnel was fully reopened in 2001. Boats are now powered through not by the traditional method of bargees hauling their boats by "legging" – using their feet along the side of the canal walls to push the barges forward – but by fume-free electric tug. Visitors can now take a guided trip into the tunnel from a well-lit and heated boat from what is now **Standedge Tunnel and Visitor Centre** in the old canalside cottages at Tunnel End.

The canal tunnel also allowed the easier building of the three parallel rail tunnels. This involved two single bore tunnels opened in 1848 and 1871 and finally the present twin tunnel in 1890 built by the London and North Western Railway to cope with the ever-increasing amount of Trans-Pennine freight and passenger traffic. The canal tunnel massively reduced the costs of building the parallel rail tunnels by providing access by linked passages that enabled the removal of spoil, and transport of brick and lining materials for building the tunnels by barge.

Though the small single rail tunnels are currently closed, plans for upgrading the Trans Pennine railway could eventually result in these closed tunnels, which are kept under repair, being rebuilt and rebored to have a new lease of life.

Marsden remains an attractive town, rich in Pennine history, its town hall a lively focal point of cultural activity. This includes the town's links with the Luddites. In 1812, on nearby Crosland Moor, Marsden millowner Robert Horsfall was murdered by Luddites, hand loom weavers protesting against the new powered looms, constructed by local blacksmiths James and Enoch Taylor, that were taking their livelihood away. Three Marsden men were eventually hanged for the murder.

The town is also a centre for exploration of nearby Marsden Moor, the huge 6,000 acre estate, once hunting lands of the Lords of Pontefract, crossed by the medieval Rapes Highway, Metcalf's pioneering turnpike road and the more modern Pennine Way. The Moor is a Site of Special Scientific Interest, owned and managed by the National Trust, and is an important habitat for bird and other wildlife. Tragically moorland fires in recent years, a result of the moor drying out in warm, dry weather, but started by irresponsible users of barbecues and even fireworks, have severely damaged much of the moorland which will takes decades to fully recover.

Close by is the Wessenden Valley, a narrow gorge and side valley of the Colne, dominated by three great reservoirs, the track by the reservoirs leading up to Wessenden Head where until 1956 there was an isolated inn known as the Isle of Skye. This area, though a typical South Pennine moorland and reservoir landscape, is just within the northern boundaries of the Peak District National Park, the area known for self-evident reasons, as the Dark Peak.

Marsden is also the birthplace and former home of poet laureate Simon Armitage who has celebrated the fact with a 42-mile walking route between Marsden and Ilkley through some of the finest landscapes of the South Pennines. In his sequence of poems known as **Stanza Stones**[5], each stanza is carved on a different rock placed at a strategic point, to be discovered and read on the journey, like a waymark shrine on a medieval pilgrimage.

Saddleworth's Yorkshire heritage

But an important part of the old West Riding of Yorkshire lies at the far side of Standedge – Saddleworth and its surrounding villages of Delph, Dobcross, and Uppermill. Though physically closer to Oldham and Greater Manchester and now part of the South Pennines, strong, ancient cultural affinity to Yorkshire remains. This older identity emerges during the annual **Saddleworth Rushcart Festival**. This originated in a single ceremony when rushes were gathered each summer for drying and use on local churchyard floors. It has developed into a major local event, held over an August weekend. A suitably decorated cart with two tons of rushes presided over by an appropriately dressed Morris man is hauled by two teams of Morris men and women. It starts from Saddleworth itself where the Uppermill Rush Dance is performed outside the church, accompanied by local brass bands and Morris dancing, plus much beer drinking; the cart is then taken to other villages where similar outpourings of merriment take place.

Eleven of the thirteen Saddleworth villages also play host to a major event in the national brass band scene – the **Saddleworth Whit Friday Brass Band Competition,** where up to 100 brass bands participate from all over the UK, and even from as far away as Germany, Sweden and Iceland, including many nationally known (Yorkshire) names such as Brighouse & Raistrick, Black Dyke and Grimethorpe. They are drawn to the picturesque South Pennine villages to compete for one of the most prestigious prizes in the world of Brass Band music.

The Holme Valley

But closer to Huddersfield, on another tributary of the Calder, the Holme, is another distinctive part of Yorkshire's South Pennines, the Holme Valley. This is another typical, perhaps gentler part of the South Pennines, centred on the town of Holmfirth. The area is served by the scenic Penistone Line railway between Huddersfield, Penistone and Barnsley, which crosses the Colne valley near Lockwood by an impressive viaduct, and its string of local stations serving Holme Valley villages also provides access to much fine countryside.

The two important branches of the line to the mill and moorland towns of Meltham and Holmfirth closed many years ago as did the branch to Clayton West, kept open until the 1980s when it still served a local colliery, which now carries a narrow-gauge tourist line, the **Kirklees Light Railway**.

Holmfirth was for a time, at the turn of the 20th century, a pioneering centre of the film industry which morphed into another unique industry – comic postcards. Between 1911 and 1990 Bamforth's became the world's largest producers of saucy postcards to delighted, and perhaps maybe mildly shocked, visitors as a part of every traditional British seaside experience.

Holmfirth has another claim to fame – being the town which featured in the world's longest running television situation comedy. **Last of the Summer Wine**, written by Roy Clarke, who was born in Austerfield near Saddleworth, went through an amazing 31 series between 1973 and 2010, with episodes being exported to 25 different countries. The appeal of the series, filmed in several locations in the South Pennines, was essentially that of a group of characters who in their speech and dry humour were totally Yorkshire. In fact, they were all brilliant actors. Bill Owen who played Compo came from London, as did Peter Sallis, who played Clegg. Sallis also provided the inimitable Yorkshire voice of Wallace in the Wallace and Gromit cartoons. Kathy Staff, better known as Norah Batty came from Cheshire. But the important point is that the series celebrated, internationally, the distinctive landscape and a charming, if at times a nostalgic and slightly sentimentalised aspect of Yorkshire culture on a world stage.

The series totally transformed the fortunes of Holmfirth which became a living film set, with visitors coming in their thousands by coach and car to recognise individual buildings around town. A former shop adapted for film use in the series as Sid's Café actually became a real-life Sid's Café, an example of life imitating art.

Beyond Holmfirth, the road up Holme Valley goes through the little village of Holme then climbs over the steep pass of Holme Moss out of the Holme Valley and into the Peak District, at 1,719 feet or 524 metres above sea level one of the highest roads in the Pennines, and a magnificent viewpoint in fine weather. The radio transmitter at Holme Moss is the highest transmitter in England.

Upper Calderdale

The very best place to begin to understand what the Yorkshire part of the South Pennines is all really about is Upper Calderdale, that narrow, steeply sided, twisting valley between the open moors, carved by ice and glacial meltwaters. Towns such as Sowerby Bridge, Mytholmroyd, Hebden Bridge, share the narrow valley floor between the River Calder, the Rochdale Canal, and the railway line which divides at Todmorden from Halifax to both Burnley and Manchester.

The Rochdale Canal, dating from 1804, is another wonder of the canal age – its complex engineering requirement including sourcing of water supplies for its locks from several different moorland becks and reservoirs. All required skilled engineering and impacted on the landscape. Its 32 miles length led from Sowerby Bridge, at the canal basin and interchange with the Calder-Hebble Navigation through the heart of the Pennines and industrial England, linking Halifax with Hebden Bridge, Todmorden, Littleborough, Rochdale and Manchester. For a period until the opening of the Lancashire & Yorkshire Railway in 1840 this was a commercially successful waterway, providing a stimulus for economic development on both sides of the Pennines. Sowerby Bridge for example became a centre of heavy engineering as well as textiles, especially for heavy duty woollen blankets, serviced as it was by both canal and railway.

After its closure in 1952 and years of decay and dereliction, it was rescued by a whole variety of different environmental, job creation and economic recovery programmes, including studies that foresaw the

Canal as a major engine of economic recovery for the Calder Valley. The reopening duly took place in 2002, and the canal is now a major visitor and leisure attraction in its own right, managed and promoted by the Canal & Waterways Trust as part of the South Pennine Ring of Canals.

Sowerby Bridge also lies at the confluence of the River Calder and the River Rye, the latter forming another narrow, well wooded cul-de-sac valley dominated by the small town of Ripponden and ending at another steep moorland pass that crosses the open moorland summits to Rochdale and Oldham.

Among unspoiled side valleys, that have retained their typical South Pennines character are Luddenden, including the pretty woodland of Luddenden Dean, and, south of Mytholmroyd, the steep, and densely wooded valley of Cragg Vale.

Calderdale has in recent years attracted numerous film makers and writers, none more successful than multi-Award-winning Huddersfield dramatist Sally Wainwright whose dark thriller **Happy Valley** and more whimsical **Last Tango in Halifax** use both the inspiring and more threatening sides of Calderdale landscapes. Her recent hit **Gentleman Jack** based on the life story of Anne Lister (1791–1840) celebrated diarist and feminist of Shibden Hall, uses both **Shibden Hall** and local landscapes as an essential and powerful aspect of this historical drama. There is even a Gentleman Jack walking trail from the Hall now available through typical South Pennines landscapes.

Mytholmroyd has a small but important place in literary history, being the birthplace of one of Yorkshire and England's greatest poets, Ted Hughes (1930–1998). Few writers have ever captured the Pennine landscape better than Hughes. His poetry reflects the raw power and even violence of the Pennine landscape, its natural world and its wild creatures. A deep sense of belonging to Yorkshire runs through much of Hughes' greatest verse. One of his famous poems, **Six Young Men** was inspired by a photograph of six local boys all killed in the First World War, a few months after the photograph was taken. A small memorial plaque at a waterfall and pool in Crimsworth Dean recalls a place where the six often came – and that Hughes knew well. His collection of poems **Remains of Elmet**, published in 1979[6] in partnership with photographer Fay Weldon, is deeply inspired by the history and landscape of Calderdale.

Todmorden at the far end of the valley in a curious way blends both Lancashire and Yorkshire. For many years its Town Hall actually lay across the West Riding-Lancashire boundary. Not only will you hear a Lancashire burr in local speech but some of the best black puddings, a Lancashire delicacy, to be had anywhere can be bought on Todmorden market. Like its neighbour Hebden Bridge, Todmorden is a town also proud of its Pennine heritage and also deeply engaged with ideas of conservation and social and economic regeneration. Even its railway station car park and station platform boast the Incredible Edible herb garden, where people are invited to pick health-giving herbs.

Todmorden has something of the atmosphere of a town in a deep mountain pass. The crossroads in the town centre offer routes northwards to Burnley or south to Rochdale; the former though Cliviger Gorge, the latter over Summit pass by road, or by rail through the Summit tunnel to Littleborough.

The great 121-foot-high stone obelisk of Stoodley Pike, originally erected in 1814 to commemorate the Battle of Waterloo, but rebuilt several times after lighting strikes and other incidents, looks down from the summit of the moors above the town, as it does much of Upper Calderdale. The 250-mile Pennine Way, passes the Pike on its journey from the Peak District to Scotland, crossing the South Pennines, through the Bronte Country and Airedale, to Malham and Ribblesdale.

Hebden Bridge, with its almost perfectly preserved Lancashire & Yorkshire Railway Station, Rochdale Canal wharves, restored cinema and community-owned Town Hall, is perhaps the town in the South Pennines that most sharply reflects the forces of change now affecting the whole of the UK, not just Yorkshire.

Space is so tight in this part of the valley, that many of the terraced houses of Hebden Bridge are built one on top of the other, with separate street entrance at different levels. Steep roads zigzag from the valley floor to reach hill villages such as Old Town and Heptonstall high above the valley floor. Narrow paved tracks and stone steps twist up the thickly wooded hillsides, which are penetrated by steep gills, many containing the remains of now secret ruined mills with their complex ponds and water courses.

Just a short way up the tributary valley of the little River Hebden, beyond the end of the cul-de-sac lane where the valley splits into the upper

Hebden Valley and Crimsworth Dean, is **Hardcastle Crags**, one of the most stunningly beautiful places in Yorkshire, now owned and managed by the National Trust. In 1969 the upper part of the Hebden valley was only narrowly saved from flooding for a huge new reservoir. A 200-foot-high concrete dam would have been constructed, overshadowing the famous Crags. Mercifully the scheme was defeated but only after vigorous protest.

The steep and wooded hillsides and gills radiating from both Hebden and Crimsworth valleys are a paradise for naturalist, photographer and walker. Halfway up the valley is **Gibson Mill** still with its great mill pond, and chimney from steam days. It closed in the 1890s. But by then Hardcastle Crags was already a popular visitor destination, within an easy walk of Hebden Bridge Railway Station served by frequent trains from Manchester, Rochdale, Halifax, Bradford and Leeds. Gibson Mill was transformed into an "entertainment emporium" with the old weaving shed converted to a dance hall and roller skating rink, with a popular café, and boats on the mill pond. After this enterprise closed in the 1950s, it was acquired by the National Trust, who now own and manage much of the valley. It has now become a heritage centre and café, the whole enterprise linked to the theme of sustainability and conservation. The 1926 water turbines that replaced the original waterwheel have been restored. The energy requirements of the whole complex are provided by the turbines, supplemented by solar panels. Local spring water is used for all purposes and composting toilets provide useful fertiliser rather than a wet sewage disposal problem.

Heptonstall, on the end of a ridge high above the Hebden and Colden valleys, is perhaps the most spectacular of all the hill villages of the Pennines, a collection of weavers' cottages and large houses dating back to the 16th century. There is also a pioneering 18th century Methodist Chapel, a small Piece Hall, an old grammar school, two inns and a ruined medieval church – the latter abandoned when the larger Victorian church was built.

The village is also one of several in both Lancashire and Yorkshire to celebrate Pace Egging – and Pace Eggs Plays. These are a kind of secular miracle play, performed around Easter by Pace Eggers in lurid costumes, acting out mock combats, and accompanied by folk songs, in anticipation of gifts of decorated eggs and maybe the odd tankard of ale, from grateful villagers and by-standers.

Heptonstall has also become something of a cult place for people with alternative views and lifestyle, a trend perhaps accelerated by the churchyard containing the grave of the young American poet Sylvia Plath (1932–1963) whose poems, short stories and novels have transformed her into an icon of feminist thinking. She was married to poet Ted Hughes. Some people believe that the at times difficult relationship between the two highly gifted individuals, so poignantly recorded in Hughes's sequence of poems **Birthday Letters** (1998), may have contributed to her untimely death.

The Pennine Heritage Story – and Pennine Prospects

Hebden Bridge, in the heart of Calderdale where several of these small tributary valleys meet, is also the epicentre of much that has happened and is happening in the South Pennines.

By the mid–1960s Calderdale and Yorkshire's textile industry was in terminal decline. Outside certain high-quality producers of worsted yarns and fine woollen cloth for suits, mainly concentrated in the Huddersfield area, all the great mills of the Pennines were closing. They were either seeking new tenants for light industry, warehousing or were being converted for residential use or being demolished. Hebden Bridge was a place of falling property prices and decay.

But thanks to a few remarkable individuals, by the early 1970s things were about to change. It was one individual, a young polytechnic lecturer named David Fletcher who in the 1960s was the catalyst. A keen walker, in the late 1960s he published a book of beautifully drawn local walks **Pennine Walks around Hebden Bridge** in conjunction with his local Civic Society. This helped raise the profile of the town as a great place to visit, work from and indeed live, within easy access as it was of Manchester where David lectured, but also the cities of West Yorkshire. In 1973 David and his wife even showed their commitment to the town by buying a small derelict mill, Bridge Mill in the centre of town, to develop it into a small boutique shop to cater for the new generation of visitors now coming to the town.

Over the next few years David, with a lecturer colleague David Ellis, and a third David, a local accountant, the late David Shutt (who

later became the liberal peer Lord Shutt), established what they called
Pennine Heritage as a charity.

One of the earliest campaigns of the new body was to prevent
the demolition by securing the listing of one of the town's finest old
mills, Nutclough Mill. This mill, dating from the late 18th century, but
much rebuilt, was taken over in 1873 by the Hebden Bridge Fustian
Manufacturing Society, one of the world's first producer-co-operatives
largely supplying Co-operative shops over the whole of the UK, via
the Cooperative Wholesale Society (CWS), with fine quality fustian
cloths, hard-wearing twill cloth often used for corduroy manufacture.
It was one of the last of Hebden Bridge's textile mills to close in
1967. The building now houses the audio electronics company Calrec
Audio, which is a very appropriate reuse of the historic building for 21st
communications technology.

When, in 1979, a former local Baptist Chapel on the hillside, Birchcliffe
Chapel, became redundant, Pennine Heritage raised sufficient cash
locally to buy the fine old building. From 1979 this became the
headquarters of the new charity. Over the next 40 years the charity has
become a major centre for the interpretation and safeguarding of the
heritage of the South Pennine area, but more importantly a mechanism
for raising awareness of the special identity of this part of Yorkshire in
terms of its geology, natural history and local history. Birchcliffe Centre
is used for lectures, seminars, workshops, producing a range of profes-
sionally researched publications, printed and in electronic format. Most
recently Pennine Heritage have created the **Pennine History Digital
Archive** containing thousands of documents and images detailing
many aspects of the area's rich cultural heritage.

Pennine Heritage also helped create the locally-authority led **Pennine
Prospects**, whose full title is the Southern Pennines Rural Regeneration
Company. In effect this is a cross-boundary quango supported by all
local authorities over a wide area, plus the water companies, the National
Trust and Northern Rail and other agencies. Its prime purpose is to
"promote, protect, and enhance the built natural and cultural heritage"
of the area, and these objects are delivered through a small professional,
team, under the chairmanship of Pam Warhurst, a leading local conservationist from Todmorden. Crucially Pennine Prospects works across
local authority boundaries and jurisdictions and also draws funding

from a wide variety of Government and non-Governmental sources, such as the Heritage Lottery, to fund major projects. An example is the **Watershed Landscape** project, an award winning multi-dimensional educational project that ran between 2010 and 2013. Work with local communities and schools helped raise awareness of the special qualities of the local environments and encouraged engagement and enjoyment of the area's special qualities management.

South Pennines Regional Park

One key early aim of Pennine Heritage was to get the South Pennines designated as a National Park or, pointing to the North Pennines, at least an Area of Outstanding Natural Beauty.

The trouble is that the South Pennines do not easily fit into those categories which are essentially for wild, unspoiled landscapes, not the heavily populated, heavily industrialised South Pennines which have, in some areas, suffered massive degradation from air and water pollution from which it will take decades to recover. Equally supporters of the South Pennines have pointed to the fact that renaturing and recovery can happen with quite amazing speed. Ever since the terrible polluting industries which poisoned the air, the land and the streams and rivers of the South Pennines have largely ceased, recovery of much that natural beauty has been taking place. It is now the joint mission of bodies like Pennine Heritage and Pennine Prospects to accelerate that process. This can best be achieved they believe at grass roots level, which is why creating understanding, awareness, and pride in local environments throughout the region is so important. This will ultimately translate into the kind of Government, local authority, private sector, and voluntary action needed to transform not only the South Pennines but the whole region.

The current suggested name for this most important cultural sub-region of Yorkshire – but also of Lancashire and Greater Manchester – is a new one, the **South Pennines Regional Park**. "Park" is now used to mean far more than green space but an area of particular activity or interest as in "Business Park". Whilst having no legal status, it is nevertheless a useful way of understanding and uniting a sub-region which in this case crosses local authority and regional boundaries. It includes such fine outliers of the South Pennines as the West Pennine Moors, which as they culturally and geographically belong to Lancashire, are therefore outside the scope of this study, but could most certainly be part a South Pennines Regional Park.

The South Pennines and Climate Change

But just as Calderdale more than anywhere else has been the focal point for the social and economic renaissance of the South Pennines, it is also in the forefront of the impacts of Climate Change. This has taken the form of a series of catastrophic floods over recent years. Since 2000 there have been 20 flooding incidents in Calderdale, varying from the relatively minor to the utterly major, damaging homes, businesses, workplaces, resulting in often appalling damage and loss. Many properties along the valley are now uninsurable.

This also means that the South Pennines, with its steep, winding valleys, many scoured by glacial torrents, processes too easily replicated by the heat-induced global storms of the 21st century, is also an area where resilience is most needed, and is being found.

Actions on the ground includes engineering features for flood defences, strengthening and raising walls on the Calder and tributary streams, making sure that homes and business can better withstand flood waters by for example storing vulnerable equipment and belongings in first floor rooms. Long term however, it requires far better management of the peat moorlands, much of them important water catchment areas, but also including the still extensive areas of heather grouse moors. A huge programme of investment in tree planting to both absorb and mechanisms to store rainwater, in catchment ponds and underground storage reservoirs is required. Vital too are ways of protecting peat against erosion, and above all from burning whether by accidental moorland fires or so-called traditional ways of heather management. The catastrophic fires experienced on Marsden Moor in 2019 and 2021 were an ecological disaster but also increased the likelihood of severe flood damage down the Colne Valley from future storms.

Already much is happening in the South Pennines to give optimism. So-called "leaky dams" of timber and brushwood are being built in the woods along the becks, sykes and runnels to slow down the speed of water of the tributary streams that flow into the Calder. Drainage ditches are being filled on the open moorland. Sphagnum moss is being planted to allow areas of carbon-capturing peat bog to recover. **The Northern Forest** is a major, cross-regional, visionary project to plant 50 million trees across the North, including the whole of the Pennines, to both reduce the impacts of flooding but also as a major mechanism for carbon sequestration.

It is quite likely the South Pennines will be taking a key role in the work of the newly established **Yorkshire Climate Commission** in seeking new techniques and active participation in ways of both adaptation and mitigation of the impacts of climate change in our Region.

In this and in many other ways, what is taking place in the South Pennines is likely to become a blueprint for what needs to happen throughout Yorkshire – and indeed England.

Notes

1 Kellett Arnold 1998: *On Ilka Mooar Baht 'At – The Story of the Song* Smith Settle Ilkley

2 Petyt K.M. 1983 *Emily Bronte and the Haworth Dialect* Yorkshire Dialect Society Brighouse

3 Hughes Glyn 1975: *Millstone Grit* Gollanz London

4 Goddard Christopher 2021: *The West Yorkshire Woodlands Part II The Aire Valley* pp xvi – xxxvii Gritstone Hebden Bridge

5 Lonsdale Tom & Armitage Simon 2012 *Stanza Stones Poetry Trail Guide* Ilkley Literature Festival Ilkley

6 Hughes Ted & Weldon Fay 1979 *Remains of Elmet* Faber London

West Yorkshire: Wakefield, Kirklees, Bradford and Calderdale

In the local Government changes of 1974, the heavily industrialised central parts of the former West Riding, the fourth most densely populated urban area of the United Kingdom, was designated as the Metropolitan County of West Yorkshire.

But a decade later once it was clear that West Yorkshire and other Metropolitan Authorities were not merely there to rubber-stamp Westminster's wishes, they were all abolished and under the familiar Westminster "divide and rule" principle. West Yorkshire was divided into the five Metropolitan Boroughs, Leeds, in population terms by far the largest, Bradford, Wakefield, Kirklees (essentially Huddersfield and Dewsbury) and Calderdale (greater Halifax).

A new unity

A great strength, but also weakness of West Yorkshire, compared with say Greater Manchester, is the vitality and sense of independence not only of the main cities of Leeds and Bradford – between which there are long and ancient rivalries – but also of the smaller towns and centres of population. This has made working together to create a single united voice for West Yorkshire, let alone the wider Region of Yorkshire, at times difficult and even fractious. Greater Manchester, with no major rival satellite towns, has been able to attract far greater central Government support. Its outspoken Mayor, Andy Burnham, has earned the title of "King of the North", Manchester too often being assumed to be only city of consequence in The North.

So far, various attempts to achieve regional coordination on strategic planning and transport issues, including the setting up of a West Yorkshire Combined Authority, have produced meagre results. The closure of even the residual Government Office for Yorkshire & Humber Region in 2012 has added to a growing sense of injustice. This has impacted even on Leeds, the most economically successful of Yorkshire's cities missing out on basic investment, most notably in public transport. Leeds is now the largest conurbation in western Europe without a modern mass transit system, leaving the city suffering from severe problems of traffic congestion and poor air quality.

However, things have changed dramatically since the election in 2021 of the West Yorkshire Mayor. This means that the former Metropolitan County of West Yorkshire, with a total population of 2.3 million, now has for the first time since 1986, a single, democratically elected leader. There is every hope this will result in this crucial part of Yorkshire having a stronger regional and national voice, especially as seems likely, a strong partnership can also be developed between the two most heavily populated, and economically strong parts of Yorkshire, West and South Yorkshire, which already has its own elected Mayor. Hopefully similar strong, mutually supportive relationships will be eventually developed between the West and South Yorkshire Metro Mayors and their colleagues in rural North Yorkshire and East Yorkshire including their two component cities of York and Hull, as and when these two equally important parts of Yorkshire are able to elect their own Mayors, hopefully in 2023.

In this chapter, therefore, I want to examine some of the key common factors that created the great but distinctive cultural landscapes of these two parts of the old largely industrial West Riding, before looking in greater detail at some of the specific contributions to West Yorkshire made by the historic towns of Wakefield, Halifax, Huddersfield and Bradford. I have allowed coverage of the great Metropolitan city of Leeds however to be dealt with in a separate chapter, before a final chapter on the very different cultural landscapes of South Yorkshire, including the great city of Sheffield.

The growth of industrial West Riding

So why has West Yorkshire, together with its sister, the former Metropolitan County of South Yorkshire, grown so much in population over the last two centuries, with a current combined total of 3.6 million, and also in industrial and economic might, compared with other parts of Yorkshire?

The answer is threefold. First was communications and trade. The larger towns and cities of West and South Yorkshire were first established at the highest points of their respective rivers where a decent sized cargo boat or barge could penetrate, especially when, in the 17th and 18th centuries, the rivers were deepened, widened and mill dams by-passed by locks and sometimes new "cuts" or canal sections to provide what were known as Navigations.

Leeds was to become dominant through trade. It was the highest point in West Yorkshire on the River Aire, later the Aire & Calder Navigation, which could be accessed by sea-going boats or large barges. The other major towns also did so but not on the same scale – Wakefield on the Calder, Halifax on the Calder-Hebble Navigation. Bradford only enjoyed massive economic growth when the Bradford Canal, a branch of the Leeds Liverpool Canal reached the city centre in 1774, likewise Huddersfield when the Broad Canal was opened in 1776. The railways – often constructed parallel to the canals – only continued the process that the canals had begun.

The second major factor, which has only recently become more evident and honestly acknowledged, was the impact of the Slave trade. Britain benefited enormously in the 17th, 18th and early 19th centuries from the so-called "slave triangle" of slaves transported in British ships from West Africa to the Caribbean, the sugar from British-owned sugar plantations in the Caribbean back to the UK and finally manufactured goods, including textiles, brought from Britain to Africa to pay for the slaves.

When this obnoxious traffic in human lives was finally ended in the 1830s, it was at a price of massive financial compensation to slave owners to end the trade. The Government borrowed £20 million, the equivalent of several billions at today's values. This is turn released a huge amount of capital for middle and upper class people and institutions to re-invest in the rapidly booming industrial expansion of Northern cities, including the railways, mines, factories and mills of Yorkshire.

As many historians have also pointed out[1], the Empire itself, even after slavery was formally abolished, was based on a system of exploitation of cheap labour and captive markets. Textiles from Bradford, railway locomotives and traction engines from Leeds, steel products and cutlery and tools from Sheffield, sold to the closed markets of the colonies, produced the income to create the wealth and power that made the United Kingdom the world's first great industrial superpower.

The third factor was black gold – coal – an immense source of cheap and abundant energy was locally available in West and South Yorkshire to power the mills, factories, forges, railways and heat homes.

In Yorkshire the Lower Coal Measures of the Carboniferous era were relatively easy to access in the Bradford area and in the lower Aire valley south of Leeds. Further south around Wakefield, Barnsley and even as far east as Selby, the Middle Coal Measures were deeper and harder to access, but of higher quality and more abundant. The development of geological science and ever more sophisticated deep mining engineering in the 19th and 20th centuries enabled these riches to be exploited.

There was a heavy social and human price to be paid for the wealth so generated. Coal smoke led to appalling air and soil pollution, with towns and cities literally blackened from the soot and smoke of domestic, mill and steam locomotive chimneys. This pollution on a huge scale resulted in killer winter smogs. These continued right until the late 1950s and the impact of the passing of the Clean Air Act in 1956. This pollution contributed massively to chronic lung disease, illness and premature death in the crowded towns and cities of the West Riding, adding to the impacts of poor housing and lack of effective sewage and clean water systems. This resulted in diseases such as cholera, typhoid and tuberculosis spreading on an epic scale. As always, it was the poorer people who paid the price, the wealthier moving out of the industrialised valleys to higher, greener suburbs served by the new suburban railways and tram systems, where air was fresher and water purer.

Coal is also one of the principal fossil fuels that with oil, has contributed to the process of rapid global heating which will, over the next century, be a major threat to human survival.

But after the First World War, itself a result of intense industrial-imperial rivalry between the great European nations, Britain never regained its lost industrial supremacy. The twentieth century was a period of long, slow decline, accelerated by the two World Wars, which have left their marks on the landscape and turned many of the symbols of former industrial might into sites of nostalgic industrial and social heritage.

This process of change has had a profound impact on the landscape in an area such as West Yorkshire.

The majority of the countryside of West Yorkshire reflects what is best described by that ugly but accurate term "peri-urban", where the landscape outside the town and city centres is dominated not so much by the few surviving "heritage" mill chimneys or mill buildings, but by sprawling estates, warehouses, retail and business parks surrounded by huge car and lorry parking lots. Motorways, slip roads, and by passes also take up much precious land and space.

But not entirely. What makes the difference in West Yorkshire are the precious areas of Green Belt which even if increasingly threatened by various developers, supported by successive slavishly pro-development national Governments, and weakened local planning authorities, provide green space between the conurbations. Often these contain precious networks of footpaths and bridleways, some of great antiquity, and pockets of ancient amenity woodland. Public parks, some of them extensive also provide the towns and cities of West Yorkshire with extensive green lungs. Many of these were provided by far-seeing social reformers of the second part of the 19th century, concerned to improve the health and mental well-being of the urban population.

Despite some dreadful civic vandalism in the 1960s (central Bradford was a notorious victim) many of the towns and city centres of West Yorkshire have kept their essentially Victorian hearts. We look at our first four key West Yorkshire towns and cities in turn.

Wakefield

Wakefield, the county town of the old West Riding, is one of the oldest towns in Yorkshire, its origins in an Anglian settlement, perhaps originally known as Wake's field, or maybe a field where a watch or "wake" was held on a low hillock north of an important crossing of the River Calder, where eventually a bridge was built. A wooden motte and bailey castle was constructed in the 12th century by William De Warrenne Earl of Surrey, at Lowe Hill, north of the river, on land in what is now Thornes Park. Because it was not rebuilt in stone, nothing of this original Wakefield Castle survives. However, the De Warrennes, the powerful Norman barons who controlled the huge medieval manor of Wakefield, also owned and rebuilt Sandal Castle, a mile south of the city, as their local family seat and military base. This is a fine example of what was originally a Norman wooden motte and bailey castle converted to stone in the 14th century.

In the 13th century the town was granted rights by William de Warrenne, for a weekly market and by King John and King Henry III for the two annual fairs in the 13th century, whose accompanying sporting and other activities held on fair days reputedly gave the town its medieval name of Merry Wakefield. The little wooden Anglo-Saxon church built on the hillock above the river was rebuilt in stone several times over the ensuing centuries, most notably in the 15th when an elegant spire was added, and again in the 19th when the present fine building and its landmark tall spire, the highest in West Yorkshire, was restored by Sir George Gilbert Scott between 1858 and 1874, prior to it becoming Wakefield Cathedral, at the same time city status was given to Wakefield in 1888.

The three medieval streets of old Wakefield, Westgate, Kirkgate (after which the town's two stations are named) and Northgate, and the streets and alleyways between them, formed the core of the old town. On the old Chantry Bridge over the Calder, now dominated by the traffic-pounded concrete bridge carrying the A638 close by, is one of only four chantry bridges surviving in England, built in 1350 in elaborate Gothic style, but heavily restored in later years.

The Wakefield area also saw a good deal of action in the Wars of the Roses with the Battle of Wakefield taking place in 1460 near Sandal Castle, where Richard Duke of York was killed. The Castle was a Royalist stronghold in the Civil War, captured and destroyed by the Parliamentarians led by the Yorkshire general Sir Thomas Fairfax, in 1643.

Wakefield flourished from Tudor times onwards as an important inland port with access to the Humber and the sea which was greatly improved by the Aire & Calder Navigation, completed in the early 18th century. Large quantities of grain, especially from the surrounding countryside, were exported by barge from the little port, as large surviving grain storage warehouses by the old city wharves on the river still testify. But equally important was also coal from the huge numbers of mines opened in the area, as well as leather from the local tanneries and locally produced wool textiles. So important was this trade in the 18th century that it rivalled Leeds. The city had its own Cloth Hall for trading in textiles, and a huge local cattle market. During the coaching era it also became a significant service centre on routes to Leeds, Manchester, Sheffield and London.

This prosperity was reflected in the growth of the northern part of the town in Georgian and Regency times, with elegant terraces and villas and the handsome St. John's Church. The railway arrived in 1840. The first Leeds-Manchester line along the Calder valley served the town from the now beautifully restored neo-classical Kirkgate Station. But in the latter half of the 19th and well into the late 20th century, coal mining became the town's prime industry. In terms of employment, this was overtaken in importance by local Government administration by the middle of the 20th century as the huge County Hall, serving the whole of the West Riding, was established together with County law courts, after West Riding became a County Council in 1889, taking Wakefield as its headquarters.

Despite some unsightly development from the 1960s onwards, Wakefield has retained something of its charm in its compact city centre, with attractive pedestrian areas around the cathedral and central streets. The area around Westgate station, the city's main railway station, totally rebuilt in 2013 to replace 1960s brutalism, has enjoyed a major revival with galleries, cafes, theatre and the city's museum and library with an alternative café now occupying a fine new building known as One Wakefield and developing as a focus for the city's cultural life.

Wakefield enjoyed a brief period in the national literary limelight as one of the hotbeds of the 1960s New Wave of northern writing and film making, associated with what were initially labelled the Angry Young Men of post-war England. These were writers, many of them from working class backgrounds, producing work that challenged conventional middle-class values and attitudes.

Stan Barstow (1928–2011) born in Horbury near Wakefield. With **A Kind of Loving** (1960) with its anti-hero Vic Brown, Barstow achieved national fame through John Schlesinger's powerful 1962 film, albeit with the original location changed to Manchester. A Kind of Loving was the first of a successful trilogy, but Barstow was also a gifted writer of short stories and his collection **Desperadoes** (1961) is a modern classic, as is his sensitive novel of childhood at the start of World War Two **Joby** (1964).

In 1960, Wakefield author David Storey (1933–2017) also scored a major hit with **This Sporting Life**, a powerful and earthy novel loosely based on Wakefield Trinity Rugby League team (Storey was himself a former Rugby League player) and the declining fortunes of fictional team star Frank Machin. In 1963 this also became a highly successful film directed by Lindsey Anderson. David Storey went on to write several other acclaimed plays, screenplays and additional novels including **Saville** that won the Booker Prize in 1976.

The City and Metropolitan Borough of Wakefield includes the towns of Castleford, Pontefract and Ossett, and several former mining villages extending towards the boundary with South Yorkshire. Among particularly interesting green spaces is **Heath Common** a lovely expanse of open common land close to the village of Heath, and **Thorpe Park** close to the city centre,

Newmillerdam close to the city is a popular country park noted for its wildlife, but also of exceptional interest is **Nostell** about 5 miles south west of Wakefield, a fine 18th century neo-Palladian country house in extensive grounds, described by the National Trust who manage the estate as "one of the great treasure houses of Northern England", with interior designs by Robert Adam, furniture designed by Otley born Thomas Chippendale (1718–79), as well as a rare Georgian doll's house and a clock by the great clockmaker John Harrison. Harrison (1693–1776) was born in the village of Foulby, near Nostell, where his father was a carpenter on the estate. John followed his father's trade but went on to be a remarkable clockmaker. During the 1730s and 40s, he developed several versions of marine chronometers and sea watches, inventions that were to revolutionise navigation throughout the world. His statue stands in Leeds City Square.

Pontefract

Pontefract is another town with a seminal role in English history, and one with an intriguing name – Norman French for broken bridge. There are various theories about how the little market town got its name, as there is no bridge nor river crossing in the town. There were originally two Anglo-Viking villages, Tanshelf and Kirkby on what was the original paved Roman Road between Doncaster and Castleford. The Castle was probably given its name by the powerful De Lacy Family, who had control of the huge Honour of Pontefract, as it was close to a more recognised crossing of the River Aire, probably near Ferrybridge where indeed a bridge eventually replaced a historic ferry. This bridge might have been destroyed in 1069, according to one story, by Anglo-Viking fighters trying to defend their Kingdom and city of Jorvik against William's army as it marched north to destroy York during the Harrying of the North and retained the name ever since.

More certain is the story of the still impressive ruins of the castle that still dominate the town. Pontefract Castle was the stronghold of various barons and Kings during the Wars of the Roses, the most famous prisoner there being King Richard II who according to various sources was murdered either by starvation or as recorded by Shakespeare by the sword in its dungeons.

The Castle also had a major role in the English Civil War as a Royalist stronghold, before being finally demolished by General Lambert in 1659 to ensure it never troubled Parliament again.

Pontefract, or Pomfret as it was known in Tudor times, continued to flourish as a market town but discovered another useful skill – sweet making. It is said that liquorice was first brought back to England from the Middle East during Crusades in the 12th century, but more likely it was Dominican monks who later brought and cultivated the plant in Yorkshire. It was soon successfully grown in Pontefract with great success. Many household names such as Dunhills, Barrets and Wilkinsons were established in the town by the 1930s, producing the celebrated Pontefract Cake with the castle as its emblem. After various takeovers, the German company Haribo is now based in the town, where it continues to make the famous Pontefract cakes, as well as many other popular sweets in the town, as does the Bon Bons company.

Local commercial liquorice growing disappeared from the area in the 1970s, with just a few struggling plants left in local parks and gardens. However there has been a recent important local revival. **Farmer Copley's**, a local independent family-owned, award winning farm, food production company, events venue, shop and café, based between Featherstone and Pontefract, is once again growing Yorkshire liquorice on a small scale. The farm also acts as an important retail outlet for locally produced, high quality liquorice sweets and drinks (based on an amazing variety of recipes including liquorice flavoured gin and beer) as well as a wide variety of locally based, Yorkshire grown organic farm produce.

Pontefract retains its pattern of medieval streets, many with their original names, even if less than sympathetic modern development has changed the character of the town. The town also lays claim to having the oldest flat racing racecourse in continuous use in Europe, since the 1720s.

Castleford, on the River Aire, on the site of a Roman army settlement long vanished under urban development, has a quite different cultural significance as being the birthplace of the great English sculptor Henry Moore (1898–1986). Born into an impoverished coal mining family, as an alternative to going down the pit, Henry managed to get a place at his local Grammar School, where his talents were recognised. World War I intervened, in which he served and was injured. After the Armistice, Moore trained at Leeds School of Art where rebelling against classic traditions, he developed his interest in primitive and abstract art. Combining a teaching role in London with his work as a sculptor, he soon became one of the best-known sculptors in Britain. By the 1950s he was internationally recognised. His massive semi-abstract figures in marble and bronze have become instantly recognisable in squares and precincts in many world capitals. He was also a skilled artist in other media. His drawings of Londoners sleeping in the underground during the blitz have become part of the iconography of World War II.

Two triangles

A fellow student at Leeds School of Art, now Leeds Art University, was Barbara Hepworth (1903–1975), born in Wakefield who though a very different artistic personality, also became a world figure through her own amazing abstract sculptures in a variety of materials, the use of pierced forms being her signature technique. The award-winning Hepworth Gallery, a stunning building on the banks of the River Calder, houses several of her most impressive works and drawings, and a recreation of her studio, in addition to the permanent collection of the work of local and contemporary artists as well as changing exhibitions.

The personal friendship and rivalry between England's two greatest sculptors of the 20th century have been brought together in what is now known as the **Yorkshire Sculpture Triangle** – the **Henry Moore Gallery** in Leeds, **The Hepworth Gallery** in Wakefield and the great **Yorkshire Sculpture Park** in West Bretton, in the magnificent, landscaped park setting of Bretton Hall. As well as the largest collection in Europe of sculpture by Moore, and several monumental works by Hepworth, the Galleries and Park host work of internationally known sculptors in constantly changing indoor and outdoor exhibitions and displays.

Wakefield also enjoys a very different kind of Triangle which is also an intriguing footnote in horticultural history. The city lies at the apex of what is known as the Rhubarb Triangle, which flourishes in the semi-urban farmland between Wakefield and the towns of Morley and Rothwell. Rhubarb, technically a vegetable but treated like a fruit, is frequently grown in long, windowless heated sheds, using artificial heat and light to force the strong, pink-red long shoots to grow rapidly. Long considered a Yorkshire speciality, requiring skill to cultivate, it was for a time used as a secret ingredient for improving the taste of champagne, and trainloads of rhubarb once left Wakefield to take the night crossing to France at the appropriate season. Rhubarb is now enjoying a remarkable revival as a tasty delicacy, even being used to flavour gin, and once abandoned rhubarb sheds and fields are being restored to meet new demands resulting from changing taste.

Halifax

Halifax, like Wakefield has a history as old as Yorkshire. It was a thriving town and commercial centre when Leeds and Bradford were still modest villages. Situated on the River Hebble, a navigable tributary of the Calder, within the foothills of the surrounding Pennines, it was well known as a market town and centre of local clothing manufacture from the 13th century. Its Parish Church, now **Halifax Minster**, was dedicated to St John, the patron saint of weavers, dates from this period, though most of the building, including the great tower, dates from the 15th century and is in Perpendicular style. But its grandeur, on the scale of a cathedral, reflected the importance and wealth of the town at this period. As well as fine wooden ceilings from the 17th century and Georgian memorials, an unusual feature is a wooden life-sized effigy of Old Tristram, a local beggar, a familiar figure seen standing outside the church in the late 17th century. For many years his effigy acted as the town's poor box, collecting alms for the needy.

The most breathtakingly and impressive building in Halifax, however, is the magnificent **Piece Hall**, built in 1775 in classical style, with its grand, two storey colonnades, surrounding a huge piazza. This is where hand loom weavers from the Pennine villages surrounding Halifax brought their rolls or "Pieces" of finished cloth produced on their handlooms for sale to local merchants. A Piece was defined as a 30-yard length of woven woollen fabric.

As handloom weaving declined, the building found other roles, most notably as a wholesale market, but into the 20th century suffered decades of neglect. It has now received the accolade of Grade I listing for its historic and architectural importance, the last surviving building of its kind in the UK. In recent years it has enjoyed a triumphant revival as a major regional centre for cultural events, heritage and the arts.

The two great industries that sustained Halifax through much of the 20th century, carpet making, and confectionary manufacture have now declined to virtual extinction with the closure of the huge Mackintosh and Crossley's Carpet factories near the town centre. Another change has been the Halifax Building Society. First established in the town in 1853 it soon became a byword for Yorkshire thrift, honesty and reliability, Britain's largest mutually owned building society and leading mortgage provider. In 1997 it was "demutualised" and became a bank and was subsequently taken over by Bank of Scotland plc., though the name Halifax lingers on as a bank and familiar credit card logo.

But Halifax, the town, has redefined itself in different ways. The town centre has been revived and pedestrianised, its lovely indoor market with its iconic clock restored. Several older buildings and inns survive, as does the remarkable Magnia Via paved medieval way that leads out of the town to the summit of Beacon Hill above the town, site of the town's ancient lookout beacon. The fine town hall designed by Sir Charles Barry, of Houses of Parliament fame, remains a high Victorian showpiece. A short distance out of town is Wainhouse Tower, a richly decorated 253 feet (77 metre) high former chimney that once served Wainhouse's dye works, is now a local landmark. The superbly named **People's Park** is a Victorian formal garden, laid out by Joseph Paxton, designer of London's Crystal Palace.

Shibden Hall, in the Shibden Valley, close to the town centre, and former home of the remarkable Anne Lister, is a beautiful half timbered 17th house and the town's principle museum with collections that include historic carriages and restored craft workshops. It is also Halifax's largest park, with gardens, woodland walks and a boating lake.

Impressive in a different way is **Dean Clough**, the gigantic former Crossley carpet factory complex that dominates the northern side of the town. Occupying a massive 116,000 square metres of indoor space, it now houses around 150 large and small enterprises and hi-tech companies, the **Crossley Art Gallery** and smaller commercial galleries, the remarkable Yorkshire-proud **Broadside Theatre Company**, Phoenix Radio and much more besides. Described as one of Britain's most remarkable urban regeneration schemes, Dean Clough has brought new energy and life into Halifax, economic and social revival which spreads not only into the rest of the town, but into the towns and villages of the adjacent South Pennines, a fascinating example of culture-led economic revival.

Dewsbury

The adjacent Metropolitan Borough of Kirklees takes its name from the relatively obscure 12th century Cistercian Abbey of Kirklees, of which only part of a gatehouse survives, and even that on private land. The choice of the name of the Abbey was perhaps to avoid a spat between the two most likely contenders – Dewsbury and Huddersfield.

Legend has it that the Christian missionary St Paulinus preached in a settlement above the River Calder that is now Dewsbury, in that crucial year of Anglo-Saxon conversion to Christianity, 627AD. The site of his first preaching cross is where the present Dewsbury Minster now stands. Dewsbury became the centre of a huge ecclesiastic parish which extended across the Pennines as far as the Lancashire border. The Minster itself dates back to the 13th century, with fragments of an earlier Anglo-Saxon church embedded in its stonework. The present building, which has a fine 18th century tower designed by John Carr of York, was heavily restored in the 1880s. It houses "Black Tom", a bell rung at Christmas Eve. It is tolled once for each year since the birth of Jesus Christ, a tradition going back to the 15th century and known as the "Devil's Knell". The bell was given to the church by local squire, Sir Thomas de Soothill, allegedly as penance for murdering a servant boy.

The town's popular market, one of the largest in Yorkshire, dates its charter back to 1318.

Growth of the town during the Industrial Revolution was stimulated by the Calder-Hebble Navigation, opened in 1770 linking the town with Leeds and by 1812, with the two Huddersfield canals, through to Huddersfield and Manchester. It became, with Batley, Heckmondwike, Morley and Ossett, and towns along the Spen Valley, the Yorkshire centre of what became known as the Heavy Woollen industry. "Heavy Woollen" is the term used essentially for thick blankets and heavy fabric for items like military uniforms. The other key textile product for which mills in the Dewsbury area developed unique expertise was shoddy – a mixture of new and recycled wool often reclaimed from rags – suitable for a range of hardwearing purposes, and also mungo based on recycling finer, tougher fibres. "Shoddy" rapidly became a word used for poor quality garments, less desirable than those made with new wool, despite the fact that we now regard any form of recycling as highly desirable.

Like Bradford, Dewsbury's textile industry was kept alive in the 1950s and 1960s by successive waves of immigrants from the Indian subcontinent, which has created both opportunities and challenges. The area has suffered a degree of economic decline over recent decades, and despite some success stories such as local biscuit and confectionary manufacturing and light industry, is an urgent candidate for new investment.

Dewsbury has also strong links with the Brontë family. Patrick Brontë was curate at All Saint's Parish Church, now the Minster, between

1809–11 before moving on to Hartshead, Thornhill and finally, in 1821 to Haworth, where he remained the Vicar of the Parish for 40 years. But in later years the Brontë sisters used local settings in several of their novels. This was most notable in Charlotte's 1849 novel **Shirley** set against a background of Luddite Riots in the Spen Valley around 1813. The Red House at Birstall, home of the Taylor family, friends of Charlotte, are immortalised as the Yorke family and their home as Briarmains. Sadly, the Red House is no longer open as a museum.

Huddersfield

Huddersfield contrasts with Dewsbury in being fortunate in having a wider economic base, including a fine new University established in 1992, developed from the success of the former Huddersfield Polytechnic. The University, with its main campus at Queensgate, close to the Huddersfield Broad Canal, also has outstation campuses in Oldham and Barnsley. It has rapidly built up a reputation of excellence, especially in scientific and technical subjects, including biomedical sciences, engineering and physical sciences, but also in the social sciences and arts and humanities. With a total of around 17,000 students, the University is estimated to contribute around £300 million per year to the local economy.

Though Huddersfield like other Pennine towns grew out of the success of the woollen industry, albeit suffering especially badly in the early years of mechanisation because of Luddite Riots, it also diversified at an early stage. This was a process helped by enlightened local landowners, the Ramsden Family, who had the foresight in 1770 to build a just under 4-mile-long canal from Cooper Bridge on the Calder-Hebble Navigation to Apsley basin on the Huddersfield Narrow Canal. Known as the Huddersfield Broad Canal or Sir John Ramsden's Canal, this opened the door to major new industrial development. The Ramsdens also welcomed the railways, with the direct London and North Western Railway line opened in the 1840s, between Manchester and Leeds, through Standedge tunnel serving Huddersfield.

Huddersfield's link with the traditional woollen trade continues into the 21st century with fine worsted cloth manufacture. Some of the finest lengths for Saville Row suits come from top quality Huddersfield manufacturers. But over the last two centuries it has also diversified into tractors, textile and electrical engineering, agro-chemicals, and in more recent years electronics, the town taking advantage of its good rail and M62 motorway links to access either side of the Pennines and the rest of England.

Harold Wilson, (1916–95), Prime Minister between 1964 and 1976 perhaps the most successful Labour politician since Clement Atlee, was born in Huddersfield. Wilson's statue stands proudly in George Square, opposite the magnificent neo-classical entrance to Huddersfield Station.

It is interesting to note that once Wilson became the official Labour Party candidate for Prime Minister in 1964, he took up pipe smoking, dropped his Oxford, but cultivated his childhood Yorkshire accent, to prove he was a man of the people who could be trusted.

Huddersfield has kept its pleasant essentially Victorian town centre with the beautiful restored Byram Arcade and notable Market Hall. The rather grand Italianate Town Hall, built in 1878, has a notable claim to fame in being the home of one of the world's most celebrated choirs – that of the Huddersfield Choral Society, whose annual renderings of Handel's Messiah have passed into classical musical folklore. Nowhere better illustrates the Northern deep love of choral music, which rivals that of Wales, than Huddersfield, though there are several other excellent choral societies in Yorkshire most notably those of Leeds, Sheffield and Bradford, as well as celebrated male voice choirs – Wales has no monopoly – for example the Colne Valley, Honley or Steeton Male Voice Choirs. The town also has a remarkably good **Art Gallery** in Alexandra Walk with work by such British notables as L.S.Lowry, Francis Bacon, Henry Moore as well as work from contemporary artists from the region. The excellent **Tolson Museum** in Ravensknowle Park has many items relevant to the South Pennines as well as Huddersfield, including a rare packhorse saddle. As well as its superb displays of local geology, archaeology and early and industrial history, it is especially notable for its transport gallery with several unusual exhibits of regional and national interest.

Huddersfield also has its elegant Victorian and Edwardian suburbs, where the captains of industry could enjoy their fine gardens on the high land above the towns, whilst their workers at least had the open spaces of **Greenhead Park** and **Beaumont Park** with its fine views of the great Lockwood Viaduct on the Penistone line, for Sunday recreation.

A celebrated viewpoint immediately south of Huddersfield, near the village of Almondbury, is **Castle Hill** a prominent sandstone ridge on which there was a late Bronze Age or early Iron Age hill fort, and later earthworks. For centuries Castle Hill was a popular place for people of Huddersfield to meet, take the air and enjoy the impressive views, with a local tavern (now demolished) to meet their refreshment needs. In 1899 the 106 feet high (32.3 metre) Victoria Tower was completed to celebrate the recent Diamond Jubilee of Queen Victoria, extending the height of the hill to just over 1,000 feet, to create a notable Huddersfield and West Yorkshire landmark.

Bradford

"Pity poor Bradford". These were the words according to legend uttered by a ghostly lady in a dream to the Earl of Newcastle where he slept in **Bolling Hall** on the night of July 3rd, 1643 before his Royalist troops pillaged and ravaged the little town which had supported the Parliamentary cause.

The Parliamentary forces under Fairfax and Cromwell ultimately won, but from time to time Bradford has, over the centuries, suffered undeserved ill-fortune.

This included one of the worst tragedies in British sporting history, when on 11th May 1985, rubbish under an elderly wooden stand at Bradford City's Valley Parade football stadium accidentally caught fire, the flames soon spreading to the roof. The conflagration resulted in the death of 56 spectators, with a further 265 people suffering serious injury.

Bradford made a relatively late entry to the great growth of the Yorkshire wool industry in the medieval period, compared with towns like Beverley, Ripon and Halifax. But it soon became a focal point and market for the scattered villages and hamlets in the Pennine foothills where the traditional Pennine dual economies of subsistence hill farming supplemented by spinning and weaving made a reasonable living possible. By Tudor times, the little town, centering on the three streets of Ivegate, Westgate and Kirkgate above Bradford Beck, became increasingly prosperous, with the yeoman-clothiers building handsome houses built in Bradford and surrounding villages. **Bolling Hall** was bought by William Bolling in 1316. Built in the 15th century it was fortified as a defensive Pele Tower, but over ensuing years was extended into a fine yeoman's mansion. It now houses Bradford's main Museum, even if still reputedly haunted by that mysterious lady who spoke to the Earl of Newcastle.

Bradford continued to grow after the deprivations of the Civil War, though inadequate transport links made it a poor relation of Halifax, Leeds or Wakefield.

But major changes were about to happen, perhaps driven more than anything else by the opening of the Bradford branch of the Leeds-Liverpool Canal in 1774 which, together with the rapid growth of worsted spinning in new steam powered mills released a huge period of economic growth – the population leaping from just 4,506 in 1780 to 52,493 in 1855 and over 100,000 by 1900. This growth was not just in Bradford itself but in outlying villages.

Remarkably even by 1851 there were an estimated 1,117 handloom weavers still producing cloth in the traditional way in Bradford[2]. The last hand loom weaver in the area was reputed to be Timmy Feather, who died in Stanbury near Haworth in 1910 aged 85.

Change when it came was rapid. Soon Bradford was one of the leading centres in the UK of textile dyeing. By 1900 Bowling Dyeworks had become the largest textile piece dyeworks in the world.

The key factor stimulating this huge period of growth and investment was international trade. Exports to the rapidly expanding cities of Germany attracted inwards investment. By the 1840s no less than seven German merchants had moved into the city, building fine warehouses and showrooms over the next few decades in part of the city near the Cathedral still known as "Little Germany", and now an important Conservation Area. These entrepreneurs and their families brought capital, expertise and energy to invest in the city.

One of the families was that of Frederick Delius (1862–1934). Born Fritz Delius, his parents were successful wool merchants from Bielefeld, Westphalia, who saw Yorkshire as offering an ideal location to base their business in the international wool trade. Young Fritz attended Bradford Grammar School, but his love of music encouraged by his cultured family background overtook his willingness to follow a career in the family business. He became one of England's greatest composers, developing his own particular impressionistic, post-romantic style in such masterpieces as **A Village Romeo Juliet** and such popular orchestral works as **Brigg Fair, The Florida Suite, On hearing the first Cuckoo in Spring**. Although very much a European composer, much of his early work was, however, inspired by the landscape of Yorkshire, particularly the Dales. This included such fine works as **North Country Sketches**. In the last years of his life, when he was both blind and partially paralysed, the young Scarborough composer and pianist Eric Fenby worked with Delius in Paris to make possible the composer's last works.

The new steam powered mills erected in the city, suburbs and in outlying villages and towns, brought highly efficient mechanisation replacing manual labour to spin, weave and dye worsted yarns. This transformed the size of the emerging city and its nearby villages at an unprecedented rate. Ample coal supplies from local mines close to the town boosted iron production in areas like Low Moor and Bowling. But wool was to dominate. Thanks to improved communications, Bradford became the major trading centre for woollen and many other textiles for the whole of the West Riding and indeed England.

This industrial and economic success came at huge human cost. The thousands of workers and their families that came in from the surrounding countryside were forced to work long hours for pathetically low wages, even children suffering 12- or 13-hour days being usual. Housing conditions were horrific, families packed into cheaply quickly built slums and courts with poor or non-existent sanitation. Pollution was so bad on the canal that it is recorded that the water was so full of concentrated chemicals it frequently caught fire, and the stench was intolerable. It was even said that on hot days silver coins in the pockets of workers turned black with the acid pollution of the air[3]. During 1848–49 over 400 people in Bradford died of cholera. The Bradford Canal had to be filled in and the Bradford Beck culverted. The Canal was later rebuilt, shorter in length and with better water quality and waste control, but it did not survive long into the railway age.

By the 1840s social reformers were creating awareness of the horrific conditions and major changes that needed to take place and which were implemented during middle years of the century. This included the creation of the Bradford Corporation in 1847 and the Bradford Improvement Act of 1850 to establish a police force and tackle problems such as poor housing and sanitation, including building a desperately needed new sewerage system for the city. Civic pride was emerging. Peel Park and Underhill Cemetery were created. St George's Hall, in Hall Ings, still the city's principal concert hall, was opened in 1852, and the magnificent City Hall inspired by the architectural styles of the Italian city of Florence, in 1873.

Bradford had also become a centre of the banking industry with several banks established in the city from the late 18th century onwards. One of the country's first mutually owned Building Societies, the Bradford Equitable Building Society, was established in 1851.

By this time many industrialists in Bradford were becoming extremely rich. Samuel Cunliffe Lister (1815–1906) typified the entrepreneurial spirit, turning his family's great mill in Manningham into a multi-million-pound business, partly through the invention of the Nip Combe, a device that separated and straightened raw wool and speeded the spinning process. In 1870 he sold Manningham Hall and its grounds to the Corporation of Bradford for half its real price to be developed as a park. When he returned in 1898 and discovered the poor state of the Hall, he repaid the money for the sale to the city to build what is now **Cartwright Hall**, named after Edward Cartwright (1743–1823) whose invention of the powered loom had contributed so much to Bradford's prosperity. It is now the City's magnificent art gallery. A statue of Lister stands at the entrance of what is now **Lister Park**.

An equally impressive benefactor to the city was Titus Salt (1803–76) the extraordinary textile manufacturer who after he inherited his family mill in the centre of Bradford developed alpaca, a fine fabric created from the wool of alpacas brought from South America, as well as mohair from the wool of angora goats. Concerned about the need to expand his business, and the health of his workers in the increasingly polluted air of Bradford, in 1850 Salt moved his entire venture and its workforce out to a greenfield site along the River Aire, the Leeds-Liverpool Canal and new Leeds-Bradford railway. He built a huge new mill but also a carefully planned village for his workers, complete with a fine town hall, unitarian church, school, public park and boat house, but no public house to reduce the risk of alcoholism among the workforce. He named it with suitable lack of modesty Saltaire, and its streets after his children. It is now a World Heritage Site.

By the 1870s Bradford was the recognised leading centre of the worsted industry in England, and the city as it officially became in 1897, was known as Worstedopolis. The price of wool worldwide was fixed in the grand neo-gothic Wool Exchange on Market Street.

Bradford Industrial Museum in the former Moorside Mills, a Victorian worsted mill in Eccleshill, opened in 1875, provides insight into Bradford as it was at the height of its industrial and economic success, with working exhibits demonstrating aspects of the textile, printing and engineering industries, and examples of the tram and trolley buses that once animated the city's streets. Space is given to the famous Jowett cars once made in the city, and also Scott motorbikes. Pride of place is a Scott bike actually owned and ridden by national hero and icon Captain Sir Tom Moore, who was born in Keighley in 1920.

When Moorside Mills were new, new offices and shops were being opened throughout the growing city. Brown Muffs, which began in 1814 as a small draper's shop, by 1870 opened a fine new department store to meet the new demand from middle class shoppers brought into town from outlying suburbs by the railways. The magnificent Alhambra Theatre opened in 1914 to serve a similar market for plays and shows.

William Forster, (1818–86) co-owner of the massive Greenholme textile mill on the River Wharfe at Burley in Wharfedale, which employed around 3,000 workers producing the navy-blue serge cloth used for Britain's police forces, became a leading Liberal MP. His 1870 Education Act brought universal primary education and literacy for all children in the British Isles. Forster Square and Bradford's first railway station are both named after him.

Bradford was also the centre of a new radicalism The Bradford Labour Union which arose out of a five-month strike at Manningham Mill in 1891, became one of the proponents of the new Independent Labour Party which had its inaugural meeting in Bradford in 1893. A year later perhaps the most influential Bradfordian of the 20th century was born in Manningham: John Boynton Priestley (1894–1984) – prolific essayist, novelist, dramatist and broadcaster.

His plays such as **An Inspector Calls** (1945), **When We Are Married**

(1938) and **Eden End** (1933) are still in the repertoire, and of his many novels **Good Companions** (1929) and **Angel Pavement** (1930) are still regarded as modern classics. But his greatest influence was perhaps as a wartime broadcaster when his regular talks on the BBC offered hope and new ideas for a better post-war future. His broadcasts, with that warm Yorkshire accent, became so popular, second only to Churchill, that it was rumoured that Churchill was jealous and resented his democratic socialist ideas to a point when he ordered the broadcasts to be pulled at the BBC[4]. Undeterred Priestley continued to produce essays, novels, plays and film scripts. There is little doubt his influence on public opinion and on the post-war settlement, the Attlee government and the creation of the Welfare state was massive, and enduring.

A larger-than-life bronze statue of Priestley stands outside the National Media Museum overlooking the city centre he so loved, though not all the changes that took place in his lifetime met with his approval.

Priestley's love of the Edwardian city in which he grew up illuminates all his writing, even when, in a play like **Eden End** he regrets its passing. It was a time when new suburban train services and electric trams, and in Bradford's case a network of clean, silent electric trolley buses, allowed people to live not just in the outlying suburbs but surrounding villages and towns on the edge of the Dales and commute into the city by train or tram. Spectacular houses like Heathcote in Ilkley was designed by Sir Edwin Lutyens for Bradford wool magnate John Hemingway in 1904, or Cliffe Castle in Keighley, which was transformed into a neogothic palace for the Butterfields, local textile magnates.

It is estimated that in the 1920s you could travel all the way from Leeds to Liverpool using different town and city tramway systems, though changing trams at places like Queensbury above Halifax where tram tracks had a different gauge, and with only a short walk between networks across the central Pennines.

There was even a funicular tramway in the outskirts of Saltaire built in 1895 to carry day trippers up what was named Shipley Glen to Brackenhall Green on the edge of Baildon Moor where for many years there was a fairground funfair and gardens. **The Shipley Glen Tramway**, beautifully restored continues to this day.

But two world wars and gradual loss of the captive markets of the British Colonies were soon to change things. Cheaper imports from the same now independent countries with low wage economies or, more ominously, who had been able to invest in new state-of-the art machinery, including the ability to handle the many new low-cost man-made fibres, meant that competition was fierce. There was also a tendency, in many wool manufacturing families, for the second and third generations to leave the soot of Bradford for greener, leafy surroundings where the air was clean, perhaps in Surrey or Buckinghamshire and spend the family fortune on good living. It became easier to make money by investing money in the stock exchange than rebuilding a woollen mill struggling to survive in an increasingly hostile, competitive environment.

One of the first Angry Young Men to describe the changing mores of post-war life in Yorkshire was Bradford-born John Braine, who was a librarian in Bingley when he wrote his novel **Room at the Top** published in 1957. Braine cleverly uses the topography of Airedale, where the posh suburbs like Eldwick or Gilstead on the hillsides above the smoke of the valley, served as a metaphor for an aspirational lifestyle. It was where you could live if you married the boss's daughter and made your money that way, living "at the top" in the literal as well as the figurative sense. It became one of the first of the New Wave films in 1959, using both Bradford and Halifax for locations, and won several awards for its acting and directing.

Another successful New Wave film shot in Bradford was based on Leeds author and journalist Keith Waterhouse's darkly comic novel of a teenage fantasist **Billy Liar** (1963). It starred Tom Courtney and Julie Christie. Director John Schlesinger used the soot-black buildings of central Bradford as the setting for many scenes. These included shots of properties being demolished to make way for soulless new concrete development, a process that echoed the film's plot of its central character desperate to escape the stultifying background of his family and personal circumstances.

A later film success was **Rita, Sue and Bob Too** (1987) a darkly funny yet powerful picture of the tragically restricted lives of two teenage girls from Bradford in the 1980s. This was based on the Royal Court premiered play by the young Bradford playwright Andrea Dunbar (1961–90) who grew up on Bradford's Buttershaw housing estate. Dunbar's early death robbed English theatre and Bradford of one of its outstanding talents.

The success of these and many other films over following decades in locations from around the city and in the neighbouring countryside, including the South Pennines, was a major factor in the city gaining, in 2009, the accolade of becoming a UNESCO's City of Film. So important has film making become to the Yorkshire economy that a company **Screen Yorkshire** has been established to work with film and television producers and directors, worldwide, to help them find locations in the Region to meet their needs.

The textile mills of Bradford that survived into the 1950s and 60s did so by working their assets harder, and one way of doing this was to bring in sufficient workers for extra night shifts. This required a new workforce not available locally, so increasingly factory owners looked to the "New Commonwealth" countries, most especially from the Indian subcontinent. By 1971 it was estimated that there were 30,000 people from the new Commonwealth living in the city; by 1987 this had grown to 64,000 from Pakistan and Bangladesh, and 15,800 from India. These were ambitious, hardworking people determined to create a better life for themselves and their children, bringing new cultures to the city. A recent study has suggested that by 2015 there were no less than 72 mosques in the city, and their characteristic domes and minarets were now making a difference to the architectural profile of the city[5].

But they also came from different communities, backgrounds and faiths – Muslim, Hindu, Sikh. Some were well educated, keen to get into higher education for entry into the professions or start their own business. Others who came from poorer and less privileged backgrounds found it difficult to integrate in the strange new city they found themselves in, where they found it easier to stay in their own communities where they could speak their own language and understand the customs.

Their contributions to the work of the mills only delayed the process of decline of the wool trade. Whilst Bradford had for many decades diversified into many different aspects of engineering, many traditional, low paid jobs disappeared. When more difficult economic conditions emerged in the 1980s, prejudice and ignorance blamed "immigration" as a cause. Social tensions exploded in the so-called Manningham Riots of 1995 and again in 2001 with confrontation between Asian youth and the police, causing serious damage, ironically small Asian shopkeepers in the city suffering most. Thanks to huge effort by the city, community and faith leaders, community relations in the city have massively improved in recent decades. There is now increasing recognition that ethnic and cultural diversity are now a huge source of potential energy and creative strength for the future of the city.

These more recent immigrants, like those of the past, provide significant economic benefits to the city. This has become much more apparent through the recent coronavirus pandemic. A large proportion of the NHS front line workers, especially doctors and nurses in intensive care wards are of South Asian and African descent. Around 22% of the total NHS workforce are from black and Asian ethnic minority backgrounds, but if you look at senior doctors, this rises to an impressive 31% of senior doctors and 29% of junior doctors (Source NHS Workforce Statistics 2020) from Asian backgrounds. For many Asian families, passionate about education, medicine as a career is a route out of working-class deprivation. But there has been a slow realisation that so many other front line "essential" workers, particular in West and South Yorkshire, in care homes, driving buses, cleaning, driving taxis, delivery vans, are the sons and daughters of the people who came to Yorkshire in the 1950s and 60s, in search of a better life, as indeed immigrants have been doing to Yorkshire since Viking times. We owe them a huge debt of gratitude.

Not only does Bradford have a rising middle class that includes many people of South Asian heritage, but there is a recognition among these communities that you can be proud of your birth heritage and that of the land your family adopted – to belong to the country at the other side of the earth your family came from but also to England and to Yorkshire.

The establishment of a great northern University in Bradford has helped this process. In 1966 as a part of his pursuit of what he called "The White Heat of Technology", Prime Minister Harold Wilson granted the Bradford Institute of Advance Technology its first charter. Bradford University, in a new build site close to the city centre, now has around 10,000 students and 1,800 staff. It has built up an international reputation in several fields, most notably engineering and what is now called informatics, as well as life and social sciences and social and international studies. Its motto fittingly is *give invention light* and it is the world's first university to offer Peace Studies as a discipline.

The presence of the University not only makes a massive difference in terms of employment, but also attitudes. With a high proportion of international students, this also creates an ambience of cultural openness which works its way into and throughout wider society.

Cultural activity in the city has been hugely enriched by its diversity. Not only does Bradford have an international reputation for its curry houses, but this impact is felt in many other ways – in the annual religious festivals such as Eid and Diwali, as well as Christmas, celebrated in the city by lights and decorations, in theatrical performances and exhibitions. **The Cartwright Hall** has its own collection and regular exhibitions of Indian-subcontinent art. Especially indicative is Bradford's magnificent Cathedral that has developed and adopted a **Faith Trail**, along which people are invited to explore and understand different faiths, and how many common values they share. **Kala Sangram**, based at St Peter's House in Forster Square, in the heart of the city, is a multi-cultural arts hub, with a focus on south east Asia, which encourages and supports a wide range of visual and performing arts activity in the city, including events, performances, exhibitions and outreach work.

A particular series of planning decisions, however, has left an unfortunate, indelible impression on the city. In the early 1950s the city adopted what was then considered a pioneering and radical plan to divide the city centre into zones and build a road system to serve those zones with new roads to speed up traffic flows and remove congestion. This led to a programme of destruction which in Bradford exceeded anything done by Hitler's Blitz. Despite the protests of many people including J. B. Priestley and the Victorian Society, much of the historic heart of Bradford including its Kirkgate market, Swan Arcade, much of Forster Square including its grand station entrance, was replaced by modern concrete office blocks of unrelenting mediocrity, many designed by the notorious 50s architect John Poulson. Worse, huge new dual carriageways were driven through the heart of the city, with pedestrians trying to cross the city centre forced into under-passageways, so-called "people sewers" in which few people feel safe, especially at night. Go for an evening play or musical show at the beautiful and recently restored Alhambra Theatre, and outside the exit door you are faced with a horrific, polluted dual carriageway, forced to wait at the traffic lights for a chance to cross.

Further development focused on the convenience of the motorist has forced many shoppers away from the narrow, hilly streets of the city centre. The Forster Square development in the old station post office/ good yards offers large warehouse type shops next to huge car parks. This has left old city centre streets round Ivegate struggling to survive.

Bradford also suffers by being too close to its major rival Leeds, a mere 9 miles or short train journey away. Faced with a choice between the now carefully managed ambiance of refurbished Victorian streets and arcades, and Bradford's traffic-filled town centre, people have voted with their feet. Even the new Westgate Centre faces a tough future with the closure, post-pandemic of so many chain stores, including Debenhams that occupied a prime part of the complex.

The present generation of planners are doing much to mend the damage. **Centenary Square** opposite City Hall with its water feature is a delight, and already a favourite with people of all backgrounds. There are imaginative plans to revive Ivegate area with small specialist shops and coffee houses, no doubt with the involvement of many Bradfordians of different backgrounds. The former art-deco Odeon Theatre has narrowly escaped demolition and will hopefully soon be reborn as a major centre for popular music events. The city still has some lovely old Victorian pubs such as Jacob's Well and The Corn Dolly, as well as modern bars and night clubs.

Will Bradford in the decades ahead get the investment it needs? Much help in recent past has come from the EU via the Regional Development Fund.

This includes what is now the **National Science and Media Museum**, one of the most popular visitor attractions in the North of England and a major educational facility for the region. Its prime foci, over seven floors, are photography, film, television animations, video gaming and the internet, including an exploration of the scientific principles behind the phenomena of light and colour. There are regular events and Festivals, including the annual **Bradford Film Festival** linked to the Museum and in other film venues in the city. The existence of the Museum in the city together with its links with the Bollywood tradition within the city's Asian community, was also a major factor in UNESCO recognising Bradford as the first World City of Film. There is also the annual **Yorkshire Gaming Festival** based at the Museum.

Another huge success story on the outskirts of the city is that of **Salts Mill** in Saltaire. Part of the Mill has been turned into a huge exhibition area, shop, cafe and art gallery with an unrivalled collection of David Hockney prints (Hockney was of course born in Bradford) but part of the complex is also devoted to new IT developments. PACE electronics, makers of digital communication systems on a worldwide scale began life in Saltaire. It is now part of the international Arras group.

Will Bradford, faced with the loss of EU regional funding, get new support from the Government's ill-defined "levelling up agenda", or will it, once again, be at the back of the queue for investment in the new service economy?

Maybe its greatest asset is the environment. In particular, now that the smoke, soot and filth of the first industrial revolution has passed and a green recovery continues, Bradford could become an increasingly attractive place to live and work, especially in a new greener, post-Covid economy. Because of its changing demographics, Bradford is now one of the youngest cities in Britain in terms of the average age of its population.

Much will depend on the ability of its citizens and their elected representatives to harness the energy, drive and diverse cultures of these younger people, to engage with each other and with the city they live in. This might be through the mechanism of small businesses, and new set-ups with communities who have a strong enterprise culture, quite possibly helped by existing and new links with the University. It might be through new community effort, through mechanisms for cooperation and mutual enterprise. The city is still the home of one of Britain's most successful and fully mutual Building Societies, significantly known as the Yorkshire Building Society. It is also the home of Morrison's, one of Britain's most successful and best loved supermarkets.

If somehow the tradition of thrift and caution of the past can be married to the energy and enterprise of youth, Bradford could have a great future.

Notes

1 Sanghera Sathnam 2021; *Empireland* Penguin/Random House London
2 Firth Gary, 1997: *A History of Bradford* Phillimore Chichester p64
3 Ibid pp58–9
4 Hanson Neil, 2008: *Priestley's Wars*; Great Northern, Ilkley p290
5 Sheeran George 2015: *The Mosque in the City* PLACE York p12

West Yorkshire: The City of Leeds

Wellington Webb, the former Mayor of Denver and past President of the U.S. Conference of Mayors, once memorably said: *"The 19th century was a century of empires, the 20th century a century of nation states. The 21st century will be a century of cities."*

The city of Leeds, with a population of just over 800,000, is the region's largest city and according to some estimates, the fourth largest city and metropolitan area of England. It is also the region's great commercial and cultural capital and the one that has adapted most successfully from being a great manufacturing to a service centre and a major metropolis of the 21st century.

Medieval village to Georgian centre of trade

Like Bradford, Leeds was a relatively insignificant market town in medieval times. Its name suggests its origin, latinised as Loidis, was a semi-independent area within the ancient lower Airedale Celtic kingdom of Elmet, a name perhaps echoed in the popular name for an inhabitant of the city as a "Leeds Loiner". In reality in early medieval times it was only one of several modest villages in the lower, more fertile part of Airedale, with a mixed economy supported by hand loom weaving, with sufficient fast running streams in areas like the Meanwood valley to drive early corn and later woollen mills.

Leeds received a major boost with the establishment in 1152 of Kirkstall Abbey. A few years earlier a group of 12 Cistercian monks were granted land at Barnoldswick by the Norman baron in control of the great Honour of Pontefract, Henry de Lacy, in order to establish a daughter house of Fountains Abbey. However, the site proved unsatisfactory, so they petitioned De Lacy to help them acquire land from local landowner Walter de Poitou in a sheltered, wooded riverside in Airedale, about two miles upriver from the village of Leeds. Over the following decades, the monks and lay brothers acquired more land and established a network of granges and outlying farms. They also brought knowledge and skills to exploit the natural resource of the area – farming, forestry, mining, smelting, tanning, brick, ceramics and tile making as well as wool spinning and weaving, activity which continued in the area long after the Dissolution of the Abbey in 1539.

The tradition of pottery and tile making in Leeds may have originated from this monastic influence, with locally rich sources of fireclay near coal seams, suitable for both brick making and tile making, as well as other ceramic manufacture. This industry reached its zenith in Leeds in later Victorian and Edwardian times, with the growth of Burmantofts Pottery whose richly decorated tiles can be seen in many buildings throughout the city, for example in County Arcade, and in the Leeds Pottery, based in Hunslet with its celebrated creamware.

Another important local industry that can be linked to the Abbey, is quarrying and stone masonry. Seeking suitable hard, workable local stone for their proposed Abbey, the brothers opened a quarry at Bramley Falls, about half a mile upstream. This was accessed by a weir which still exists, above Kirkstall Bridge, that raised the river level sufficiently to enable the high-quality millstone grit to be floated on small barges downstream to the site of the Abbey. The quarry remained in use for centuries afterwards, eventually served by the Leeds-Liverpool Canal, as a source of high-quality building stone for public buildings, bridges and balustrades, eventually transported as far away as London for use on London Bridge and even the south coast for Martello towers.

The ruins at Kirkstall are the best preserved of any Cistercian Abbey in England and have long been a source of fascination for artists and writers including such celebrated seekers after the picturesque as Horace Walpole, John Sell Cotman, Thomas Girtin and J.M.W. Turner. The former Abbey gatehouse is now the **Abbey House Museum** whilst the ruins themselves form the centrepiece of a popular city park.

The River Aire is crucial to an understanding of Leeds. The city had the good fortune to be sited where the industrial Pennines meet the agricultural Vale of York. It is also highest navigable point on the River

Aire where merchants could bring their ships to buy Yorkshire wool. By the 18th century, Leeds was already established as the country's most important trading centre for textiles. Daniel Defoe in his **A Tour Through the Whole Island of Great Britain** published in 1726, has a detailed description of the great market for woollen cloth held on Leeds Bridge and extending along what is still Leeds' principal shopping street, Briggate. Merchants and buyers were attracted to Leeds market not only from London but as far away as Leipzig and Hamburg, trade being especially important with the Netherlands.

To provide shelter from the Yorkshire weather, the first White Cloth Hall for trading in undyed fabrics was built in Kirkgate in 1710, the surviving portions of which are currently being rescued. This was followed by the great Coloured or Mixed Cloth Hall built on a site between what is now City Square and Infirmary Street. This was demolished in 1888, and by three more larger White Cloth Halls all now lost.

By the middle of the 18th Leeds was already a successful trading and manufacturing centre with elegant squares of Georgian houses appearing and the handsome Holy Trinity Church on Boar Lane. There was even a small spa and baths filled with mineral springs, just across the river in Hunslet. The town's once fashionable Assembly Rooms, originally an elegant ballroom for Georgian dances and card games, can still be seen – and is still in use as a night club, a somewhat similar purpose but a rather different clientele.

An indication of sophistication of life in 18th century Leeds was the career of the very successful landscape and portrait painter, Julius Caesar Ibbetson (1785–1817), his somewhat splendid name a result of him being born by caesarian section. Growing up in Farnley, Leeds, he was given an excellent education by local Quakers and Moravians, probably at the local Fulneck School that still thrives in the outskirts of the city. He became a brilliant watercolourist, renowned for both his rural landscapes and early industrial scenes. He was a close friend of both Wordsworth and Coleridge, and is buried in the churchyard in Masham. His work is exhibited in several Yorkshire galleries.

The heart of old Leeds still reflects its 13th century layout. The Parish Church of St Peter that dates from the 15th century (though largely rebuilt in the 19th) at the end of a lane, now a central city street, that has kept its

Anglo-Viking name of Kirkgate. Kirkgate leads to another equally ancient street, Briggate, as its name implies leading to Leeds Bridge. Close by were the town's old wharves, known as The Calls, with Swinegate, presumably the site of a pig market, heading westwards. Across the top of Briggate was a narrow lane known as Head Row, beyond which was the 17th century church of St John's. On each side of the road behind Briggate were narrow plots of land or Burgage Plots allotted in 1207 to his tenants by Maurice Paynel, Lord of the Manor, for houses and workshops for which they paid an annual rent of 16 pence per year. Between these individual plots ran narrow courtyards or alleyways. The owners of these plots were also given half acre "tofts" of land on which to grow vegetables, a medieval version of an allotment, in the area on the edge of the town centre known as Burmantofts to this very day[1].

Amazingly several of these ancient courts or yards such as Queen's Court or Hirst's Yard have survived, despite constant rebuilds. Some have old city inns in their narrow courts that still function, such as The Angel, The Packhorse, The Ship and The Turk's Head, the latter a perfectly preserved Victorian city inn and luncheon house, with a richly tiled interior. It is better known as Whitelocks.

The coming of industry

When the Leeds-Liverpool Canal was opened during the 1770s, connecting as it did with the Aire-Calder Navigation in Leeds Basin, this accelerated the growth of Leeds as a major inland port and trading centre. Kirkstall Forge was established in the 17th century by the Spencer family, taking advantage of a medieval goit fed by a side stream down the Hawksworth valley. Later another dam was constructed across the river at Newlay to increase the water supply. The Forge grew to become a major manufacturer of wrought iron in the 18th and 19th centuries, which continued production of heavy engineering items, such as vehicle axles right until the late 20th century. Though the great iron works have long vanished, thankfully fragments of the 17th century workshops have survived, with 17th and 18th century tilt or helve hammers and a slitting mill, once driven by a water wheel, in a small conservation area within the centre of major new office and housing development, close to the new railway station known appropriately as Kirkstall Forge.

Further down the river are Armley Mills, now the **Leeds Industrial Museum**. The original mill was sited to take advantage of huge waterpower from the falls in the river but was also perfectly positioned also for coal, raw materials and finished goods to be transhipped along the Canal. The present mill replaced a large fulling mill on the site destroyed by fire 1799. In 1805 the mill was rebuilt by local landowner Benjamin Gott of Armley Park and was at the time the largest mill in England with some of the most advanced engineering and structural features. The Museum has exhibits including working looms that vividly recall the great heyday of the woollen industry in Yorkshire, but also a range of galleries and exhibits devoted to engineering, tanning, and printing.

So important is the Leeds riverside heritage that in the 1980s, a six mile stretch of the towpath and riverside from Leeds's superbly refurbished Canal Basin from City Square to Rodley was designated **The Museum of Leeds Trail**. It offered several excellent examples of early and later industrial development and construction easily seen and in some cases visited from the canal towpath, starting from the City Square and the Station, the Dark Arches and Victoria Bridge and ending at the remarkable former Smith's Steam Crane Works at Rodley.

South of the city, 2½ miles down the towpath of the Aire-Calder Navigation and on a small island on the River Aire is **Thwaites Watermill**, a museum in an 18th century mill used for a variety of purposes – crushing seeds and wood for the dyeing industry, then flint and china stone for industrial processes and finally, up until 1975, for the making of putty. Reputed to be one of the finest preserved water-powered mills in the UK, it is now a Leeds City Museum offering a wide range of exhibits and displays relating both to industrial history and the local environment.

Railway history

Part of this industrial heritage is the city's railway history. The world's oldest continuously operated railway line is in Leeds – the **Middleton Railway**. Initially it was just a wooden wagonway built for Charles Brandling, to carry coal in horse drawn waggons from his coal mine at Middleton down to the wharves on the river Aire. In 1812 it was converted to steam, using one of the world's first steam locomotives designed by engineer Matthew Murray, using a rack and pinion rail system devised by mine manager John Blenkinsop. After years as a freight branch, from 1960 the line was taken over by the Middleton Railway Trust volunteers who continue to manage it as a heritage railway with regular public steamings. There is also a small museum of railway memorabilia.

The success of Murray and Blenkinsop's work led to Leeds developing into one of the major centres for the manufacture of steam locomotives in the world. Great company names whose work continued well up to the second half of the 20th century included Hunslet, Hudswell Clarke, Kitson, and Manning Wardle, all engineering firms whose locomotives can still be seen in use on heritage railways at Middleton and elsewhere in Britain.

But perhaps the most significant name of all was John Fowler. Fowler, though born in Wiltshire, came to Leeds to establish his factory in Hunslet to make mobile steam traction engines for use on public roads for haulage, but also mobile power units to enable the mechanisation of agriculture. Though he died in a hunting accident in 1864, the business was continued by his son Robert Fowler and his partner Robert Eddison, who established the company as John Fowler & Co of Leeds. This grew into the world's largest builder of steam and ploughing traction engines, power units once a familiar sight at fairgrounds and on farms, as well as the ubiquitous heavy steam rollers which used to surface and repair Britain's roads.

More orthodox passenger carrying railways arrived in 1834 with the Leeds to Selby line, which terminated in Marsh Lane, but in the 1848 a second station Central Station was built in Wellington Street to connect with the new lines west and south. The decision was taken in 1865 to connect the two stations across the city, demolishing many important buildings and homes and running across even the church graveyard, some of whose memorial stones are still stacked by the railway embankment. The new extension also required the building of the great atmospheric arches across the river under what is now City Station and the Dark Arches.

Reviving the historic riverside

For generations, this part of the city was a neglected decaying slum. In the 1960s, with the city fathers proudly claiming Leeds to be "the Motorway City of the 70s" there was real fear that the centre of Leeds might face Bradford's fate with massive new roads and demolition schemes especially of the city's great Victorian heritage.

Mercifully this did not happen. This was largely thanks to the work of several individuals and organisations, including the Victorian Society and Leeds Civic Trust. Highly influential was the work of Dr Patrick Nuttgens, outspoken architectural critic and historian, and Director of Leeds Polytechnic (now Leeds Beckett University). In his writing, broadcasts and lectures Nuttgens suggested that Leeds "the back to front" city had turned its back on one of its defining features, its river and this needed rectifying with a totally new approach[2].

And so it came to pass. **The Leeds Waterfront** as it is now proudly known, and promoted as a tourist destination, is a combination of the imaginative restoration and conversion of many former warehouses and wharf areas into a combination of residential, office and hospitality areas, with bars and restaurants, riverside promenades waterside apartments. Its effect has spread into the rest of the city centre. Recent retail development such as the Trinity Centre and the Victoria Quarter has kept in scale with the rest of the city centre, with linked pedestrian areas and arcades making Leeds an exceptionally attractive city for visiting and shopping. Leeds was one of the first major cities in England to adopt pedestrianisation of city centre streets with the conversion of Briggate to a traffic free zone in the 1960s.

A huge boost to the city came in 1996 with the relocation of part of the national Royal Armouries collection in the new **Royal Armouries Museum** in a superb new waterfront purpose-built building, with an arena for outdoor displays. This all now forms part of the Clarence Dock development.

But at its heart Leeds remains an essentially Victorian city. By the middle of the 19th century, engineering had taken over from textiles as the major source of employment. By 1900 Leeds' population had grown to almost 500,000, compared with around 50,000 in 1800.

Cuthbert Brodrick and the Victorian city

The huge new wealth of the city meant it needed a suitably grand Town Hall. Funds were raised and a site chosen at the end of what eventually became a widened Headrow leading to the fine new Victoria Square. The architect chosen after a competition was an unknown 29 year old architect from Hull, Cuthbert Brodrick. Brodrick was a genius. Almost everything he created was a masterpiece, with **Leeds Town Hall**, opened in 1858 perhaps his greatest achievement. The mixture of classical and baroque styles, with its dramatic central dome has become an icon on television screens when any news item relating to Local Government in England is discussed. The magnificent space of the Victoria Hall within the building is both the city's main concert hall and a focal point of all major civic events. The seat of civic governance in Leeds however is the **Leeds Civic Hall** in Millennium Square, built in 1933 in pale Portland stone. Incredible as it seems now, the building was commissioned in part as a job-creation project to help provide work in Leeds for those many people thrown out of work because of the 1929 world financial slump.

But Brodrick's work in Leeds didn't end with the Town Hall. He went on to design the amazing **Corn Exchange** opened in 1863, an insufficiently recognised, nationally important tour de force of Victorian engineering and architecture, with its extraordinary dome, conceived around the mathematical concept of the ellipse. Its central floor area held small wooden desks where buyers and sellers of a variety of grains from all over the North of England and indeed importers from overseas could meet and discuss prices. Some of the grain was milled in local flour mills. The merchants also had their offices around the balconies.

The Corn Exchange remained in use for its original purpose until the 1960s. It has been imaginatively converted to various small, more specialised restaurants and food and retail outlets, yet the building seems to demand some even more prestigious future role.

Brodrick also designed the splendid Mechanics Institute, opened in 1868 with a large lecture theatre and library for the education of working men and women. In later years it became the city's Civic Theatre, home for much semi-professional and amateur theatre productions. Appropriately enough, and after imaginative re-adaption, it now houses the excellent **Leeds Museum**, which over several floors tell the story of various aspects of the city, from its geology and natural history, to its emergence as a major regional capital and cultural centre.

Brodrick, having created a handful of masterpieces in his native Yorkshire, moved to France in 1870. He retired in 1875 and spent the next 30 years of his life painting and tending his garden, drifting into obscurity as Yorkshire's forgotten architectural genius.

For many years these great Brodrick buildings, like all other public buildings in the cities and towns of West and South Yorkshire were soot black. When they were finally cleaned in the smoke-free air of the 1970s to reveal shockingly pale sandstones, this engendered mixed feelings, as their "traditional" appearance had changed, with some people even suggesting Leeds Town Hall should remain black as a memorial to Leeds' industrial past.

Victoria Square is shared by another prominent Victorian building, **Leeds Art Gallery**. Built between 1886 and 1888 to the designs of W.H.Thorp, it now houses an outstanding collection of Victorian and Edwardian paintings. Its 20th century British art collection is considered to be of national importance. Part of the building now houses the **Henry Moore Gallery** with examples not only of Moore's work but of other 20th century sculptors. His great bronze **Reclining Woman: Elbow** stands in the piazza outside the entrance. The exquisitely tiled café on the ground floor has become a popular Leeds rendezvous.

One of the people on the original advisory committee for the design of the Leeds Gallery, whose work is now on display in the gallery, was John Atkinson Grimshaw (1836–93). Atkinson was born in a back-to-back terraced house in Leeds. He worked as a clerk for the North Eastern Railway until he was 24. He became a talented self-taught artist, whose extraordinary intense and beautiful, twilight scenes of cities, suburbs and harbours, most notably in Leeds, Scarborough, Whitby and London, are now recognised as being masterpieces of their kind. His work drew the admiration of no less an artist than James McNeil Whistler for their brilliance in capturing urban moods, colour and dusk light.

Commerce and the contribution of mainland European immigrants

The other civic building which is very special to Leeds is Kirkgate Market with its great neo-Venetian indoor Market Hall. Built to the design of London architects John and Joseph Leeming, the building has echoes of the Crystal Palace, with stunning tilework and decorative details in wrought iron. Opened in 1904, Kirkgate Market is the largest market of its kind on a single site in Europe, extended as it is by the large outdoor market to its rear.

One of the traders with a stall in the market was Michael Marks (1859–1907) a Jewish refugee from Poland who spoke little English. On his arrival in England, Marks was offered a job by a company who employed Jewish migrants. He borrowed £5 from a friend to start his Penny Bazaar in the market in 1884. In 1894, when Marks acquired a stall in the covered part of the old market, he invited Skipton accountant Thomas Spencer to become his partner. In the century that followed Marks and Spencer grew to become a great British institution, for many years selling almost only British produced goods.

Michael Marks was only one of the many refugees who came from Central and Eastern Europe. Many were Jewish families fleeing to escape antisemitic pogroms. They brought with them tailoring skills. This pool of skills, within a few decades around the turn of the 20th century, attracted companies to establish themselves in the city, such as Hepworths, Burtons, and Price – the Fifty Shillings Tailor – fifty-shillings (£2.50) being the price of a ready-made suit in the 1930s – an equivalent of £90 today.

This established Leeds as the centre of the ready-made clothing industry. Montague Burton, (1885–1952), born Meshe Osinsky but shrewd enough to change his name to a familiar English-sounding "Burton", was another Jewish refugee from Russia, in what is now Lithuania. Burton moved his clothing manufacturing business to Leeds because of its available skilled workforce. By 1934 the Leeds factory had a workforce of 10,000, 90% of whom were female, who worked in the company's fine new art-déco factory in Burmantofts, Leeds, to provide for its nationwide chain of 500 ready-made clothing shops.

The Jewish community also brought a new middle European culture to the city, and successful business, legal and entrepreneurial skills which were to transform the life of the city in so many ways. The Burton family, for example, became major benefactors and contributors to both the University and the arts over more than one generation.

Another example is the life story of Jacob Kramer (1892–1962). From a family of Jewish refugees from Ukraine, who arrived, penniless in Leeds, Kramer won a scholarship to attend Leeds Art School. After war service Kramer won a second scholarship paid for by a Leeds Jewish educational charity which allowed Kramer to study at the Slade School of Art. Kramer developed into one of Britain's finest portrait painters and illustrators. He returned to Leeds at the Leeds School of Art, which was named the Jacob Kramer College before becoming Leeds Arts University.

Leeds by this time was a centre for radical ideas in art, philosophy and politics. The Leeds Arts Club formed in 1904 became a focal point for people like Kramer and his friend, influential writer, art-critic and poet Sir Herbert Read who also studied in Leeds.

Leeds' three Universities

By 1874 Leeds already had its own prestigious Yorkshire College of Science which was amalgamated in 1884 with the Leeds Medical School to become the Yorkshire College. In 1887 it became part of the curious federal Victoria University, a status shared across the Pennines with colleges in Leeds, Liverpool and Manchester. Finally Leeds was given its own royal charter by King Edward VII in 1904 to become the University of Leeds. Its iconic art deco/Greek revival style Parkinson Building built of white Portland stone, was because, of wartime issues, only finally completed in 1951. The 57 metre tall Clock Tower soon became a local landmark. There have been no less than six Nobel Prize winners among its distinguished alumni, and political figures to have studied there include Jack Straw, Baroness Warsi and Sir Keir Starmer, the present Leader of the Opposition. The University has now grown to become one of Britain's top ranking education institutions, with a total of 36,000 students.

If you add to that the 23,000 students in what is now **Leeds Beckett University**, formerly the highly regarded Leeds Polytechnic, with its greater focus on vocational education, and now one of Britain's top institutions for Olympic standard sports, sports science, tourism studies and much more besides, and a further 1,850 at **Leeds Arts University**, Leeds student population totals over 60,000. Many of these students are from overseas. The three universities make a huge contribution to the economic and social life of the city, giving the city a young and dynamic, temporary and permanent population. Whole areas of the city, especially around Hyde Park and Headingly, for good or for ill, are now dominated by student accommodation and facilities, a transformation of what were pleasant working-class suburbs into huge student-dominated quarters, with student flats, apartments and house shares.

Opportunities and challenges for the 21ˢᵗ century

But this huge population of bright young undergraduates and post-graduates has also encouraged the transformation of the city in another way, helping to secure its place as the second city outside London for financial, insurance and business services. Many international investment companies now have their North of England base in this now cosmopolitan city, with over 30 national and international banks with offices in the city. The Bank of England has recently indicated that its Northern Hub, principle outstation of the Bank outside London, will be located in the city, reinforcing its importance as a national financial centre. It is also a major legal centre with over 150 firms including those specialising in company and business law, now established in the city.

Another rapidly growing industry is digital gaming, with both Leeds and Sheffield becoming major centres of the new, rapidly growing industry.

However, Leeds with its good road and rail connections and even a local airport with regular flights to mainland Europe, as well as holiday destinations, remains an important manufacturing centre, the third largest in the UK, with an emphasis on hi-tech engineering, printing and publishing, and chemical engineering. Around 50% of the manufacturing activity in the UK lies within 50 miles of the city. Even though railway locomotives are no longer made in Leeds buses are – or almost so. Optare, a company which had its origins at Cross Gates, in east Leeds, is now located in a large industrial park at Sherburn in Elmet, technically just outside the city boundaries. Optare are now the leading manufacturer of state-of-the art buses in England and pioneers of single and double deck electric powered buses now rapidly appearing in Yorkshire cities.

A city of social contrast

By Victorian times, the areas to the south of the city were already dominated by the smoke of heavy industry. The better off middle class escaped to the greener north side of the river, largely splitting the city economically, socially and politically in two, the south side of the river still being dominated by heavy industry, motorways and warehousing, the north the leafy suburbs extending to Headingley, Moortown, Alwoodley and out into the satellite villages such as Shadwell, Horsforth, Bramhope or Scholes.

Like Bradford, Leeds has also attracted significant numbers of workers in the past from Ireland, and more recently from Eastern Europe, the Commonwealth and even the Far East to meet the growing demands of heavy industry and the service industries, especially in the 1950s and 60s. Amongst these were numerous people from the West Indies, including many from the Windrush generation. Many settled in the older areas of Victorian and Edwardian "back-to-back" areas of dense terraced housing in the Chapeltown area, and people from South East Asia in Harehills. As in Bradford these communities have suffered decades of the negative consequences of poverty, unemployment, discrimination, racism and social unrest, leading for example to the Chapeltown Riots of 1981. But these same communities have made major contributions to the city, as in Bradford providing a major input to core health and care industries. There is no better illustration of their positive cultural contribution than the annual Leeds West Indian Carnival, when communities of Caribbean background join everyone else in Chapeltown and other areas of the city in a day of brilliantly coloured costume, traditional music, dance, warm humour, friendship and distinctive cuisine.

But like too many cities in England in the first decades of the 21st century, Leeds is a divided city, with in some inner city areas, and on outer suburban housing estates, serious levels of poverty and deprivation, resulting from a decline in many of the traditional manufacturing industries replaced by low paid jobs, often part time or part of the "gig-economy".

It took one of Britain's greatest living writers, poets and dramatists Tony Harrison, to explore this deep cultural divide in the city. Harrison was born in a working-class district of Leeds, south of the river, getting a scholarship to Leeds Grammar School and then to Leeds University, where he studied classics. He combined an academic career with brilliant translations and adaptations both of Greek Plays and the York and Wakefield Miracle Plays, the latter exploiting the power and beauty of Yorkshire speech and language. Many of his verse plays have been performed at the National Theatre and around the world, but he is also a poet of international renown.

His powerful and justly celebrated poem "V" was published in 1985 and broadcast on television to much controversy and outrage by politicians and self-appointed moralists, shocked as much for its earthy language as its content. The poem, in carefully crafted stanzas, was stimulated by discovery of the disfigurement of his parents' grave in Hunslet cemetery. In beautifully controlled rhymed quatrains, Harrison imagines a discussion between his present self, grammar school boy now world-famous poet, meeting what might have been his other self, his *doppelgänger*, a skinhead, the person he might have become, were it not for his gifts of intelligence and education that became his passport into a very different, privileged world of intellectual freedom and pan-European culture. It is a powerful, humorous and moving indictment of our divided nation.

The recent decade-long period of so-called austerity, which in fact meant constant, debilitating cuts to public services, have left many areas of the city with communities suffering from unacceptable levels of poverty and even destitution. Too many people are now dependent on charity for their physical survival, most especially on food banks managed by dedicated volunteers. These differences have been made more acute by the coronavirus epidemic, albeit with corresponding unbelievable acts of kindness, compassion and support by members of the community given to those most in need. But there is a growing awareness that meeting those needs should not be dependent on charity.

Urban transport – a failure

One source of weakness which inevitably reinforces deprivation in the city has been inadequate and increasingly expensive public transport. Despite having, in the 1950s, a comprehensive if seriously neglected local urban rail network and one of the best and most modern street tramway systems in Britain, including a dedicated light railway to the huge overspill housing estate in Middleton, until recently most decisions about transport have been dominated by the needs of one mode and one type of user, the motorist. The unspoken priority since 1960s has been to largely ensure continued unrestricted access into and across the city, offering ample low cost parking, despite the inevitable consequences of this in implicitly encouraging rising car usage that quickly overtook any increased road capacity, with dire impacts on the city's air quality.

Plans to build an underground railway or metro were scrapped at the start of World War II. Pressure by drivers to rid the city of the cheap "old fashioned" trams that were alleged to be causing traffic jams, led to their replacement by diesel buses. Beeching rail closures in the 1960s removed many local suburban lines, for example key branches to Wetherby and Otley.

Nevertheless, in the 1970s and 80s West Yorkshire Passenger Transport Executive made highly successful efforts to revive the West Yorkshire rail network. However since the 1980s, continued underfunding and poor decision making by Westminster politicians, from both Labour and Conservative administrations, has steadily undermined much of this progress.

Leeds is now the only metropolitan region in western Europe without a modern rapid transit system. Three attempts for a Super Tram, LRT or even a modest trolley bus-based system have been thwarted by decisions by Westminster bureaucrats and politicians mainly to cut costs. There are now new current proposals from WYCA for a West Yorkshire Mass Transit System to bring Leeds into the 21st century in urban transport terms. It is planned to be open by the mid 2030s – if indeed there are not yet further delays, financial cutbacks and cancellations.

Traffic congestion now makes travel into, from and across city at peak times slow and difficult, with buses becoming both victims of and a cause of traffic congestion. Rising bus fares now make bus travel unaffordable for many poorer people. It is often cheaper to take a taxi than catch a bus especially if there are two people travelling together. The consequences are additional traffic congestion and air pollution which at peak times in the city reach levels which are both illegal and are a huge threat to human health, especially on people on lower incomes living in inner-city areas. It is not yet known if the change to home working, post-pandemic will ease the situation or drive even more people back to the perceived "safety" of their cars.

These problems are now being vigorously tackled by the City Council and West Yorkshire Combined Authority, with the development of new cycleways and pedestrian and bus priority schemes, electric buses, charging points for electric cars and an increasingly effective bus-based park and ride scheme from outlying car parks, such as Stourton or Elland Road football ground, into the city centre. Clean Air Zones are also planned, but at time of writing private cars are still largely excluded from these restrictions.

There is still a feeling that what is happening is too little and too late. What is urgently needed is, like Manchester, Nottingham and Sheffield, a clean, efficient metro system for Leeds and other cities in West Yorkshire, segregated from road traffic, to allow Leeds and Yorkshire to catch up with the rest of Europe.

Green space – a Leeds success

But one dimension where Leeds scores highly is in its green spaces. Like Sheffield, Leeds is one of the greenest cities in England in terms of parks and open spaces. A major attraction of establishing a business or taking a job in Leeds, is the closeness of the city to some of the finest landscapes in the British Isles, with not only the Yorkshire Dales National Park on the doorstep, but the North York Moors and the Lake District within a couple of hours' drive or bus and train ride. Even more important perhaps are the many areas of public green open space within the city itself.

Temple Newsam with its magnificent Jacobean house, spectacular gardens and parkland is reputedly the largest urban park in Europe. **Roundhay Park**, nationally famous for its gardens, lakes, glasshouses, large collection of tropical plants and an amazing butterfly gardens, was first acquired for the city through an amazing local initiative. When in 1872 it had been made clear that the city could not legally pay the £180,00 required to buy the park, its visionary mayor Sir John Barran persuaded several wealthy citizens to loan the cash to the city. Soon afterwards the city's pioneering electric tramway was extended to serve the Park.

Other notable parks and opens space include **Golden Acre Park** to the north of the city, a former pleasure garden of the 1930s acquired by the city when it was in a derelict state after World War 2. It is now a fine botanic garden and public woodland, notable for its areas of wetland, arboretum, national collection of syringas (lilacs) and hostas, and much more besides. **Otley Chevin Forest Park** is a magnificent area of semi natural and plantation woodland and crags on the great ridge overlooking the town of Otley in Wharfedale. Much of this woodland was given to the city in the 1960s by the Horton-Fawkes family of Farnley Hall near Otley, distant relatives of Guy Fawkes. Turner was a frequent guest of the family and paid for his stay with exquisite drawings and watercolours, many of which are still in a private collection at the hall. One of his most famous oil paintings **Hannibal Crossing the Alps**, painted in 1812 and now in the Tate Gallery was actually inspired by the great gritstone crags seen in a snowstorm at Caley Crags on the Chevin. This was one of many paintings and drawings he made in the Leeds area including vistas of Kirkstall, Farnley, Harewood and a celebrated 1816 view of Leeds from Beeston Hill at a time of its industrial awakening.

Leeds Green Belt is not only important as precious green space, farmland and woodland, accessible by footpath and bridleway, including the 62-mile **Leeds Country Way** around the city, but because such green lungs physically separate the many small industrial villages and even quite large towns such as Yeadon, Guiseley and Rawdon that over the few decades have been absorbed into the City. A particular threat in the north of the city is the major expansion of the Leeds-Bradford Airport between Yeadon and Otley, whose proposed expansion would not only be in contradiction of international Climate legislation, but also require new roads, parking areas and distribution warehouses in the Green Belt, all generators of road traffic.

The area south and east of the city, particularly into the lower Aire valley was, until quite recent times subject to mining activity, including in later years open cast coal seams near the surface. At one time even part of the **Temple Newsam Park** was exploited albeit with careful restoration work by the National Coal Board. Some areas closer to the river, also subject to subsidence as underground seams collapsed and were left as "flashes" or expanses of open water.

By happy chance some of these such as **Fairburn Ings** and **St Aiden's** were also situated close to seasonal migration routes of many species of birds that cross the British Isles, and both stretches of water, together with their surrounding stretches of woodland, wet grasslands and lagoons having become nationally important RSPB bird reserves, now attract up to 100,000 bird watchers a year. An amazing 280 different species of birds have been recorded at the site, including the elusive bittern.

Unfortunately central Governments have increasingly interpreted Green Belt legislation as advisory rather than mandatory, and the very attractive physical qualities of north Leeds extending into Wharfedale, are now a threat to the survival of the Green Belt. Massive pressure for new homes, mainly so called "executive" homes with prominent car ports, is now resulting in planning permission for new residential estates in the Green Belt being granted largely on hypothetical (and changing) population trends often against the wishes of local communities and local politicians. This demand to move to north Leeds is increasingly driven by a national awareness of the beauty of the nearby Yorkshire Dales and surrounding areas.

The pandemic has also emphasised new opportunities to work from home and only visit a perhaps distant office once or twice week or for freelance workers not at all. This is putting unsustainable pressure on areas like Wharfedale, forcing local authorities to concede piecemeal urbanisation of the Green Belt without any corresponding investment in transport, educational, medical or other facilities. The Council for the Protection of Rural England is leading a valiant campaign to change Government policies to protect our surviving areas of Green Belt and switch housing development to focus more on social housing and start up accommodation in town and city centres, close to services, to meet escalating housing needs rather than building middle class homes for escapees from the overcrowded south east.

Harewood

One spectacularly beautiful part of the Leeds Green Belt, overlooking the great ridge that divides Wharfedale from the city, is Harewood, the great estate of the Lascelles family, Earls of Harewood. **Harewood House**, was built between 1759 and 1765 to the designs of John Carr of York and Robert Adam, who was largely responsible for the interior design. It is one of the great country houses of England, noted for its sumptuous interiors, Chippendale furniture and great display of paintings including old masters and portraits by Joshua Reynolds and Thomas Lawrence. There are also splendid gardens and walks, a Bird Garden, a Planetarium, an extensive area of parkland landscape designed by Capability Brown, a ruined 13th century castle, and a disused church; the village it served was removed as an eyesore and rebuilt at a more convenient site on the nearby A61 Harrogate road.

Edwin Lascelles (1713–95) first Earl of Harewood, builder of the house, inherited his immense wealth from his family's West Indian businesses and plantations, and so indirectly from slavery. In an era of Black Lives Matter, the Harewood estate have rightly not attempted to deny the past, as history cannot be changed. Rather the Estate and family have taken a positive view by not only having exhibition material in the house which faces the cruel facts of the past, but also supporting a variety of worthwhile education schemes. This includes support for visits to the Estate by new generations of British citizens, including local children of Afro-Caribbean descent, to enjoy the magnificent works of art and landscape which their ancestors helped to create. This recognises a common heritage that is equally available and accessible to everyone. Significantly the main 36 Leeds-Harrogate bus stop outside the entrance drive to Harewood Park also picks up from the centre of Chapeltown in Leeds. The Lascelles family have also donated a significant amount of documentation and materials to the Borthwick Institute of York University in the Lascelles Slavery Archive so that people interested in the story of their ancestors or the wider issues of slavery can access primary source materials.

Film, television and the creative arts

One interesting use of The Harewood Estate is ITV Yorkshire's **Emmerdale**. One of the most popular television drama series in the world, Emmerdale began life in 1972 as a popular drama about life in the Yorkshire Dales, first filmed around Arncliffe in Littondale, the old name for which is Amerdale. When it was clear that the popularity of the series was causing logistical problems, including loss of privacy for local communities, the series moved to a more accessible location, Esholt, near Shipley. Even this proved unsatisfactory so a deal was struck with the Harewood Estate to build an entirely artificial "filmset" village on private land within the Estate to which access could be strictly controlled. Indoor scenes are recorded at what was formerly Yorkshire Television studios in Kirkstall Leeds, now ITV Yorkshire.

Emmerdale is only one example of the major financial contribution the creative arts make to the economic and social success of Leeds. The city is a centre of excellence for countless television and film productions, and the city and West Yorkshire provide locations for a huge variety of programmes and series, for example **A Touch of Frost** with David Jason, created by the ITV Yorkshire studios in Leeds and filmed on location in West Yorkshire.

Leeds also has the good fortune to be the home and workspace of one of Britain's most exciting talents in the form of director, screen and stage play writer Kay Mellor. Mellor's vivid portrayals of the lives of ordinary West Yorkshire people, in BBC television series such as **Bands of Gold**, **Fat Friends**, or **The Syndicate** have an authenticity which few of her contemporaries can match. Her stage and screen plays combine humour with the exploration of the lives of ordinary people being overwhelmed by sometimes tragic circumstances beyond their control, writing with a powerful sense of social justice and compassion. At the same time there is a sense of real theatrical moment strong enough to grip any audience – popular television at its very best.

Two other nationally known writers born and brought up in Leeds are dramatist Alan Bennett, of **History Boys** fame, and whose televised "Talking Heads" monologues, almost always with a Leeds accent, have perfected this art form, but also novelist Barbara Taylor Bradford whose 1979 international best seller **A Woman of Substance,** partly set in Yorkshire, also made a hugely popular TV series.

With the coming of the headquarters of Channel Four to Leeds, to add to the existing ITV and BBC Studios, the city is now at the cutting edge of the creative arts, which though Governments do not always realise this, are major creators of wealth for the UK economy.

In terms of the musical performing arts, the most thrilling development of recent years has been the establishment in the city of **Opera North** which has developed into one of the most exciting opera companies not only in the UK but in western Europe. Much of this was due to the work of George Lascelles 7th Earl of Harewood (1923–2011), the Queen's cousin. The Earl was a leading, world authority on opera, a music impresario, and a former Director of both the Edinburgh International Festival and The Royal Opera. In 1977 he persuaded Government to establish an outstation of English National Opera, English Opera North to the city, which eventually became the fully independent Leeds-based opera company, Opera North.

The company since its formation has been based in the superbly refurbished **Grand Theatre** in Leeds. This now includes rehearsal rooms and the **Howard Rooms**, its own special recital theatre area. As well as touring to other northern cities, the Company also does a huge amount of educational work in local schools. Nor is the company just about the more rarefied medium of classical opera. The Orchestra of Opera North is now a regular performer at concerts throughout the region. There is also an Opera North String Quartet.

Opera's sister art of ballet is astonishingly well represented in the city by two outstanding dance theatre companies. **Northern Ballet** began life as Northern Dance Theatre in Manchester, but frequently performed in Leeds. Since 2010 under its current Director David Nixon, it has moved to be part of the Leeds Cultural Quarter at Quarry Hill in purpose-built studios, teaching areas and studio theatre. Over the last few decades Northern Ballet has presented an astonishing range of award-winning work, using ballet as a brilliant means of storytelling.

Northern Ballet shares its studios with **Phoenix Dance Theatre**. Phoenix is a hugely exciting contemporary dance group and has an amazing history. It was first established in Harehills, a deprived part of the city by three young black dancers – David Hamilton, Donald

Edwards and Vilmore James who had their love of dance sparked by the tuition they received from their teachers John Auty at Intake High School and Nadine Senior at Harehills Middle School. Phoenix now has an international reputation for its edgy, culturally diverse work in the medium of dance.

Since 1963 Leeds has also been host to the **Leeds International Piano Competition** established by the extraordinary Fanny Waterman (1920–2020) which has helped the careers of so many outstanding young pianists. The city is also a centre for the study of music – performance and composition. As well as being the music department to Leeds University, the former College of Music is now the Leeds Conservatoire, with courses in jazz and popular music as well as classical. The Conservatoire, based in what is now known as the Cultural Quarter of Leeds on the site of the old Quarry Hill Flats, and the University jointly promote the **Leeds Lieder Festival** each year, which as well as public performances in the Recital Theatre, include a concert where poets and composers work together to create memorable songs for voice and piano.

There are also current plans to revive the once highly respected **Yorkshire Symphony Orchestra**, disbanded in 1955. This will be a way of supporting and releasing the creativity of the large number of gifted freelance classical musicians based in the Region to become a focal point of a wide range of musical activities. Though serving the whole of Yorkshire, the orchestra will be based in Leeds.

Leeds is also a significant centre for popular music. The Kaiser Chiefs, an indie rock band established in 2003, are just one of several groups from the Leeds area to achieve national and even international success and fame. Much new talent is encouraged by the annual **Leeds Festival** which takes place in the idyllic surrounds of Bramham Park on the outskirts of Leeds every August Bank Holiday weekend. The city also now has the massive 13,000 seat **First Direct Leeds Arena** in the centre where national and international groups and singers can perform to huge audiences.

Leeds also has a vibrant traditional theatrical scene. The beautiful, red plush and gilt and tiled **Grand Theatre** opened in 1878, is one of England's finest high Victorian theatres, an architectural masterpiece in its own right, with a fascinating history of great performances and actors. As well as opera and a variety of musical shows, it hosts major touring theatre productions. The Grand is now one of the three Leeds Heritage Theatres, the second being the delightful **City Varieties**, opened in 1865, a perfectly preserved small theatre housing the world's longest continuously functioning music hall. It was given fame with the television series **The Good Old Days**, an adaptation of Edwardian music hall for television which ran between 1953 and 1983 attracting huge audiences. The third is the **Hyde Park Cinema**, an Edwardian Picture House, dating from 1914, in a student suburb near the University, now an independent cinema.

The former West Yorkshire Playhouse at Quarry Hill has now been totally refurbished and renamed **The Leeds Playhouse**, reflecting its earlier origins in temporary buildings in the University, paid for by local fund-raising efforts in the 1970s. Essentially this is a Repertory Theatre with its own company but also offering space for touring productions. It is really two theatres in one, the larger 750 seat Quarry Hill Theatre, suitable for larger productions and the smaller Courtyard Theatre for more intimate theatre or more experimental productions. Amateur, alternative and experimental groups also have a score of performing venues around the city.

Metropolitan English University cities of the North, with younger, better educated populations, such as Manchester, Liverpool, Newcastle, Leeds, and Sheffield, and in Yorkshire to only a slightly lesser extent Hull, Bradford, Huddersfield and York, are now in the forefront of changing liberal and progressive values. Many of these values are at odds with the nostalgic, imperial, isolationist view of the past which is currently and constantly being presented by central Government and the popular press.

Only by means of Devolved Administrations in the English Regions will the voices of their younger citizens be heard and their creativity fully realised. It is within such great progressive cities, such as Leeds, that the future of Yorkshire, and of England, resides.

Notes

1 Brears Peter, Grady Kevin, 2007: *Briggate: Yards & Arcades* Leeds Civic Trust
2 Nuttgens Patrick 1979 Leeds: *The back to front, inside out upside down city* Stile Books Otley

9

South Yorkshire

In its brief existence between 1974 and 1986, the Metropolitan County of South Yorkshire, with a population of 1.36 million people, earned the nickname of "The People's Republic of South Yorkshire" for its unashamed left-wing policies and resistance to Government decisions on such issues as cheap bus fares and social housing.

Indeed, it is generally thought that it was primarily to get rid of South Yorkshire that Margaret Thatcher's ministers abolished the Metropolitan Counties of the North, even relatively politically moderate ones such as West Yorkshire and Greater Manchester.

South Yorkshire became four Metropolitan Boroughs – Barnsley, Rotherham, Doncaster and the city of Sheffield. These include some of the most densely populated parts of Yorkshire, a conglomeration of once busy mining towns and villages, or towns dominated by great steel works, some still functioning, others semi derelict or demolished. Towns and suburbs often merge together in ribbon development, but are often separated by fine areas of green space and precious linear woodlands, or renatured and recovered landscape. These green, often Green Belt areas, are vitally important for the future.

The decline of coal

South Yorkshire was once the heartland of industrial Britain, its wealth based on two once hugely important commodities, coal and steel. The shift away from Britain's once world supremacy as a manufacturing nation, to primarily a nation supported by the service sectors, occurred over the last decades of the 20th century. That process of change was, in South Yorkshire, especially brutal and harsh, particularly on the mining and steel communities of the region.

It also led to what was, for all intents and purposes, a Civil War.

Even by the 1970s it was clear to most people that coal mining no longer had a viable future. There had already been some pit closures during the 1960s, but Britain was still overwhelmingly dependent on coal for the production of electricity. National strikes to improve miners' pay and conditions took place in 1972 and 1974. The 1974 strike forced the Heath Government into the Three-Day Week to conserve dwindling energy supplies. In February 1974 this led to the fall of the Government and the election of a minority Labour administration.

But a decade later, with Margaret Thatcher as leader, it was a different story. Thatcher enjoyed huge popularity from the defeat of the Argentinian junta in the patriotic Falklands War of 1982. This time the key issue was the survival of the mining industry, with the rationalisation of the industry and proposed pit closures being planned by the National Coal Board. Yorkshire was easily the largest and most significant coal mining area in the UK, and its miners had a reputation of militarism. The President of the National Union of Mine Workers in 1984 was left-wing firebrand Arthur Scargill, from Worsborough near Barnsley.

Scargill made a number of crucial mistakes, including not having a national ballot before starting the strike, and in deciding to strike when coal stocks were high and power cuts less likely. He also refused to accept a compromise solution and underestimated the support that Margaret Thatcher enjoyed outside South Yorkshire.

Feelings ran high and came to a head in June 1984 in what is now sometimes called the Battle of Orgreave. Orgreave is a small village near Sheffield, where there was a British Steel coking plant, providing essential high quality coke for the steel industry. When NUM secondary "flying" pickets attempted to stop coal supplies reaching the plant, armed police, including mounted units from many different parts of the UK, arrived to prevent this, and a physical confrontation took place with violence on both sides and many arrests and serious injuries. Public opinion was divided between those who believed the police were only acting in self-defence and upholding the law of the land, and those who saw this as example of brutal "legalised state violence" against working people who had been branded by the Prime Minister as "the Enemy Within". Subsequent legal inquiries have concluded that the police may have exceeded what might be considered to be reasonable action albeit in difficult circumstances. The event was widely seen as a demonstration of the Government's determination to assert its authority.

Orgreave was by no means the only such incident. At nearby Maltby Pit a young miner was killed. By February 1985, after the Government had offered huge financial incentives for striking miners to return to work to break the strike, the NUM were forced to admit defeat. It was a victory not just against the miners but the whole trade union movement, a change in the relationship between Government and Unions, which laid the way to legislation that was to weaken their powers and influence, and change the way Britain, not just Yorkshire, was governed, forever.

The strike had continued for months, resulting in extreme hardship for the mining communities, despite almost heroic support given by the wives of the miners to their menfolk and their families, as well by the wider community.

Scargill's worst fears were indeed surpassed with the wholesale closure in the late 1980s and 1990s of all but a handful of deep, highly automated coal mines. But even these few post-strike coal mines were doomed as, even before the recognition of dreadful impact on the climate of burning fossil fuels, coal was seen to be an expensive and filthy fuel, environmentally damaging. Kellingley Colliery, just over the boundary in North Yorkshire, closed in December 2015, the last deep coal mine in Britain.

Despite all the deep bonding and camaraderie between miners and within the mining community, underground coal mining was a filthy, dangerous, health-damaging and inhumane way of earning a living and the closure of the last deep pit was in many respects a relief. You can still experience a taste of what coal mining was like by visiting the **National Museum of Coal Mining**, at Caphouse Colliery, Overton, near Wakefield, just across the boundary into West Yorkshire. But the fact remains that the closing of the South Yorkshire mines, without adequate alternative employment opportunities being offered, resulted in dreadful social costs.

Orgreave has passed into folklore. It has inspired several novelists and poets. For example, the Yorkshire poet Steve Ely, in his poem **Harrying of the North**, part of his collection **Engeland** published in

2015, draws parallels with what happened after the miners' strike in the mining areas of Yorkshire, with what William the Conqueror did to Yorkshire in 1069.

The overall industrial and social decline of South Yorkshire at that time also stimulated some powerful responses by writers and film makers. Barry Hines (1939–2016) was a novelist from Hoyland, near Barnsley. His most famous novel, **Kestrel for a Knave**, (1968) was made into an equally powerful film **Kes** in 1969 by Director Ken Loach. It is set and filmed in the Barnsley area. It explores the world of a young teenager Billy Casper, a drop-out at his secondary modern school. For Billy much of the standard, quasi-academic school curriculum is meaningless, yet when it comes to caring for the kestrel he rescued close to his home, he reveals sensitivity and intelligence which orthodox education, with the notable exception of his English teacher, had failed to perceive. Both novel and film are powerful works of protest about the failures of education for working class children.

The film **Brassed Off** from 1996 had a more specific link with pit closures. Closely associated with the reality of declining industrial communities, is the thinly disguised story of Grimethorpe Colliery Band. The film relates, with the help of such stars as Peter Postlethwaite, Tara Fitzgerald and a young Ewan McGregor, of how a mining community, devastated by the closure of their pit, succeeds through their magnificent brass band. The band outlives its colliery as a symbol of the creativity and talent that is there in the post-industrial communities of South Yorkshire and elsewhere.

Also a comedy, but perhaps even darker in its message, was the 1997 film **The Full Monty**, screenplay by Simon Beaufoy, in which a group of unemployed Sheffield steel workers decide, in despair, that the only way to earn a little extra cash would be to organise a musical strip show to attract the women who in many ways now had become the main breadwinners, taking what jobs there were in the area such as telesales and care work. The film is as much about the humiliation of working-class men resulting from the loss of the skills of the industrial crafts that once defined them, as about poverty. The film has enjoyed a worldwide success. In reverse of the usual pattern, it has now also become a popular stage play. Ironically, its powerful social message and protest has rather become eclipsed by a curious quasi-feminist agenda

– women can now enjoy the spectacle of naked male flesh in a shared and jovial context that seems thoroughly respectable.

Inevitably, as time has passed, this has all become an over-simplified picture. The site of Orgreave Coking Plant is now occupied by The Advanced Manufacturing Park, financed in part by the European Union, with high tech industries including one project engaged in nuclear fission energy production, and by new housing estates. Roberts Radio, based in the former mining town of Mexborough near Doncaster, is now one of the world's leading manufacturers of digital radios. There are many other examples of companies in South Yorkshire achieving excellence in manufacturing and engineering, and the new digital industries. There are also several examples of business parks and start up schemes which are helping communities in South Yorkshire to recover socially and economically. But as always, these measures may be too little, too late.

If you travelled across South Yorkshire little more than a generation ago, you would have been looking at a smoke-polluted landscape dotted by slag heaps and pit head winding gear, busy rail sidings and access roads, factories and forges. Villages were often dominated by drab ribbon development of housing along the roads linking the mines. A generation later the only hint a huge coal mine may once have existed is a low, long hillock carefully planted with conifer trees. Business parks, distribution centres and new housing estates have now sprung up on what was derelict, industrially ravaged land. Miners' social clubs and welfare institutes and even pubs, have been demolished or repurposed.

The area is cleaner. There has also been a notable regreening and renaturing. Former "flashes" caused by mining subsidence are now bird reserves, slag heaps are transformed to wooded parks with nature trails or riverside walks, or as on the Trans Pennine Trail, abandoned rail trackbeds are cycle routes or walking trails. Older landscapes are slowly beginning to remerge.

But in the process, it is almost as if a whole, formerly dominant way of life, in Yorkshire as in other coal mining areas of Britain, has never existed. Coal mining has, within a few short years, been wiped off the map, reduced to memory, black and white photographs, a few "heritage" monuments.

In some ways the disappearance of coal mining has been a blessing.

Human beings should not be exposed to such dangerous, life-shortening activity as a source of employment. But equally, what has been lost has been pride in skilled, well paid, secure employment which once mattered crucially to the nation. Equally lost are the comradeship and communal solidarity which the "gig" economy or work in a distribution centre, can never replace. Little wonder there has been anger and despair within mining communities, a sense of being thrust, like their lamps, picks, drills and helmets, on the scrap heap, a loss of identity which will take years to heal, a process that has social, economic and political consequences.

A recent report[1] by the British Association has highlighted how the pandemic has *"exposed, exacerbated and solidified existing inequalities in society"*. This is especially true for many communities in the less affluent areas of towns like Barnsley, Doncaster and also Rotherham, which has a significant ethnic minority population. Concerted action to help economic recovery and resilience, and to tackle urgently needed issues such as health, education and housing inequalities, is needed not just in South Yorkshire, but over the whole Yorkshire region.

Unlike coal mining, steel remains a major economic player in South Yorkshire, particularly the production of top-quality specialist stainless steels for key industrial processes and manufacturing, though even in such areas survival has been tough, with a privatised steel industry suffering constantly changing foreign ownership and subject to the variability of world markets and shifting trading conditions. Modern, fully automated state-of-the art steel plant and rolling mills also employ far less workers than the old labour-intensive steel works.

Like West Yorkshire, South Yorkshire is making the transition to a more varied and balanced economy, in which high tech industry and electronics have replaced outdated production methods. Niche markets are still there to be filled, especially in the new greener technologies. South Yorkshire has the skilled and younger workforce, and technical training institutions, to adapt to meet these emerging needs. Sheffield has already become a national leader in research and development of hydrogen technology, including pollution free hydrogen fuel cells to fuel cars or as a source of domestic and commercial heating.

And with its beautiful backdrop of hills, particularly the Peak District National Park which lies within the boundaries of both Barnsley and

Sheffield, and the "renaturing" and greening of so many former mining and steel production areas, South Yorkshire, like West Yorkshire, is truly becoming an excellent place to live, work and establish a new business.

Barnsley

Barnsley might have been the epicentre of the Yorkshire coal industry in the past, but the modern town is about far more than a heritage of coal. Close to its new Transport Interchange is a pleasant town centre with a Victorian Arcade and famous market, home of the celebrated cut of lamb the Barnsley Chop. The Market has been relocated into a fine new two storey building, linked by a glass walkway into a major new retail and leisure development known as **The Glass Works**. This underscores Barnsley's links with another major industry, glass making. Barnsley's imposing white Portland stone 1930s Town Hall provides, as well, as its main civic functions, the **Experience Barnsley** local museum.

Also in the centre is the **Cooper Gallery**, an art gallery and creative workspace given to the town in 1914 by local colliery owner Joseph Cooper to display his own art collection "for all to freely enjoy" .

Barnsley has produced some of Yorkshire's most recognised personalities. Maybe it is to do with the very typical, local version of the Yorkshire accent, well spiced with dialect words, recognisable in the speech of people like broadcaster Michael Parkinson, Cricket Umpire "Dickie" Bird and the poet and broadcaster Ian Macmillan "The Bard of Barnsley", who are all from the town.

Though coal mining has vanished, glass making remains an important industry in the town, together with food production, Barnsley claiming to have the largest cake baking factory in Europe. It is also, close to the M1, a major centre for the UK distribution industry.

Around 9% of area of Barnsley District lies within the Peak District National Park, an area dominated by huge areas of treeless gritstone moorland characteristic of the Dark Peak, including Thurlstone, and Langsett Moors above the Derbyshire's Upper Derwent valley. Dunford Bridge, above the little town of Penistone and close to the entrance of the now disused Woodhead Rail tunnel, lies where moorland streams from high on Holme Moss and Thurlstone Moors meet to form South

Yorkshire's main river, the Don. This is the river which runs through the edge of Barnsley and then through the three other South Yorkshire boroughs, Sheffield, Rotherham and Doncaster, becoming an important navigable waterway before joining the Ouse at Goole. The River Don and its many tributary streams also provided power during the crucial early years of the Industrial Revolution for countless iron foundries and forges. It is also fed by Barnsley's own main river, and major tributary of the Don, the Dearne.

West of the M1, Barnsley is indeed mainly rural, the undulating foothills of the Pennines intersected by narrow streams and shallow valleys. It is a landscape pockmarked by old mine workings, and disused railway lines, for example around Silkstone and Wentworth, their slag heaps now largely naturalised with grass and shrubs, and their scars healed as they disappear into the landscape, leaving their former villages to recover their rural charm.

To the north, just above the village of Cawthorne, is **Cannon Hall**, a fine 18th century house, now one of Barnsley's most attractive Museums. It was the former home of the Spencer family who made their fortune as local iron founders. It now is home to an impressive collection of furniture, paintings, sculpture and ceramics, including examples of the work of the De Morgan family. As well as extensive gardens, the wider landscaped park forms **Cannon Hall Country Park,** a beautiful area of open parkland, with a farm open to visitors nearby.

Worsbrough Mill Country Park, just to the east of the M1 and south of Barnsley, covers 240 acres of parkland and lake, with a cluster of buildings that includes a rare 17th century working water-powered flourmill, and former 19th century steam powered mill. The waterwheel takes its power from the nearby little River Dove, not the reservoir, which is now a noted bird sanctuary and local nature reserve.

A couple of stops on the railway to Sheffield from Barnsley's fine new transport interchange is **Elsecar Heritage Centre**. This is a largely 18th and early 19th century industrial village built to serve the mines and ironworks of Earl Fitzwilliam. At the terminus of the Elsecar branch of the Dearne and Dove Canal, the Centre has its own short section of heritage steam railway complete with a reconstructed station, exhibition areas, galleries, shops and cafes. But pride of place is the only surviving steam-powered Newcomen Beam Engine in the world still in its original engine house. The engine was constructed in 1795 to drain water from the deep shafts of nearby Elsecar New Colliery.

Rotherham

Two miles south east of Elsecar, across the boundary into Rotherham, lies the village of Wentworth and great country estate where the wealth of Earl Fitzwilliam was spent. **Wentworth Woodhouse** was started in 1725 by Thomas Watson-Wentworth 1st Marquis of Rockingham and continued by his son, using a variety of different architects, in both Palladian and baroque styles. It was not finally completed until 1790 when it came into the ownership via marriage, of the Fitzwilliams.

The House and its Park are now regarded as one of the great undiscovered treasures of England. The immense eastern façade is reputed to be the longest of any country house or chateau in Europe, and there are an estimated 300 rooms. The gardens and extensive parkland with their fantastic stone follies and great mausoleum were created by the celebrated landscape gardener Humphry Repton. After decades of neglect, including being used as a training centre for intelligence officers in World War II, and the destruction and use of much of the estate for open cast coal mining and eventual restoration, it became the Lady Mabel College of Physical Education. After more changes in ownership, the house, by then in urgent need of repair and restoration, was eventually acquired in 2017 by the Wentworth Woodhouse Preservation Trust. There are plans to eventually restore the building, the gardens and estate to their full glory, using funds from a variety of sources. Already the building has been used for several film and television period dramas including such popular successes as **Pride and Prejudice** (as Pemberley), **Mr Turner, Downtown Abbey** and **Darkest Hour.**

Rotherham, situated at the confluence of the Rivers Rother and Don, is an industrial town which is in fact of both considerable antiquity and heritage. Its magnificent parish church of All Saints, now has the status of a Minster, and occupies a site used for Christian worship for at least a thousand years. The present building dates back to the 14th and 15th century, and is regarded as one of the finest examples of English Perpendicular architectural style. Its splendour reflects the wealth of the town in the 15th century. It stands close to the compact town centre which has pleasant squares and pedestrianised shopping precincts, covered areas and a popular indoor market.

Much of the film **Brassed Off** was filmed at locations around the town.

Rotherham also shares with Wakefield, a rare example of a chantry bridge, the little carefully restored chapel on the town's old bridge dating from the 15th century. **Boston Castle** in Boston Park is a small hunting lodge built between 1773 and 74 by Thomas Howard, Earl of Effingham to commemorate the Victory of the Americans in the war of Independence. It now contains a small museum. The town's main museum is in the handsome 18th century house in **Clifton Park**. This features items from the town's long history as well as examples of locally made Rockingham pottery.

The South Yorkshire Transport Museum at Parkgate reflects Rotherham's more recent history. It has a fleet of vintage buses, offering rides to local attractions plus a wealth of vintage transport exhibits from scooters to bicycles, motor bikes, cars, army vehicles and even an electric milk float.

Rotherham from the mid–18th century onwards became a major centre for cast iron and steel production. It was the combination of plentiful local supplies of coal and iron ore plus the improvements in the River Don in 1751 to create the Sheffield and South Yorkshire Navigation that was to act as the blue touchpaper. Over the next decades many iron foundries and glass works were being established in Rotherham and surrounding towns. Rotherham was a focal point for this growth during the 19th century. The cannons used on Nelson's Victory were manufactured in the town. The Parkgate Iron works, established in 1826, made iron plates for Brunel's pioneering steamship The Great Eastern in 1851. Iron and later steel were produced in the town in huge quantities, accelerated by the growth of the railways. Glass making was also of major importance in the town, an activity which continues to the present day. It still has one of the largest surviving steel works in South Yorkshire, Liberty Steel.

Much of the story of steel making is told at the award-winning **Magma Science Adventure Centre** opened on the site of the former huge steel works at Templeborough near Rotherham. Using the theme of the four traditional elements, earth air, fire and water, aspects of scientific and technological research are explored. Particularly spectacular is an audio-visual experience to replicate the different stages of steel making.

Among recent distinguished sons of Rotherham are former Conservative party leader William Hague and the educationalist, writer, and author Gervase Phinn. Phinn's richly entertaining books about children and their teachers in the classrooms of the Yorkshire Dales and Vale of York, such as **The School at the Top of the Dale,** have become best sellers.

Doncaster

Doncaster, like Rotherham, has a history going back to Iron Age and Roman times, a town and fortress known by the Romans as Danum, guarding the vital crossing of the River Don on what was the alternative great Roman road, Ermine Street, between London and York avoiding the treacherous Humber crossing. In 1971 the remains of a shield belonging to a Roman soldier was found in the ruins of the fort under the Minster. Now known as the Danum Shield, it is on display alongside a carefully recreated replica, in Doncaster's Museum in the new **Danum Heritage** complex.

In later centuries Danum was anglicised to Doncaster, the castle by the Don. An entry in the Doomsday Book, generally presumed to be about Doncaster, indicates that by 1089 the little Anglian settlement by the river crossing had a church, probably wooden, on the site of what had been the Roman fort, and also two corn mills. Until it was improved for the purposes of navigation, Doncaster was also important as being the highest point that boats of any size could travel from the Humber and Ouse up the River Don, so it became like York, Leeds and Wakefield an important river-served inland port.

The use of "gate" for several of its streets also suggests an Anglo-Norse presence – for example Frenchgate, presumably the street of Norman-French or simply foreign traders. Intriguingly the little town was given to Scotland in a treaty dated 1136 agreed between King Stephen of England and King David I of Scotland. That treaty was never legally rescinded so in the event of Scottish independence, Doncaster inhabitants might be able to claim their free passage to Scotland.

Nigel Fossard, the Norman Lord of the Manor, fortified the town, with earth ditches and embankments, probably topped by timber palisades, but in later years more substantial stone gates were erected. Richard I gave the town a charter in 1194 and a full market charter was granted in 1248. The church was rebuilt in Norman times and this survived until 1853 when it was destroyed by fire. It was replaced in 1854–8 by Sir George Gilbert Scott's magnificent neo-Gothic Minster. This recreated some features of the original church, whose vaulted crypt still remains below the vestry, but is far grander in scale. Doncaster Minster, as it is now known, is crowned by a splendid 170-foot tower which has become a major local landmark.

By the later Middle Ages, Doncaster was an important market and commercial centre, becoming the largest town in the southern part of the old West Riding. It continued to flourish as an important coaching town on the Great North Road through the 17th and 18th centuries. Several very attractive Georgian houses survive in the town. Most splendid of all is the rather grand Mansion House, dating from 1748, designed by the noted architect James Paine (who was involved with the design of Wakefield's Nostell Priory) to serve as the prestigious residence and entertaining rooms of the town's mayor. It is now owned by Doncaster Council and used for a variety of civic functions. **Cusworth Hall**, another fine 18th century country mansion, in what is now a small country park two miles north of the town, contains Doncaster's main local museum.

Brodsworth, about six miles northwest of Doncaster, was the chosen rural retreat of the Thellusson family, London bankers of French Huguenot origin. In 1860 they used their formidable wealth to rebuild **Brodsworth Hall**. This became an elegantly designed and sumptuously decorated and furnished country house, set in particularly lovely gardens. It is one of the finest houses of its period in the North of England in the ownership of English Heritage. The family benefited from allowing nearby Brodsworth colliery to mine their land, close to and underneath the estate. They also rented out land nearby for a well-planned village at Woodlands, for miners and their families, funding the erection of the church.

Doncaster Racecourse immediately to the east of the town, first attracted horse racing on what was the town moor in the 16th century.

In 1600 the town tried to ban the annual horse races because of the "ruffians" it attracted. But it was decided in later years to mark out the course and profit from the many racegoers who would come to spend their money in town. It is now one of the most important racecourses in Britain, hosting the celebrated annual St. Leger stakes, first run in 1778.

Like other towns in South Yorkshire Doncaster grew rapidly in the 19th century as a centre of industry. Most of the town centre including the Corn Exchange dates from this period. A key event was the arrival of the great Northern Railway from London in 1849 on route to York, which was to eventually become the East Coast Main Line. Within a decade, Doncaster had become a major railway junction with lines to Hull, Lincoln, Sheffield, Leeds. In 1853 reflecting the importance of the town as a rail hub, the GNR moved its main locomotive building and repair works from Boston to Doncaster.

Over the next century, Doncaster Locomotive and Carriage Works became pioneers and innovators of railway carriage and locomotive design. Britain's first railway coaches with through corridors were built in the workshops, plus the first dining and sleeping cars. It was also the home of great classics of steam locomotive design such as the elegant Stirling Singles and Ivatt Atlantics. In the 20th century, as part of the London and North Eastern Railway, Doncaster Works became the birthplace of the celebrated Gresley Pacifics, including perhaps the world's most famous steam locomotive **The Flying Scotsman**, and a few years later the equally iconic streamlined **Mallard**, the world's fastest steam locomotive whose record of 126 miles per hour on the East Coast Main Line in 1938 has never been beaten. When the building of steam locomotives came to an end in Doncaster in 1957, having constructed 2,000 locomotives over a century, the Works, now part of British Rail Engineering, switched production to diesel shunters and freight locomotives, plus some electric locomotives.

Sadly rail locomotive construction, in the land that invented railways, no longer takes place in Doncaster and what is left of the huge works site, not taken for housing, is now occupied by Wabtec Rail Works for passenger fleet maintenance and refurbishment. But Doncaster has also become the focal point of important developments in rail research and training opportunities managed by a cluster of several different companies.

Doncaster Rail Heritage Centre now forms part of the new **Danum Gallery**, Library Heritage complex now open in the town. Whilst Flying Scotsman and Mallard are inevitably part of the national collection in York National Railway Museum, two Doncaster built locomotives, Ivatt Atlantic 251 and K1 Green Arrow form the centre of the display.

But Doncaster's heritage isn't just about industrial development. Four miles south west of the town is spectacular **Conisbrough Castle**. Built on a rocky spur of magnesian limestone in a prominent position above the Don valley, the first fortress was built in the late 11th century by the Norman, William de Warenne. A century later it came into the hands of Hamelin Plantagenet. He and his son William built the huge castle in local stone as a defensive fortification.

By the 16th century the walls of the castle had suffered from damage by subsidence, and it therefore had no effective role in the Civil War. It remained in ensuing centuries as a romantic ruin, and provided the inspiration for Sir Walter Scott's 1819 novel **Ivanhoe.** The Castle is now owned and managed by English Heritage.

Four miles east of Doncaster, near the village of Branton on the site of a former farm and visitor centre is the **Yorkshire Wildlife Park**, a 110-hectare zoological park, conservation and educational centre established in 2009. The enclosures house important collections of large mammals from all over the world, many rescued from poachers or endangered species such as polar bears being bred for reintroduction into the wild.

Just three miles south east of Doncaster and 19 north of Sheffield is Doncaster-Sheffield airport that serves South Yorkshire but also the wider region, accessible by a new spur road off the M18 and a projected new rail link. It utilises the former Finningley RAF station site, built on former agricultural land. It was opened in 2005, and for a time was known as Robin Hood Airport. In 2019 it carried about 1.9 million passengers, compared with around 4 million carried by Leeds-Bradford. Whether future climate concerns will allow domestic and holiday travel to continue to grow at previous rates, is an open question. Unlike Leeds-Bradford, built on a hilly ridge and often closed because of bad weather, Doncaster-Sheffield is in the less exposed and windy lowland, and is further away from densely populated areas. It also has a runway capable of taking larger trans-Atlantic aircraft.

North of Doncaster is a riverine landscape of meandering streams rivers, canals and wetland through richly fertile farmland, punctuated by former mining villages such as Stainforth, Hatfield and Thorne, birthplace of celebrated Yorkshire soprano Lesley Garrett.

In the 17th century, Hatfield Chase, as its names implies, was an area of forest and marshland rich in wildlife and the favourite hunting terrain of King Charles I. However, the area frequently flooded. Charles therefore employed the great Dutch land engineer Cornelius Vermuyden (1595–1677) to drain and reclaim the fenland. This Vermuyden duly did, one of many such land reclamation schemes in eastern England that earned him both a knighthood and British citizenship.

At Hatfield, the solution was to build a new deep section of artificial river or navigation to carry excess water and drain the fenlands, in effect connecting the River Don to a wide bend in the River Ouse near a hamlet known as Goole, where a bridge was built over the new section of river.

Goole

What turned out to be the real benefit of the new waterway was the hugely improved navigation along the lower level of the Don, with improvements to the river as far as Rotherham and Tinsley, with first a road, then a canal link to Sheffield opened from Tinsley in 1819. This was a huge stimulus to the industrialisation of the whole of South Yorkshire, enabling bulk supplies of coal, iron, glass and many other finished and raw material access to and from the North Sea for onward shipment goods to and from the Continent or London.

The new waterway enabled Goole to develop what it still is today, South Yorkshire's main inland port. New docks were built on the Ouse to accommodate sea-going vessels from Hull, London and across the North Sea, with a system of locks and floating docks to allow larger sea-going vessels to berth and unload there. Cranes were positioned to unload vessels for transhipment along the narrower inland waterways; one brilliant concept being the use of small squat iron barges known as Tom Puddings that could be filled with coal and hauled behind a tugboat. At Goole, each Tom Pudding could be lifted by specially designed boat hoists or lifts and its contents loaded into larger ships or barges heading down river towards Hull or upriver to Leeds. One of the Tom Pudding Boat Hoists, last used in 1985, has been preserved as an industrial monument.

Goole also benefited from the building of the Knottingley-Goole section of the Aire & Calder Navigation opened in 1826. The coming of the Lancashire & Yorkshire Railway in 1848, and the short-lived Hull and Barnsley Railway in 1885, created even better access between the Yorkshire coalfields and the port of Hull than the canals could offer, though the waterway still scored on the cheaper carriage of heavy bulk material such as coal and minerals. This is evidenced by the construction of The New Junction Canal, opened in 1905 and the last commercial waterway to be constructed in Britain, to give Doncaster even more direct access to the Aire Calder Navigation and Goole.

Goole remains an important, even growing, inland port with significant container traffic to replace coal, as well as steel and chemicals. The town was originally within West Riding but later was transferred to Humberside and is now within East Riding. Despite such confusions it retains its strong cultural (and rail) links with South Yorkshire. The town's riverside now has a small leisure marina, but sadly its fascinating Boat Museum was forced to close in 2020.

Fortunately, a sizeable area of the ancient peatlands of Thorne, Goole, Crowe and Hatfield Moors was not drained by Vermuyden, and survived land reclamation work. It remained an ancient common but until the 1980s was used as a rich source of peat extraction, originally for fuel and later for gardens. **The Humberhead Peatlands National Nature Reserve** covers a massive 2,887 hectares, the largest area of raised peat bog in the lowlands of the British Isles. The site is internationally important, both as an example of a lowland raised peat mire and for its insects, amphibians, plant life and birdlife including breeding nightjars. The Peatlands are a remnant of a large wetland that occupied the floodplain centuries ago. The peat has been cut for fuel throughout recorded history, but this usage is now strictly forbidden to allow the peatland, a major mechanism to store carbon, to recover, and to protect its habitat.

Sheffield

Sheffield, Yorkshire's second city in terms of its population, at 735,000 more than half the total of South Yorkshire, and economic importance, is, like Leeds, a modern metropolis with a great, if very different history to its West Yorkshire counterpart.

The present City and Metropolitan Borough of Sheffield covers roughly the ancient, most southerly division or skyre of Northumbria and Jorvik, known as Hallamshire, on its southern borders with Mercia. The origin of what is now Sheffield was a small Anglian settlement, probably dating from the 8th century, at the confluence of the Rivers Sheaf and Don. The Norman invaders in the 11th century built a castle on this strategic site in the Upper Don valley, close to what had been an Anglo-Saxon longhouse.

The Castle gave Sheffield, as the market town that served its garrison became known, prominence over other villages. Recent research has suggested that by late medieval times the Castle was an impressively large structure. It was deemed sufficiently secure and important to be a prison for Mary Queen of Scots in 1574. It was damaged, whether by divine intervention or otherwise, in a minor earthquake in that same year, requiring the Queen's urgent removal.

During the Civil War Sheffield was held successively by the Parliamentarians and Royalists before Cromwell's forces having gained final control in 1644, razed it to the ground. The site was later occupied by the old Castle Market, with some visible relics. These have largely been lost under modern, recent development. But the town continued to thrive long after its castle had been destroyed to become the major centre of economic activity in Hallamshire.

Sheffield is often described as a city "Built on Seven Hills" drawing comparisons with Rome or San Francisco; but some commentators have disputed this, suggesting the actual number is between five and eight. It might be better in fact to think in terms of the city's five rivers – the Sheaf (that gave the city its name), Don, Loxley, Rivelin and Porter. It was the fast-flowing water of these streams and rivers that became the prime reasons for the city's growth.

From medieval time onwards Sheffield became a centre for the manufacture of cutlery. The earliest mention of a Sheffield cutlery in a document was as far back as 1297[2]. There is even a mention of a knife from Sheffield in Chaucer's Canterbury Tales, dating from the late 15th century.

This trade grew from an abundance of local useful seams of ironstone to provide raw materials, for example the outcropping seam at Tankersley near Barnsley. Dense local woodlands provided sufficient processed charcoal to create more intense heat for smelting in small bloomeries and early forges. But better-quality steel, a more malleable alloy of iron, first developed in the Middle East, was imported from quite early times via Hull and the River Don from Germany, the Baltic and even northern Spain. From the mid 18th century onwards, coal from the rich Yorkshire coalfields around Barnsley and Rotherham could be brought along the navigable River Don and the new canals to allow significant increases in production.

The other key factor was waterpower. Along each of the five rivers, waterwheels were used to provide the power to mechanise the process of grinding and hammering of steel for knives and tools. By 1604 there were 28 waterwheels recorded in Hallamshire which had risen to 32 by 1664. But just over a century later, in 1770 just before the advent of steam power, this number had risen to 133 working rolling mills, tilt hammers and forges. This was made up by 47 on the River Don, 33 on the Sheaf, 42 on the Loxley 24 on the Rivelin, and 15 on the Porter.[3] **The Shepherd Wheel** – a small grinding mill on the Porter Beck, in Whitely Woods is a uniquely well-preserved working example.

Little Mesters – and Cutlers

Up until the 18th century, craftsmen known as Little Mesters working alone or with a couple of apprentices, in a workshop at the back of their cottage or sometimes in a shared space, would produce the entire knife, scythe, chisel or other tool. By the 18th century specialisations had taken over the process, with forgers producing the basic knife, grinders smoothing and sharpening the blade, and cutlers polishing or "buffing" the blade, putting on the handle and doing all the necessary work for the finished product.

This system of individual craftsmen in their tiny workshops continued right up until the 21st century, though most mass production from the later 19th century onwards was delivered from the larger factories that were developed in and around the city.

Even by the 16th century the cutlers had organised themselves into a trade association rather like a guild – The Fellowship and Company of Cutlers, primarily to ensure high quality standards for all Sheffield-made cutlery, to ensure apprentices were properly trained, to keep strangers away from cutlers' crafts and to keep prices stable by preventing overstocking. By 1624 the Company became legally incorporated as the Company of Cutlers headed by the Master Cutler. It operated from the handsome **Cutlers Hall**, the first such building of that name being erected in Church Street in 1638. The present fine building dates from 1832 and is used for major civic events, including the annual Cutlers' Feast. There is also a small museum with silverware and other objects relating to the work of the Cutlers in the city.

But by the 18th century, industrialisation of the process led to the setting up of major companies for the manufacture of cutlery and specialist knives and other items of kitchenware, as well as more ornate silver alloy or silver-plated decorative items, which could be made at a fraction of the price of pure silver. This process was invented in the city.

The city in fact became famed for the quality of its silverware, and a Sheffield hallmark survives in use to this day.

Culery firms such as Walker & Hall, Mappin & Webb, Joseph Rodgers, Firths thrived to become household names. A late entry was Viners, established in the city by a German immigrant Adolphe Viener in 1901. Viners grew to become Sheffield's biggest cutlery manufacture by the 1950s, until eventually defeated by overseas competition. It has been estimated that by 1891, 25,743 people were employed in cutlery and related trades in Sheffield. By this time the name Sheffield was renowned throughout the world for the high quality of its knives, cutlery and other bladed tools.

The manufacture of saws, files and other tools became hugely important for the city. Spear & Jackson's origins in Sheffield date back to 1760. It is one of the many household names to emerge from the city's great industrial past.

Iron forging and steel making became another mighty Sheffield industry, one interestingly shared with Middlesbrough at the opposite end of Yorkshire. But Sheffield, a far older town, was England's great pioneering city in terms of steel making.

The technique of creating steel by cementation, heating up alternate layers of charcoal (later coke) and pig iron in one or more stone pots inside a furnace to produce what was known as blister steel, a technique which was developed in Germany in the 16th century. This was widely used in Sheffield. Amazingly the last surviving Sheffield Cementation Furnace still survives as a small historic monument in Doncaster Street. It dates from 1848 and it would have been just one of an estimated 250 such structures in operation in the city around 1860.

But more revolutionary techniques were to come. Benjamin Huntsman (1704–76) was born into a Lincolnshire Quaker farming family. He came to Yorkshire and as a young man worked as a clockmaker in Doncaster. In 1814 he moved to Handsworth in Sheffield, where he developed a way of transforming crude blister steel into higher performance cast steel using clay crucibles and coke to achieve the necessary high temperatures. At first local cutlers refused to use Huntsman's steel because of its harder nature. He therefore was forced to sell his new type of steel in France.

However, when French cutlery makers started selling their wares in England, using Huntsman's steel, in competition with their own products, the Sheffield men panicked. They started using Huntsman's steel. Unfortunately for Huntsman he had not patented his process. The story is that one of his competitors, a local iron founder called Walker, posed as a beggar on a cold winter's night, asking the compassionate Quaker to allow him to sleep by his furnace fire. But in the night, he stole Huntsman's secret process. This was rapidly taken up by many other steel makers. It allowed Sheffield steelmaking to grow so successfully that by 1860 the city was producing 80,000 tons per year, half the total amount of steel produced in Europe.

The other great hero of Sheffield steelmaking was Henry Bessemer (1813–98). A gifted inventor and entrepreneur, Bessemer invented a revolutionary process for converting basic pig iron to high quality steel by oxygenating molten iron by blowing air through it at high temperatures. The process drastically reduced the cost of steel. Unlike Huntsman, Bessemer patented the process and soon overcame initial apathy by producing steel at between £10-£15 per ton cheaper than his competitors, who were then forced to adopt his patent, thus making a massive fortune for its inventor. The Atlas Works, owned by ironmaster John Brown, was the first to use the Bessemer process. It became one of the foremost manufacturers of armour plate for the Royal Navy and other armed services.

You can see an actual example of a Bessemer Converter outside Sheffield's **Kelham Island Museum.** This is a nationally important museum illustrating the development of the cutlery, tool making and steel industries in Sheffield and surrounding areas, from the earliest days of the Little Mesters to the present time, including a street and even actual workshops. Situated on a man-made island within the River Don, pride of place is given to the River Don Engine, a 400 ton, 12,000 horsepower steam engine, the largest and most powerful surviving in Britain today. Built in 1905 and used in a steelworks in Grimesthorpe until 1978, it is demonstrated in action daily.

Abbeydale Industrial Hamlet near the historic southern boundary of ancient Yorkshire at Dore, is more of a Skansen type open-air museum, situated on an old steel manufacturing site alongside the River Sheaf which goes back to the 13th century, the present buildings dating mainly from an 18th century steel and scythe works. There is a carefully restored and furnished Manager's House, and a nearby worker's cottage. Workshops, waterwheels, tilt hammers, an 1817 Grinding Hull and a steam engine are also on display. Of special interest is the last complete surviving crucible steel furnace.

An interesting homage to these great steel heritage museums has been paid by two very successful regional traditional real-ale craft breweries in the city that take their names from these two museums – Kelham Island and Abbeydale.

Steel making is not just about craft beer and history. In 1913 Harry Brearley, son of a Sheffield steelworker, invented a special "rustless" steel whilst he was working on the creation of new gun steels in the Firth Brown Research Laboratories[4]. Its use rapidly spread worldwide. In the later part of the 20th century and the first decades of the 21st, despite immense overseas competition, in particular from India and the Far East, and successive ways of post-war nationalisation and privatisation, Sheffield and South Yorkshire have held their own in the global manufacture of specialist steels for a wide range of technical purposes.

Several of the great Sheffield steel foundries operating as part of British Steel came together with Firth Brown in 1983 to form Sheffield Forgemasters. The company is one of the leading companies in the world of large and complex steel castings, making forged and cast steel components for the defence, engineering, nuclear, offshore, petrochemical, and steel processing industries, including some of the largest steel castings ever made.

Visitors arriving at Sheffield's recently refurbished Station, whose main entrance leads directly into Sheaf Square, are reminded of the city's great steel and cutlery heritage by the dramatic Cutting-Edge sculpture and water feature made of shining stainless steel with a leaping salmon sculpture linking the exhibit back to Sheffield's five rivers.

Sheffield's railways – and trams

Railways helped create the success of the Sheffield steel industry. Yet in terms of railways Sheffield has had mixed fortunes. In the early days of the iron road, the city was by-passed by George Stephenson's North Midland Railway between Derby and Leeds, with only a branch line connection to Masborough near Rotherham in 1838. A second important link to Manchester and Lincoln via the Sheffield Ashton-under-Lyne and Manchester Railway opened in 1841. This required the building of the first great Woodhead rail tunnel.

It was not until 1870 that Sheffield finally got its present main line station with the opening of the Midland line serving Pond Street (later Midland) station, giving the city fast frequent express trains to London via Derby and to Manchester via the Hope Valley.

However, the city also had an even more impressive higher-speed direct railway line to London – the Great Central Line opened in 1899 from Manchester to London. This ran from the city's Victoria Station direct to London Marylebone via Nottingham and Leicester, thus also connecting Sheffield with the East Midlands as well Manchester. In 1955 the northern section of the line from Sheffield Victoria via Stocksbridge (where there still is a large steel works) and Penistone to Manchester, known as the Woodhead line after the tunnel, was electrified using what became a non-standard Direct Current 15k volt system (though standard in The Netherlands). This was done to offer a far better system for freight trains, especially coal trains from South Yorkshire to the major power stations in Merseyside. A third larger twin rail tunnel was built underneath the Woodhead Pass to allow for the extra space for overhead wire catenary. Another feature was that the entire line from Manchester and Sheffield through to London was built by the Great Central to larger Berne-gauge standard, with a forward-thinking option to eventually allow the running of through trains to the Continent via a Channel Tunnel, something which was only finally built a century later. But it also provided fast and efficient express passenger and freight services between Manchester and Sheffield.

Unbelievably, in 1981 the decision was taken by the Westminster Government to close the entire line between Guide Bridge and Sheffield, (the line from Huddersfield and Penistone had to be rerouted via Barnsley), demolish Victoria Station and scrap all but a few of the modern electric locomotives which were sold to Dutch Railways. All rail traffic westwards was now forced to use the slower, crowded, winding Hope Valley line shared by freight and local trains. It is difficult to imagine any other country in the world in which a central Government could take a myopic decision to close an electrified railway between two of their country's major cities, leaving only a totally inadequate, anachronistic diesel-powered rail link between these two great centres of population and economic activity. Parts of what was one of the most modern railways in Britain in the 1950s, is now a footpath and cycling route- the Trans Pennine Trail.

On the positive side Sheffield was one of the last in Britain to retain its popular tramway network well into the mid–20th century. It was as late 1960 when the last tram ran through the city's streets. Appropriately enough, in 1994 it was one of the first to introduce a modern light rail or tram system – Supertram. This re-invention of a Victorian urban success story has grown to be a network of four lines operating from 50 stations and covering 21 miles (34.6km). Some sections of track require street running, others are on separate traffic-free reservations. The latest section to open has been the Tram-Train service to Rotherham, finally opened in 2018, a system whereby specially strengthened hybrid tram/railcars run in part on rail tracks from the outskirts of Sheffield to Rotherham.

Supertram has proved a huge success – despite the failure to regulate competing buses, though by awarding the operating contract to a bus operator, Stagecoach, this has in effect created a protective mini-monopoly as the company are major bus operators in the city. In 2019 over 10.5 million passengers were carried, many from well promoted park-and-ride termini into the city centre.

Just as important perhaps, Supertram is a visible symbol of Sheffield as a progressive modern city. Supertram links the inner and outer suburbs with the cultural heart of the city, including the main university areas, ascending the steep hillsides out of the city centre with impressive ease. Cheap, frequent, efficient trams are a superb, low-cost way of getting around the city, and to some extent have compensated for the total lack of electrification of the wider urban, regional and intercity rail network, including the long overdue electrification of the Midland main line to London.

The challenge of Meadowhall

The age of the car and the motorway network, whilst befitting the city in many respects, given the closeness of city to the M1 motorway, has had its downside, not only in the traffic jams that Supertram has since helped to relieve, but by the opening in 1994 of Meadowhall, on what had been a derelict steelworks site. Meadowhall was an early example of a highly ambitious out-of-town shopping centre, designed to serve a new car-borne generation of shoppers. It lies just four miles from Sheffield and three from the centre of Rotherham, easily reached by a spur off the M1 to feed drivers into huge multi-storey car parks. The concept was to provide a warm safe environment for a city-style shopping experience without a city, sheltered from the often-inclement Yorkshire weather. 280 shops share the complex ranging from large multi-national chain stores to smaller boutique outlets, cafes, restaurants, a multiplex cinema. The ersatz neo-Byzantine architecture of domes and piazzas offers a strangely detached experience within the post-industrial, warehouse and motorway landscape of this part of South Yorkshire. But for most shoppers easy parking, level walkways under cover, bright lights and a choice of familiar branded chain stories are what really matter.

There is little doubt that this huge new centre hit the retail economy of Sheffield, Barnsley and Rotherham in particular hard, though of course many new retail jobs were created in the centre itself. Although initially totally designed around the car, in later years a new railway station was opened and Supertram was extended from the city centre to have a terminus in what has become a major travel interchange.

Meadowhall was an important late 20th century experiment in retail planning. After the initial shock, Sheffield city centre did recover, the centre offering a different kind of shopping and cultural experience, linked to small galleries, traditional pubs, café bars, restaurants, theatres, and more independent and specialist shops. However, the damage to smaller centres such as Rotherham and Barnsley and even more so to the smaller former mining towns, may have been more fundamental and longer lasting.

Interestingly the digital revolution, accelerated by the pandemic, has also resulted in fundamental changes to shopping habits, with out-of-town retail parks beginning to suffer a significant decline. This may impact on Meadowhall. Whether Sheffield can buck that trend by offering a much more culturally focused experience, is far from clear, though the closure of the iconic John Lewis Department store, the successor to Sheffield's much loved Cole Brothers store, is not a good omen.

The Universities

One reason why Sheffield has survived the challenge of Meadowhall so well is because of its universities and large student population.

The city has two universities. The oldest, the University of Sheffield, one of the prestigious Russell Group, dates from 1905 with the amalgamation of three local colleges into a single academic institution. Over the last century it has grown to provide for over 30,000 students, a third of which are postgraduates. The University has an impressive record of academic and research achievement, particularly in the applied sciences, with no less than eight Nobel Laureates among its alumni. Amongst many highly achieving graduates to secure worldwide fame is the novelist Hilary Mantell.

The University also houses several small museums of publicly available collections such as the **Alfred Davey Museum of Zoology**, with its links to Darwin, the **Museum of Glass**, and the **Traditional Heritage Museum** with its links to popular culture, folklore and dialect. There is also the fascinating **National Fairground and Circus** archive, one of the most important UK collections, including materials, documentation and memorabilia relating to the world of the now rapidly vanishing travelling popular entertainment industries.

Sheffield Hallam University received its charter in 1982 to achieve University status, building on the success of what had already been the highly regarded Sheffield Polytechnic. The University has two campuses, City Campus in the centre of the city and in Broomhall two miles from the centre. With an equally impressive 30,000 student population, it has a vocational slant including research in technology relating to physical health and wellbeing, education, business studies, arts and design and biomedical research.

The University also hosts the English Institute of Sport, the national centre of sport training and scientific research, opened in 2003. Many UK Olympic athletes have benefited from its work.

The creative arts

60,000 students make a huge difference to the economy and cultural life of any city and Sheffield is no exception, and the city has become a major centre of both popular and classical music. The Annual **Tramlines Festival of Music and Comedy** in Hillsborough Park is now one of the biggest events of its kind in the UK. The **Sensoria Festival of Music, Film and Digital** uses different locations in the city, including clubs and pubs, for a wide variety of real life, streaming events and talks. The city also has a massive 13,000 seat O2 Arena between Meadowhall and Rotherham to present world class artists and groups. Among internationally renowned performers from Sheffield are the Arctic Monkeys and Jarvis Cocker.

Sheffield City Hall also functions as the city's main concert hall with a huge variety of group and solo acts and performance by visiting symphony orchestras and choirs. The handsome **Lyceum Theatre**, the only survivor of the city's many Victorian and Edwardian Theatres and Music Halls, is the main venue for touring products including West End shows, musicals and opera.

But Sheffield's most significant theatre is **The Crucible**. It was built in 1971 with an at that time revolutionary apron stage with the audience sitting on three sides close to the actors. The Crucible has earned a national reputation for its brilliant stage productions, classical, modern and experimental. The stage is also readily adapted for musical shows. The gifted young Sheffield-born playwright Chris Bush has established a national reputation at The Crucible for such plays as **TONY – the Blair Musical** and **The Band Plays On**, and a feminist version of the Faust legend, **Faustus, that Damned Woman**. Many of her plays, humorous and satirical, are firmly rooted in the life and culture of the city. She is now an Assistant Director of the theatre.

The Crucible is also known internationally as the venue for the annual World Snooker Championship, an event that attracts top competitors and audiences from across the globe. With the smaller **Studio Theatre** and the **Montgomery Theatre** close by, Tudor Square has become a theatre and cultural quarter. This also includes the **Graves Art Gallery**. Its permanent collection houses the work of some outstanding British artists, especially of the 20th century, as well as touring exhibitions. The Graves Gallery complements the **Millennium Gallery** adjacent to the Winter Gardens. This new gallery houses the collection of prints, drawings, artefacts and manuscripts given to the city for the enlightenment of working people by the great art-critic, painter and philosopher John Ruskin, plus the Metalwork collection and changing Craft & Design exhibitions.

Gardens and parks

Across the road from the Tudor Square and Surrey Street is Sheffield's handsome Town Hall, built in what was grandly called Renaissance style, opened by Queen Victoria in her Jubilee year of 1897, four years after Sheffield had officially been declared a city.

Close by are two of the city's major delights, the award-winning **Peace Gardens** and **Winter Gardens**.

The Peace Gardens opened in 1938 were originally known as St Paul's Gardens but took the name from the abortive attempts to secure peace with the Munich Agreement. They were restored and expanded in the late 1990s with water features added, to represent the five rivers of Sheffield and to replicate the fast flow of molten steel. The Garden is dedicated to the memory of the people of Sheffield who have died in recent Wars, including both World Wars and the Spanish Civil War.

The Winter Gardens, opened in 2003, occupy a huge modern glasshouse, 21 metres high and 70 metres long, carefully air conditioned and containing 2,500 tropical or sub-tropical plants, kept secure from the harsh Yorkshire climate, in what is in effect an indoor park. Galleries, cafes adjoin the main central corridor.

This has created a green focal point for the city's main civic, entertainment, cultural and shopping areas. This is especially appropriate for a city which can claim to contain more trees per head of population than any city in Europe, with 61% of the city being green space of some sort. A third of city is within the Peak District National Park.

Justly famous are the city's great parks. The city's oldest, **Weston Park**, dates from 1875 when it was laid out as an ornamental public garden. Weston House in the grounds became the Mappin Art Gallery and Museum. It is now **West Park Museum**, the city's principal museum, devoted to archaeology, social and natural history and with an important decorative arts collection. Among items of national importance is a rare 7th century Anglian helmet – the Bent Grange Helmet. **Meersbrook Park** contains the beautiful timber framed **Bishops' House**, erected around 1500, one of only three timber houses to survive in the city, the other being the Old Queen's Head pub in the city centre and Broom Hall.

The **Botanical Gardens** created in 1836 is an outstanding garden and park in its own right, with around 5,000 species of plants in its 19 acres, but its highlight has to be the great Victorian glass houses in the style of Paxton's Kew Garden pavilions. **Hillsborough Park** to the north west of the city, covers 50 acres, and also contains the **Hillsborough Walled Gardens** recently restored and dedicated to the memory of the 96 football fans, mainly from Liverpool, who died in the terrible nearby Hillsborough Stadium Football disaster of 1989.

Perhaps one of the real glories of Sheffield is to be able to walk literally from the city centre of suburbs directly into the Peak District National Park. For example, from Malin Bridge, the Supertram terminus a couple of miles from the city centre, a footpath leads along the Rivelin Valley past the site of several early waterwheels and out into the magnificent open landscapes beyond Rivelin Rocks, the wide open spaces of Hallam Moors or towards the great craggy ridge of Stanage.

The Peak District has for centuries been Sheffield's green lung, its special space. From late Victorian times onwards Sheffield people poured out every weekend, with boots and rucksacks, catching the morning train along the Hope Valley Railway from Sheffield to Grindleford, Hathersage, Hope, or Edale, to claim the heather moors of the Peak District as their own. Were it not for its importance to people from Sheffield and Manchester to reach Edale, the Hope Valley railway line would have closed in the 1960s.

Later generations took packed double deck buses every Sunday morning to Castleton, Bakewell or the Upper Derwent valley. Cars replaced trains and bus travel for most visitors from the late 20th century onwards, with all the resultant congestion and pollution that has caused. But excellent public transport links by train and bus between Sheffield, Barnsley and the Peak District remain.

Approximately a third of the city lies within the Peak District National Park. It is interesting to note the degree to which the existence and success of the Peak District National Park owes to key citizens of Sheffield. The great pioneering campaigner for access to the moors of the Peak District, G.H.B. Ward of Sheffield Ramblers Clarion Club, grew up in a city street in the centre of the City, as in more recent times did Terry Howard, of Sheffield Campaign for Access to Moorland (SCAM), a still very active contemporary defender of access to the moorlands of the Peak.

The Friends of the Peak District, the National Park Society that campaigns for and champions the Peak District, are also the Peak and South Yorkshire branch of the CPRE. This was the organisation that produced two of the Peak District's most influential campaigners – Gerald (1912–95) and Ethel (1894–1986) Haythornthwaite[5]. But CPRE South Yorkshire also does vital work defending Sheffield's extensive and precious Green Belt, and also that of the other towns of South Yorkshire. Their office is in central Sheffield. This reflects just how deeply Sheffield citizens feel that the Peak District National Park, not just the parts within their city's boundaries, is somewhere they belong to, their *Heimat*.

Sheffield's dilemma as a city therefore is that it looks in two directions. Historically and culturally the city, and Hallamshire, are an integral part of Yorkshire. But as a great modern metropolis, a city region, Sheffield also, economically and socially looks to the south. Its sphere of influence, including its travel to work areas, extend towards Worksop, Chesterfield, Mansfield, Nottingham, Derbyshire and the East Midlands, ancient Mercia.

Ultimately this does not matter. Being Yorkshire is a state of mind, more important than any lines on maps, economic links or political jurisdictions.

Notes

1 Shaping the COVID decade: addressing the long-term societal impacts of COVID-19 | The British Academy 2021
2 Hey David 2005 *The South Yorkshire Steel Industry and the Industrial Revolution* in Northern History XLII March 2005
3 Vickers J. Edward 1978 *A Popular History of Sheffield* pp74–78
4 Ibid p87
5 Smith Roly 2021 *Walking Class Heroes – Pioneers of the Right to Roam* Signal, Oxford

Key Sources

Regional

Atherden Margaret & Wallace Veronica(Ed): *The Future of the Uplands: Prospects for Northern England* (York: PLACE 2014)

Beck Howard: *Yorkshire's Roots* (Wilmslow: Sigma 1996)

Bradford Michael: *The Fight for Yorkshire* (York: Hutton Press 1988)

Brears Peter: *Traditional Food in Yorkshire* (Edinburgh: John Donald 1987)

Cowley Bill: *Farming in Yorkshire* (Clapham: Dalesman 1972)

Dewhirst Ian & Kellett Arnold: *A century of Yorkshire Dialect* (Otley: Smith Settle 1997)

Dewhirst Ian: *Yorkshire Through the Ages* (London: Batsford 1975)

Duckham B.F.: *Navigable Rivers of Yorkshire* (Clapham: Dalesman 1964)

Dykes Jack: *Yorkshire's Whaling Days* (Clapham: Dalesman 1980)

Elgee Frank and Harriet Wragg: *The County Archaeology Yorkshire* (London: Methuen 19330

Hartley Marie & Ingilby Joan: *Yorkshire Portraits* (London: Dent 1961)

Hebden William: *Yorkshire Battles* (Clapham: Dalesman 1971)

Hey David: *A History of Yorkshire* (Lancaster: Carnegie 2005)

Jennings Bernard: *Yorkshire Monasteries – Cloister, Land and People* (Otley: Smith Settle 1999)

Kellett Arnold: *The Yorkshire Dictionary of Dialect, Tradition and Folklore* (Skipton: Smith Settle second edition 2002)

Kendall P.F. & Wroot H.E.: *The Geology of Yorkshire* (Leeds: authors, 1924)

Morris Richard: *Yorkshire: A lyrical History of England's Greatest County* (London: Wiedenfeld & Nicholson 2018)

Muir Richard: *Old Yorkshire* (London Michael Joseph 1987)

Phillips John: *The Rivers, Mountains and Sea Coast of Yorkshire* (London: Murray 1853)

Pocock Michael: *A History of Yorkshire* (Clapham: Dalesman 1978)

Raistrick Arthur: *Industrial Archaeology* (London: Eyre Methuen 1972)

Raistrick Arthur: *West Riding of Yorkshire* (London: Hodder & Stoughton 1970)

Scott Harry J.: *Portrait of Yorkshire* (London: Hale 1965)

Scrutton Colin (Ed): *Yorkshire Rocks and Landscape – a Field Guide* (Maryport: Yorkshire Geological society/Ellenbank Press 1994)

Sheeran George: *Medieval Yorkshire Towns* (Edinburgh: Edinburgh University Press 1998)

Wood G. Bernard: Yorkshire Villages (London: Robert Hale 1971)

Yorkshire Philosophical Society (ed): *Yorkshire People and Places* (York: YPS 2001)

York

Hogarth Peter J. & Anderson Ewan W.: *The Most Fortunate Situation: The story of York Museum's Gardens* (York: York Philosophical Society 2019)

Mainman Ailsa: *Anglian York* (Pickering: Blackthorn Press 2019)

Peacock A.J. & Joy David: *George Hudson of York* (Clapham: Dalesman 1972)

Willis Ronald: *Portrait of York* (London: Robert Hale 1972)

Vale of York

Broadhead Ivan E.: *Portrait of the Yorkshire Ouse* (London: Robert Hale 1982)

Speakman Colin: *Portrait of North Yorkshire* (London: Robert Hale 1986)

North York Moors & Cleveland

Atkinson J.C.: Forty Years in a Morland Parish (Londoin: Macmillan 1891)

Bairstow Martin: *Railways Around Whitby* Vols 1 & 2 (Halifax: author 1989, 1996)

Burns Tom Scott: *Canon Atkinson and his Country* (Guiseley MTD Rigg 1986)

Carstairs Ian: *The North York Moors National Park* (Exeter, London: Webb & Bower; Michael Joseph, 1987)

Elgee Frank: *The Moorlands of North Eastern Yorkshire* (London: Brown and Sons 1912)

Elgee Frank: *Early Man in North East Yorkshire* (Gloucester: Bellows 1940)

Hartley Marie & Ingilby Joan: *Life in the Moorlands of North-East Yorkshire* (London: Dent 1972)

Joy David: *Whitby and Pickering Railway* (Clapham: Dalesman 1969)

Osborne Roger: *Rocks & Landscape of the North York Moors* (Whitby: High Tide Publishing 2018)

Rawson Peter F. & Wright John K.: *Geology of the Yorkshire Coast* (London Geologists' Association 2018)

Yorkshire Wolds, Hull and Holderness

Foster Pauline: *Forty Years in Thixendale 1871–1911* (York: York Publishing Services 2010)

Limon Martin: *The Villages of East Yorkshire* (Pickering: Blackthorn Press 2010)

Neave David & Susan: *Bridlington An Introduction to its History and Buildings* (Otley: Smith Settle 2000)

Neave David & Susan Hull: *City Guide, The Buildings of England* (Pevesner Architectural Guides) (London: Yale University Press 2010)

River Hull Valley Drainage Heritage Group: *Becks, Banks, Drains and Brains* (Beverley: East Riding Council 2014)

Sharp Lesley & Foster Pauline (ed): *The High Wolds Heritage Group Villages Book* (York: Yorkshire Publishing Services 2011)

Speakman Colin & Fleur: *The Yorkshire Wolds a Journey of Discovery* (Hebden Bridge: Gritstone 2018)

Starkey J. Hull (ed.): *Hull: Culture, History, Place* (Liverpool: Liverpool University Press 2017)

The Yorkshire Dales

Dixon Mike: *Ilkley Revisited* (Stroud: History Press 2010)

Jennings Bernard (ed): *A History of Nidderdale* (York: Sessions 1967/83)

Johnson David: *Limestone Industries of the Yorkshire Dales* (Stroud: Amberley, 2002)

Johnson David: *Ingleborough Landscape & History* (Lancaster: Carnegie 2008)

Joy David: *Painters of the Dales* (Skipton: Paradise Press 1997)

Joy David & Speakman Colin: *The Yorkshire Dales – a View from the Millennium* (Ilkley: Great Northern 2000)

Joy David & Singleton Andy: *Barns of the Yorkshire Dales* (Ilkley: Great Northern 2008

Joy David: *Rails in the Dales* (Market Drayton: Railway & Canal History Society 2014)

Hartley Marie & Ingilby Joan: *The Yorkshire Dales* (London: Dent 1955, 1980)

Hartley Marie & Ingilby Joan: *Life & Tradition in the Yorkshire Dales* (London: Dent 1968)

Harvey Adrian: *Excursion Guide to the Geomorphology of the Howgill Fells* (Edinburgh: Edinburgh Dunedin Academic Press 2017)

Kellett Arnold: *A to Z of Knaresborough History* (Stroud: Amberley 2011)

Mitchell W. R.: *Thunder in the Mountains* (Ilkley: Great Northern 2000)

Muir Richard: *The Dales of Yorkshire A Portrait* (London: Methuen 1991)

Raistrick Arthur: *The Pennine Dales* (London: Eyre & Spottiswoode 1968)

Raistrick Arthur & Jennings Bernard: *A History of Lead Mining in the Pennines* (London: Longmans 1965)

Waltham Tony: *The Yorkshire Dales National Park* (Exeter, London: Webb & Bower; Michael Joseph, 1987)

Waltham Tony: *Yorkshire Dales Landscape & Geology* (Marlborough: Crowood Press 2007)

White R.F. & Wilson P.R.: *Archaeology and Historic Landscapes of the Yorkshire Dales* (Leeds: Yorkshire Archaeological Society 2004)

White Robert: *The Yorkshire Dales: A Landscape through Time* (Ilkley: Great Northern 2002)

Forest of Bowland

Bibby Andrew: *The Forest of Bowland Freedom to Roam Guide* (London: Francis Lincoln 2005)

Mitchell W.R.: *Bowland & Pendle Hill* (Chichester: Phillimore 2004)

Shaw Helen & Stachulski Andrew: *The Forest of Bowland* (Ludlow: Merlin Unwin 2005)

South Pennines

Bibby Andrew: *The Backbone of England: Landscape and life on the Pennine Watershed* (London: Francis Lincoln 2008)

Clarke Mike: *The Leeds & Liverpool Canal – A History and Guide* (Lancaster: Carnegie 1990)

Emberson Ian M.: *Yorkshire Lives and Landscapes* (Stroud: Sutton Publishing 2006)

Goddard Chris: *West Yorkshire Woods Part I Calderdale, Part II Airedale* (Hebden Bridge: Gritstone 2017, 2021)

Keevill Graham: *Standedge Guide – An industrial Landscape of Roads Canals and Railways* (Huddersfield: Kirklees Metropolitan Council 1986)

Hughes Glyn: *Millstone Grit* (Southampton: Camelot Press 1975)

Parry Keith: *Trans-Pennine Heritage – Hills, People and Transport* (Newton Abbot: David & Charles 1981)

West Yorkshire

Brears Peter: *Leeds Waterfront Heritage Trail* (Leeds: Leeds City Museums 1993)

Firth Gary: *A History of Bradford* (Chichester: Phillimore 1997)

Giles Colum & Goodall Ian H.: *Yorkshire Textile Mills 1770–1930* (London: HMSO 1992)

Nuttgens Patrick: *Leeds: The back to front, inside out upside down City* (Otley: Stile Books 1979)

Sheeran George: *The Mosque in the City: Bradford and its Islamic Architecture* (York PLACE 2015)

Slack Margaret: *Portrait of West Yorkshire* (London: Robert Hale 2005)

Speakman Colin: *Shire County Guide West Yorkshire* (Aylesbury: Shire Publications 1988)

Linstrum Derek: *Historic Architecture of Leeds* (Newcastle: Oriel Press 1969)

South Yorkshire

Goddard Chris: *The South Yorkshire Moors* (Hebden Bridge: Gritstone 2019)

Hey David: *Making of South Yorkshire* (Bakewell: Moorland 1979)

Howse Geoffrey: *South Yorkshire* (Stroud: Sutton 2007)

Howse Geoffrey: *A Photographic history of Sheffield Steel* (Stroud: History Press 2001, 2011)

Unwin Joan: *Sheffield's Industries: Cutlery, Silver and Edge Tools* (Stroud: History Press 2008)

Vickers Edward J.: *A Popular History of Sheffield* (Sheffield: Applebaum 1968)

Index